WHAT THEY SAW...

AT THE
HOUR
OF
DEATH

Editions of *At The Hour of Death* by Karlis Osis and Erlendur Haraldsson:

India
Japan
Italy
Germany
France
Holland
Norway
Iceland
Spain
Portugal
Sweden
French Canada

WHAT THEY SAW...

AT THE HOUR OF DEATH

Third Edition

KARLIS OSIS, PH.D.
ERLENDUR HARALDSSON, PH.D.
Introduction by Elisabeth Kübler-Ross, M.D.

HASTINGS HOUSE
Book Publishers
Norwalk, Connecticut

AT THE HOUR OF DEATH
Third Edition
March 1997

Library of Congress Catalog Card Number 96-079111
ISBN 0-8038-9386-8

Printed in the United States of America

10   9   8   7   6   5   4   3   2   1

Contents

	Introduction by Elisabeth Kübler-Ross, M.D.	xi
	Introduction to the Second Edition	xiii
1.	The Mystery of Death: What We Believe versus What We Know	1
2.	Is the Idea of Postmortem Survival Testable?	9
3.	Research on Deathbed Visions: Past and Present	16
4.	The Pilot Survey: A Most Encouraging Start	28
5.	What the Dying See	34
6.	To Be or Not to Be: A Model of Deathbed Visions and How We Tested It	47
7.	Apparitions: Hallucinations of Persons as Seen by Terminal Patients	54
8.	General Characteristics of Apparition Cases in Terminal Patients	62
9.	Getting at the Roots of the Apparition Experience I	81
10.	Getting at the Roots of the Apparition Experience II	103
11.	From Depression and Pain to Peace and Serenity	122
12.	They Came Back: Reports from Near-Death Patients	148
13.	Visions of Another World: Afterlife as Seen Through the Eyes of the Dying	162
14.	The Meaning of Death: What We Learned from This Study	185
	Epilogue	212
	Evidence for Life After Death	214
	Appendixes	
	I. *Questionnaire*	229
	II. *Tables*	233
	Notes	249
	Bibliography	251
	Index	257
	About the Authors	261

Acknowledgments

Research described in this book was made possible by the help of several organizations and many individuals to whom we wish to express our gratitude. These surveys were performed under the auspices of The American Society for Psychical Research. We extend our warmest appreciation to the ASPR Board, staff, and especially to Dr. Gardner Murphy—its president at that time—and to its current president, Dr. Montague Ullman. Warm interest and encouragement from the late Chester F. Carlson and Mrs. Carlson, and their generous help through the Shanti and Code foundations, were essential for the project and are gratefully acknowledged. We are grateful to The Parapsychology Foundation for permission to quote from their publications. The Parapsychology Foundation, Inc. sponsored the pilot study; for this we owe our deepest gratitude to the late Eileen Garrett and Frances P. Bolton. James Kidd's thoughtful legacy funded most of the Indian survey. The University of Iceland was kind enough to make special arrangements for one of us—Erlendur Haraldsson—to have time off for this study. We are grateful to the team of Indian psychologists from the Bureau of Psychology of Uttar Pradesh, especially Dr. Yamuna Prasad and Parmashwar Dayal, who were of essential help in the Indian survey.

The American team concerned with interviewing and data processing included: Fern Cederberg, Dorothy C. Donath, Mary Leslie, Donna McCormick, Marion L. Nester, Theresa O'Rourke, Saija Osis, Wally Pearlman, Dr. Thomas Todd, Sarah Van Steenburgh, and others. Their dedicated work made the project succeed.

We are thankful for helpful consultations at various stages of the project with Drs. Walter H. Clark, Jan Ehrenwald, William Gardner, Hornel Hart, Herbert H. Hyman, David Kahn, Gardner Murphy, Humphrey Osmond, Jamuna Prosad, Ian Stevenson, Thomas Todd, Malcolm Turner, Montague Ullman, and others.

John White made a valuable contribution by editing our manuscript. For this we thank him.

Most of all, our warmest thanks to the doctors and nurses who kindly let us share their experiences with dying patients. We are very much indebted to the medical directors and the department heads of the Indian hospitals who arranged meetings with their staff doctors and nurses. Our special appreciation to: Prof. H. S. Bajpai, Dr. M. P. Mehrotra, Dr. Mittal, Dr. Kedar Nath, Col. M. Tajudin, Prof. K. N. Udupa, Dr. H. Vaishnava, and others.

Announcement to readers

This book describes our first scientific study on an international scale. However, much more could be done. We would like to receive from our readers reports of deathbed-visions and related experiences which may be valuable for future research. Any other constructive thoughts and help concerning future research would be appreciated. Write to Dr. Karlis Osis, American Society for Psychical Research, 5 West 73rd Street, New York, N.Y. 10023, or Dr. Erlendur Haraldsson, Faculty of Social Science, University of Iceland, 101 Reykjavik, Iceland.

Introduction

At the Hour of Death, paranormal experiences of the dying as observed by doctors and nurses, by Karlis Osis, Ph.D. and Erlendur Haraldsson, Ph.D., is primarily a book that all researchers and scientists should read if they have questions and problems with the newly flourishing and widely publicized research on death and life after death (Moody, Kübler-Ross).

Drs. Osis and Haraldsson have to be congratulated for years of hard, patient and dedicated work in an area which was still very much taboo a few years ago when this study was begun and when they could anticipate little support from the secular and skeptical world in which they live, from a society that can afford to send men to the moon and instruments to Mars to determine if there is life on another planet, but knows so little about life and death on planet Earth.

The authors' work has been done quietly and inconspicuously and—I am sure—only a small percentage of our population is even familiar with their existence. It is because of "silent workers" like them, who consciously and caringly devote years of their life to the study of man's mortal end, that we will ultimately understand that death is not an end but a new beginning, simply a transition into a higher state of consciousness.

The authors have studied hundreds of cases, both Hindus and Christians, Indians and Americans, to collect data to determine the subjective experiences the patients have had at the portal of death.

Human experiences at this moment are alike and do not much vary depending on religious or cultural backgrounds. They are more influenced by the depth and authenticity of a belief system—something that has been confirmed by our own studies.

Anyone interested in life after death should take the time to study this book and should reflect on the depth and care that went into it to show us yet another confirmation of existence after "death," or perhaps equally important, the fact that all men are alike at birth and at death, and that it is the quality and not the denominational label of our religious identity that will eventually be a contributing factor to our own peaceful transition into God's garden.

Elisabeth Kübler-Ross, M.D.
Author of *On Death and Dying*

Introduction
to the Second Edition

At The Hour of Death is a book that is different from many others
that deal with near-death experiences and have been published in
this decade. It directly approaches the issue of life after death on
the basis of a scientific evaluation of a substantial quantity of data
(1,000 cases) which were gathered in the United States and in
India. Since the first edition of this book, others have conducted
research on this subject and public awareness has emerged. We
have attempted to reflect these new findings and attitudes in this
current edition.

Many television shows and magazine articles have brought into
American living rooms interviews with men and women who almost died, were resuscitated, and who remembered extraordinary
experiences. Members of different scientific and academic disciplines have discussed the pros and cons, their beliefs and disbeliefs,
on numerous talk shows. Profound insights have been offered, as
have profane vulgarizations of a subject mankind has held as a
sacred mystery—the survival of human personality beyond the
hour of death. Whatever attempt is made to cover up the concept
of death—be it with words, abstractions, or with shining slogans—
death is still a mystery that is real and unavoidable. The despair
and sorrow engendered by the approach of our own death or that
of a loved one, shake us out of superficialities and may invigorate
the heart to feel its deepest roots of existence. Elisabeth Kübler-
Ross (1969, 1974, 1975, 1983) and others have convincingly demonstrated the degree of strength and support we need when facing
death. As the end draws near, we may require social warmth and
understanding, a spiritual outlook, or pharmacological alleviation of
pain and discomfort. Knowledge of what happens when we die,

what to expect, and what we may reasonably hope for form a vital part of such support. It is in this way that our book might be handy for those who are facing death, as well as for those who counsel the terminally ill and bereaved.

This edition of *At The Hour of Death* reflects the progress of research in this area since the book's first appearance in 1977. Although our data and evaluations are, of course, the same, we will relate our findings to some of the more recent research that has been carried out by others. What are the main issues that have been raised in the last decade, and where, in this new edition, do we consider them?

Shifts of Focus

In our study, we concentrated on experiences which occur near death, regardless of whether the patient died (which happened in a majority of our cases) or recovered. In the last decade, research has focused entirely on near-death survivors, that is, on those who were resuscitated and who lived to tell about their near-death experiences. The visions experienced by those who actually died were ignored in most recent studies. This results in a severe selection bias in the data, since only patients who did not really die are studied; the true inevitability of death might be an overlooked factor. For example, psychiatrist, R. Noyes, and psychologist, D.J. Slymen, concentrated on accident cases in which the threat of death was a real possibility, but where physical injuries were mild or absent. Noyes and Slymen contend that "in studies of this kind it appears important to distinguish between persons that were close to death physically and those that only approached it psychologically. Questionnaire responses from a small sample of persons who claimed to have been seriously ill—even 'dead'—have shown them to be quite different." (1984, p. 26) On the other hand, our impression was that the experiences of near-death survivors have similar but less clearly expressed characteristics than those of patients who died (see Chapter 12). Why? We cannot be certain but if the hypothesis of life after death is true, then the experiences of survivors could be considered as false alarms, which do not require a full response from "the other side."

Other shifts of emphasis in more recent studies included concerns of the living, such as life reviews and precognitive insights of the future. In our research, we concentrated on phenomena which exhibited apparent concern about entering the afterlife, and which, in turn, might be indicative of postmortem survival. Nevertheless, information relevant to the study of life after death emerged from research by cardiologist, M. Sabom, and also by the work of psychologist, K. Ring, concerning the presence of out-of-body phenomena in near-death experiences (1982 and 1980, respectively). This research on out-of-body phenomena is a viable new contribution to knowledge of near-death experiences, which our own data-gathering methods did not reveal (see Chapter 14).

Not All That Glitters Is Gold

What constitutes a near-death experience? Only a few kinds of events experienced by dying patients enlighten us about the mystery of death. On the basis of knowledge that has crystalized over one hundred years of debate in parapsychology and religious studies, we chose to focus on a few selected aspects of the phenomena experienced by dying patients, for example, apparitional experiences. The newcomers to near-death research included many more, and one such valuable choice was the study of out-of-body experiences. Less essential features of near-death phenomena which have recently been attended to are the experiences of a buzzing noise, travelling through a dark tunnel, and seeing colors. Raymond Moody's bestseller, *Life After Life*, emphasized encounters with a "being of light which did not have a human shape or appearance. There was only light." (1975, p. 59) The "being of light" appears in many other contemporary descriptions (e.g., Ring, 1984), but did not turn up in our data, which was collected prior to Moody's book. In our survey, there were very few experiences of light without form, and they were not construed as personified beings. Religious figures were described as having a human form of one kind or another. Maybe Moody created a new myth, or provided a newer, more attractive vocabulary for describing religious figures in this space age of ours. This illustrates a basic principle: what we "see" in near-death experiences and how we express it in words depends a great deal on our cultural background. The subjective and the objective sides are intricately interwoven, but they appear to be separable, to some extent, through comparisons between radically different cultures. Comparing the visions of American and Indian patients gave us some assurance that real gold was found, that we were not just chasing a glittering illusion or fool's gold. Readers are urged to follow closely our cross-cultural comparisons—they are essential. Our tables and statistics might seem like tedious drudgery at times, but so is washing away the sand from nuggets of real gold hidden in the mud. How else could we hope to transcend the many conflicting belief systems of our experiments? Belief is valuable in life, but it has to be transcended to gain scientific knowledge.

New Multidisciplinary Beginnings

Research on near-death experiences has attracted professionals from medicine, psychiatry, psychology, sociology, opinion polls, and religious studies. They have brought their varied expertise to bear upon near-death studies, and this has greatly enriched such research. We needed to know to what extent these experiences are affected by certain medical, psychiatric, psychological, and cultural factors, including religious upbringing. Although these new multidisciplinary approaches have greatly enriched our knowledge of many aspects of near-death experience, they have not contributed much insight into the core issue: the bearing of near-death experiences on the life after death hypothesis. While judgments on this issue are often passed, they usually do not incorporate the findings of previous studies on phenomena suggestive of afterlife. Ignorance of empirical material, and interpretations crystalized in long debates, do violate basic rules of scholarship and scientific methodology. We will discuss the new multidisciplinary contributions in Chapter 14, and keep our grounding in previous empirical studies of phenomena relevant to the afterlife hypothesis.

Philosophical Neutrality

The ideal of science is philosophical neutrality, that is, issues should be settled on the basis of objective observations and experiments. By and large, scientists live up to such ideals. However, in frontier areas concerning phenomena relevant to philosophical interpretations, objectivity is not the whole story (Collins, 1985). When it comes to dealing with parapsychological issues, such as ESP and the hypothesis of life after death, one's philosophical stance might slant one's judgment (McClenon, 1984). "Scientism," the philosophy dominant in elite scientific circles, is very influential. The ontological components of scientism (such as the reductionist viewpoint that demands materialistic-mechanistic explanations for everything) obviously clash with any positive ideas about life after death.

Scientism has influenced recent literature on near-death experiences in two ways. First of all, we see *reductionism* occurring: near-death experiences are forcefully interpreted on physiological, pharmacological, and psychiatric grounds (e.g., Siegel, 1980). We also see evidence of scientism in *tactical agnosticism*, which often utilizes the following ploy: near-death experiences cannot produce any evidence for life after death, however, I personally am convinced of it and so are nearly all of my interviewees.

In our work, we tried to avoid philosophical ploys and biases by requiring equal evidence for both hypotheses: namely, the hypothesis that accepts and the hypothesis that rejects the notion of postmortem survival. Our model (see Chapter 6) provides equal weight for observations which point toward postmortem survival and to those which construe death as the ultimate destruction of personality. We assessed our data accordingly and maintain our conclusions, as previously hypothesized. The value of this book is information, not philosophy.

As said before, the mystery of death is very personal: like love, it is not just a cognitive problem. *At The Hour of Death* provides information, as well as conveys the more subjective "feel for the experience" through patients' stories. This edition, we hope, will again furnish useful support for those who are facing death directly, or indirectly through loved ones, or who have in some other way encountered this deepest mystery of mankind.

WHAT THEY SAW...
AT THE
HOUR
OF
DEATH

CHAPTER 1

The Mystery of Death: What We Believe versus What We Know

No choice is uninfluenced by the way in which the personality regards its destiny, and the body its death. In the last analysis, it is our conception of death which decides our answers to all the questions that life puts to us. . . . Hence, too, the necessity of preparing for it.
—Dag Hammarskjöld

OUR destiny at death is probably the most important area of human experience into which we can inquire. According to the prevailing scientific world view, the destiny is a harsh one. Textbooks tell us in no uncertain terms that after the heart stops circulating blood, the brain is no longer nourished and begins to decay rapidly—within a quarter of an hour or so. At that point, the texts say, the patient's personality is simply no more. It is irreparably destroyed. The individual ceases to exist.

For centuries, medical schools have inculcated this grim, uncompromising concept into doctors and nurses—those who will be the ones to help us when we die. But has this view of human nature really been so well established as to allow of no doubt? Is it a solid truth on which we can rely in all situations?

Surprisingly, the experiences of the dying themselves often contradict the accepted medical view. What insights do we get from the dying? What do they experience? What do they "see" at the end? Doctors are starting to ask, is death, from their point of view, bleak destruction or a new beginning?

Although most patients apparently drift into oblivion without awareness of it, there are some, clearly conscious to the end, who say they "see" into the beyond and who are able to report their experiences before expiring. They see apparitions of deceased relatives and friends. They see religious and mythological figures. They see nonearthly environments characterized by light, beauty, and intense color. These experiences are transformative. They bring with them serenity, peace, elation, and religious emotions. The patients die a "good death" in strange contrast to the usual gloom and misery commonly expected before expiration. Other deathbed patients, although they report no visions, nevertheless undergo the same transformation, which sometimes includes the cessation of pain.

These striking deathbed vision cases came to our attention independently in the course of our work as researchers into the paranormal and the psychic. Both of us were deeply impressed by the uniformity of detail among anecdotal reports. Since we had a mutual interest, it was not entirely strange that circumstances should bring us together to complete a long-term study in search of answers to the questions above—a study of people on their deathbeds who were conscious during the last hours of their lives.

Our investigation is, we feel, the first truly scientific research into the experiences of the dying at the hour of death. First, we collected massive amounts of data through three extensive surveys of physicians and nurses who attended the dying. Second, our research was transcultural, drawing upon American and Indian medical people. Third, our data were collected carefully and systematically through modern sampling techniques, including questionnaires and probing interviews. Fourth, our data were subjected to elaborate statistical, pattern, and content analysis through computer evaluation.

Although we applied scientific rigor to this research, we did not neglect the experiential aspect of our inquiry. Death and dying is not just an intellectual problem. Rather, it is something which should be understood with the whole depth of our being. Therefore, we sought to examine it objectively and subjectively. Wherever possible, we obtained the direct words of the dying. This enabled us to be in touch with what actually happened in the hospital rooms.

What we found is both surprising and hopeful. This book will offer new evidence, based on observations by more than a thousand doctors and nurses, bearing on the question of postmortem survival. To anticipate our conclusions, we will state here that this evidence strongly suggests life after death—more strongly than any alternative hypothesis can explain the data. Neither medical, nor psychological, nor cultural conditioning can explain away deathbed visions. Moreover, they are relatively independent of age, sex, education, religion, and socioeconomic status. Taken in conjunction with other evidence obtained by competent research into this question—to be examined shortly—we feel that the total body of information makes possible a fact-based, rational, and therefore realistic belief in life after death.

We hasten to add, however, that our findings should not be considered as closing the issue. Indeed, we feel that it would be arrogant and misguided to pronounce this research as the final statement on the subject. Nevertheless, the total evidence for survival now offers a thoroughly plausible, though tentative, picture of postmortem existence. We feel that our research has revealed new phenomena and has given us new detail and insight into what has been called "the great unknown."

Consider, for example, the following two cases. They are quite typical of more than a thousand cases of this sort that we have collected.

A seventy-year-old patient had seen her deceased husband several times and then she predicted her own death. She said that her husband had appeared in the window and motioned her to come out of the house. The reason for his visits was to have her join him. Her daughter and other relatives were present when she predicted her death, laid out her burial clothes, laid down in bed for a nap, and died about one hour later. She seemed calm, resigned to death and, in fact, wanted to die. Before she saw her husband she didn't speak about imminent death. Her doctor was so surprised by her sudden death, for which there were no sufficient medical reasons, that he checked if she had poisoned herself. He found neither signs of poisoning nor any such drugs in the house.

Typical is the following case of a sixty-year-old woman tortured by intestinal cancer.

All of a sudden [the doctor reports] she opened her eyes. She called her [deceased] husband by name and said she was coming to him. She had the most peaceful, nicest smile just as if she were going to the arms of someone she thought a great deal of. She said, "Guy, I am coming." She didn't seem to realize I was there. It was almost as if she were in another world. It was as if something beautiful had opened up to her; she was experiencing something so wonderful and beautiful.

Such a case by itself cannot be said to prove anything. Hallucinations can be interpreted in many ways. However, if we take all such cases and let a computer sort out their characteristics, we may hope to see whether they support the notion of an afterlife or whether they indicate destruction of the personality as the final end.

In the course of our research, we quite often encountered reports of a sudden rise in the patient's mood shortly before death. "They light up," it was frequently reported. "Some inexplicable peace and serenity comes over them," others said. Why should such things occur? Is it because terminal patients are in the process of being extinguished—sitting in nature's electric chair, so to speak? Obviously not. These inner changes in patients are at times so profound that they scare some medical observers and change the lives of others. Especially shocking was the following experience. A Boston physician was called to one of his patients whose heart had stopped. After a heroic effort using modern resuscitation techniques, the patient was revived. The doctor naturally expected him to be thankful for his life. Instead, he opened his eyes and angrily reproached the physician, saying, "Why did you bring me back, Doctor? It was so beautiful!" Apparently this experience of dying was so gratifying that it outweighed the strongest instinct we suppose we have—the will to live.

Can we take such intimations of immortality at face value? That would be naive. Without knowing more about patients' medical, psychological, and cultural backgrounds, we cannot properly interpret them. For example, at terminal stages, many patients receive injections of morphine in order to alleviate their pain. Such drugs could cause bizarre experiences. Therefore, we can neither accept nor reject patients' stories without first critically studying them with scientific methods. Otherwise, we would just be adding another opinion to the already large body of contradictory views about afterlife in which the doctors say no, the ministers say yes, and the patients are utterly confused. And all—doctors, ministers, and patients alike—need to find out the facts. They need to see whether the facts hang together in meaningful patterns which might either support or contradict the afterlife hypothesis. This book is an attempt to do just that.

Of course, the investigation of death did not originate with modern studies. In nearly all cultures, life after death has been more or less assumed. The concept of postmortem survival seems to have been with us at least since the Neanderthal people began burying their dead and anointing them with reddish earth, some one hundred thousand years ago. Such primitive burial customs have invariably been associated with some organized religion—like belief in an afterlife. They are mute evidence that our hominid ancestors were not wholly materialists.

Nor are people today. According to a 1975 survey by the Gallup Opinion Index, popularly known as the Gallup Poll, 69 percent of all Americans believe there is life after death. (The survey also found that 20 percent do not believe it, while 11 percent said they don't know.) This finding supported a 1973 Roper Poll survey, which found that 70 percent of the American people believed in life after death.

Belief, however, can be rational or irrational, depending on whether or not the believer has a reasonable basis for his belief. Mere opinion is cheap, regardless of how widely it is accepted or how authoritatively it is propounded—whether by a clerical office or a school of medicine. True knowledge is much more difficult to attain than opinion or received beliefs; it must be based upon clear observation of reality. Rational belief is grounded in knowledge, in facts. It grows out of experience which has stood the test of logical examination and, insofar as possible, scientific inquiry.

The reasons for belief in survival fall into three main categories:

the philosophical, the mystical-religious, and the scientific. The philosophical approach to the problem of death offers some traditional arguments in favor of the doctrine of personal survival after bodily death. These have been usefully summarized[1] as follows.

1. The *ontological argument*, which bases immortality on the immateriality, and irreducibility of the soul substance.

2. The *teleological argument*, which employs the concept of man's destiny and function, his disposition to free himself more and more from the conditions of time and space, and to develop completely his intellectual and moral potentialities—the development of which is impossible under the conditions of earthly life.

3. The *ethical argument*, i.e., the moral demand of the ultimate equivalence of personal deserts and rewards, which equivalence is not found in life.

4. The *historical argument*, i.e., the fact that the belief is widespread and ancient, showing it to be deep-seated in human nature.

Although these arguments have been solemnly offered for centuries, it is obvious that not everyone accepts them. Why? Perhaps it is because the arguments are intellectual rather than experiential.

The evidence of mysticism and religious experiences, on the other hand, *is* experiential. The classic works by R. M. Bucke (*Cosmic Consciousness*) and William James (*Varieties of Religious Experience*) offer dozens of examples of mystical insight bypassing rational argument and intellectual debate. For those mystics, the traditional fear of death falls off like a cloak. It falls off, however, not as a result of logical reasoning but rather as an illusion that has been seen through. They report experiencing the cosmos as a living presence, a *whole*, in which existence beyond bodily death appears absolutely certain.

However, just as logic and reason by themselves have thus far been insufficient to provide sure knowledge of an afterlife, so, too, have the direct experiences of mystics proved insufficient to induce universal conviction. Is there another means by which we may put both logic and experience to the test? After all, grand logical structures based upon sheer fantasy, without any foundation in reality, can be, and have been, devised, as in paranoid delusion.

Likewise, hallucinatory experiences can seem real while nevertheless being based on some quirk of a disordered brain. What can be done to test the reality content of our logical structures and convincing experiences? Can anything be done to test the claims of philosophy and mysticism on this subject?

We feel that science is the answer. By that, we mean the *method of science*, not necessarily the prevalent opinion of scientists. We adhere to the empirical approach. Neither philosophy nor the authority of the establishment is the ultimate arbiter of knowledge for us. We would rather allow that coherent body of facts, ascertained with reasonable objectivity, to determine what is, what is not, and what might plausibly exist.

That being so, what has science to tell us about the problem of death and a possible afterlife?

The scientific evidence for afterlife can be divided into five major categories. Each of these categories contains independently derived data, and none is dependent upon any of the others. The categories are

1. Mediumship.
2. Apparitions, especially those seen by several observers.
3. Reincarnation memories.
4. Out-of-body experiences.
5. Deathbed observations.

The last category is the subject of this book. The others are derived from more than a century's investigations by competent parapsychologists. We will examine those categories briefly in Chapter 3, bringing a new parapsychological perspective to the study of death. For the moment, however, we want to return to the question of what science—aside from parapsychology—has to tell us about death.

The scientific study of death and dying is called thanatology. It began in the last decade, pioneered by psychologists and psychiatrists concerned with counseling dying people and their families. Thanatologists sought to teach the medical profession how to help terminal patients come to grips with their own oncoming death, and how to handle the problem of grief among the bereaved. They did, and are still doing, extensive work interviewing the dying and observing them as they interact with hospital staff and relatives. Consequently, we now know a great deal about the psychological processes involved and about how dying people behave.

Thanatology has been of valuable service because of its exploration into the physiological, psychological, and social aspects of death. But has the depth of its research really been enough? We think not.

Almost without exception, the work of the thanatologist is based on the implicit assumption that death is the termination of human existence, and the task of the helping professions is usually seen as one of teaching the patient to accept this termination. But what exactly are the dying being taught to accept? In the so-called scientific world view, which as noted above is deeply inculcated in medical education, ultimate destruction as the end of human destiny is taken for granted. We dare to ask, however, why the medical community is so sure that all the answers are already in.

Has science said its last word beyond any doubt? Is belief in a life after death long outdated by modern science, or is there some factual basis for such a conviction? What we need is reliable information on death and dying, which can be provided only with the help of scientific methodology, leaving the opinions and philosophy of the scientific establishment behind. Thus, in a spirit of scientific inquiry, we have taken up the problem where thanatology has left off.

It is interesting to note that one eminent thanatologist, Dr. Elisabeth Kübler-Ross, author of the bestselling *On Death and Dying*, has found the destruction hypothesis to be untenable. According to her, some kind of afterlife is evidenced by the stories of dying patients that she herself has witnessed.

When phenomena such as these come to the notice of professionals, can they be studied using the scientific method? This is not at all self-evident, but depends on the choice of appropriate methods. We will examine the questions of method in Chapter 3. For now, we would like to tell you more specifically about how we came to undertake this research.

CHAPTER 2

Is the Idea of
Postmortem Survival Testable?

☙

"**D**OCTOR, are you trying to catch a butterfly with a bear trap?" a psychic exclaimed after a tour of our parapsychological laboratory. Actually, she had a point. Some, but not all, psychical research has been that clumsy. The phenomena we investigate are very delicate, elusive, and hard to observe because of the spontaneity of their occurrence. With inappropriate methodology, the research can be hampered and brought to a standstill. Let us take a hard look at what can be done and what the unrealistic expectations and utopian ideals are.

Several basic objections to research on postmortem survival have been advanced, their nature depending on the "home base" of the critic.

1. According to the scientistic world view, the universe is exclusively material reality, built only of matter and energies known to physics. Mind and consciousness are mere by-products (epiphenomena) of the physical organism and therefore cannot exist without it. This is still the dominant viewpoint of the scientific community. Nevertheless, we must point out that this is really philosophy, not science. Scientism is a methodology based on certain assumptions (termed material monism by philosophers) and the rejection of other assumptions about the nature of reality

offered by other schools of philosophy and religion. (Houston Smith, 1976; 1982)

2. Zealous adherents to the "Law of Parsimony" have attacked survival research on methodological grounds. This law states that explanatory principles should not be needlessly multiplied, and that when choosing among hypotheses, the simplest is to be preferred. Certainly the assumption of something in the human personality like a soul that may survive death, and of "another reality" within which such a soul could continue to exist, is not simple and does "multiply the explanatory principles." We feel, however, that the introduction of such new basic concepts is justified in the face of a considerable body of coherent facts which make sense when such assumptions are made. In psychology, basic concepts of "mind" and "consciousness" were exterminated by rigid enforcement of the "Law of Parsimony." However, they were found to be necessary and made a strong comeback in the 1960s and 1970s. It is time to consider the concept of "soul" if empirical facts demand it.

3. Exclusion of all explanations of the phenomena other than postmortem survival is often demanded without regard to how farfetched and clumsy the other explanations are. Some parapsychologists have long been on a search for the "crucial experiment" which will "prove survival" so that it cannot be explained away by any imaginative stretching of the other explanations. The success of this kind of culling of the problem has been limited, for the afterlife issue may be much too complex to provide such exclusive evidence.

There are distinguished researchers, such as Ian Stevenson and Hornell Hart (Stevenson, 1974; Hart, 1959), who, in the face of the evidence, have fully accepted the afterlife hypothesis.[1] Others, such as the world-renowned parapsychologist J. B. Rhine (1960), have asserted that the afterlife problem is only inconclusively researchable—that is, it is beyond the limits where science can investigate with today's methods. Rhine, however, later suggested a new approach which he felt could be effective (1975). The eminent American psychologist Gardner Murphy (1961) declares that with his scientific world view he feels like the proverbial immovable object which has been struck by an irresistible force, when confronted with parapsychological facts indicative of an afterlife. Such slow progress might indicate the limited usefulness of the dominant research paradigm, which may very well have been as clumsy as a bear trap.

As noted earlier, there is a variety of complex phenomena suggesting life after death. Most of these phenomena, however, can only be observed in life as they arise spontaneously. They are not subject to investigation by controlled experiments. Therefore, their reality cannot be determined scientifically with a so-called crucial experiment. Research on such phenomena is more like the multidimensional problems one faces in research on personality theory. Certainly, the postmortem survival hypothesis is a personality theory. Assumptions of life after death do call for new, radical changes in the concepts of personality, provided the hypothesis is true. In psychology, as far as we know, there is no "crucial experiment"—the kind required in postmortem survival research—which would give "proof" of Skinnerian, Freudian, Rogerian, or any other psychological personality theory. Scientific efforts get so complex in research on the phenomena of personality that, by necessity, the approach must be different. Frequently, a host of phenomena, encircling the central problems, are tracked down by observational and experimental research. Then the data are organized with respect to theory. If a large enough body of facts hangs together within the framework of a particular theory, it usually gains some acceptance and assumption of validity in the mainstream of scientific psychology.

It appears to us that it would be unfair to demand the crucial, all-exclusive experiment that would give evidence for survival if such demands are neither made nor met in relation to all other theories of personality. It would be wrong to withdraw the survival problem from scientific inquiry simply because of a utopian criterion for evidence. Success in personality research indicates clearly the fruitfulness of research efforts in so complex an area as the problem of life after death. The success of large-scale explorations of the phenomena from which evidence of afterlife is claimed (deathbed visions, apparitions, mediumistic messages, reincarnation memories) indicates the fruitfulness of research in this area. Our project certainly was not aimed at providing all-exclusive evidence for postmortem survival, but rather at exploring a very central class of phenomena which has to be reckoned with in any consideration of postmortem survival. We learned a lot which we believe to be evidential and new knowledge. The purpose of this book is to share that information with the scientific community and the general public.

In a century of sustained effort and the most rigorous scrutiny, psychical researchers have uncovered a wealth of well-observed, factual data which support the hypothesis of life after death. This substantial body of facts flies in the face of the destructionist hypothesis, and no serious researcher can glibly bypass those facts. There are many scientific works of high quality that have accumulated over a century of psychical research by such distinguished scientists as William James, Henry Sidgwick, Frederic Myers, Gardner Murphy, and C. J. Ducasse. Unfortunately, however, most of these studies are obscured in professional literature and are usually unknown to scientists and the public alike. The Duke University sociologist Hornell Hart, in his book *The Enigma of Survival* (1959) and the Swedish psychiatrist Nils O. Jacobson, in *Life Without Death* (1973), provide an overview of the relevant research data, such as apparitions collectively seen by several observers, mediumistic messages revealing facts only the deceased knew, deathbed visions, out-of-body experiences, and such physical effects as messages from the dead (clocks stopping, pictures falling, bells ringing, and so on). The book *Man's Concern with Death* (1968), by the famous British historian Arnold Toynbee and others, provides an anthology of various viewpoints on death and afterlife.

Real classics providing insights into the best of early research with mediums are Myers's two volumes, *Human Personality and Its Survival of Bodily Death* (1903), and Murphy and Ballou's (1969) compendium of William James's work. Another overview of primarily British research is provided by Salter (1961), and philosophical problems related to the question of life after death are covered by Ducasse (1961). Works on evidence for reincarnation are presented by Stevenson (1974, 1975, 1977, 1980, 1983). Evidence from so-called cross correspondences, which ostensibly were messages from dead scholars given early in this century through different psychics in Britain, the United States, and India, are like scattered pieces of picture puzzles that make sense only if they are put together. These are thoughtfully discussed by Murphy (1961) and Saltmarsh (1939). More detailed insights into the pioneering British work with mediums are provided by K. and Z. Richmond

(1938) (1939). Apparitions are thoughtfully discussed by MacKenzie (1971), 1982) and Tyrrell (1962). The most balanced and objective presentation of some of the best work has been done with mediums is presented by a British psychologist, Alan Gauld (1982). This book carefully evaluates and weighs other explanations, and finds the life after death hypothesis to best fit the data on record.

Many living persons have reported so-called out-of-body experiences. In these experiences, they feel that their consciousness leaves the body, travels to another location (perhaps within the same room but often to another city, state, or even another country), moves around, observes, and operates there—away from the body. One of us performed a careful laboratory study of out-of-body experiences which explored brain processes during this state (Osis and Mitchell, 1977), and another study which focused on perception and physical indices of the out-of-body presence (Osis and McCormick, 1980). Apparitions of such out-of-body projections are not frequent, but on rare occasions they have been observed simultaneously by several persons (Hart, 1954, 1954–56; Osis and Haraldsson, 1976 [unpublished]. Apparitions of the dead[2] also have been witnessed simultaneously by multiple observers (Hart, 1953–56; Tyrrell, 1962; Haraldsson, 1985). Mediums, shamans, Yogis, and other seers all over the world have reported contact with the dead. There are, of course, a great number of claims of such phenomena which do not stand up under scientific scrutiny. However, some of the mediumistic phenomena were found under careful investigation to be strikingly impressive. One example is the cross correspondences,[3] especially the famous cases of "Lethe" and "Ear of Dionysius" (Murphy, 1961) in which very obscure sources of classical Greek literature were ostensibly communicated through an entranced woman and through other gifted sensitives who had not studied classical literature. The messages supposedly came from two dead classical scholars who had taught at Oxford, A. W. Verrall and S. H. Butcher. Stevenson's thorough research on reincarnation memories and xenoglossy (speaking in foreign languages, including extinct ones, which are not known to the speaker) also provide support to the postmortem survival hypothesis (Stevenson, 1974, 1974, 1984).

Spontaneous experiences of contact with the dead are surprisingly widespread. In a national opinion poll conducted by Andrew

Greeley of the National Opinion Research Center at the University of Chicago in 1973, the following blunt question was put to a representative sampling of 1,467 Americans: "Have you ever felt as though you were really in touch with someone who had died?" Twenty-seven percent of the American population said that they had. Greeley states: "Over fifty million people have such experiences; six million have them often." We have comparable information from one European country, Iceland, where 31 percent of the population claim to have had some kind of contact with the dead (Haraldsson, 1976). Widows and widowers, who had lost a very meaningful person, reported encounters with their dead spouses twice as often—51 percent (Greeley, 1975).

In spite of the high scientific quality of this poll, we found it very hard to believe that half of the widowed Americans were indeed "in touch with the dead." It seemed that one could not reach Heaven that easily! However, another study in Britain reached the same conclusions when using an entirely different method. The researcher, W. D. Rees, contacted all the widows and widowers that he could reach (81 percent) in selected communities and found essentially the same results: 47 percent had, at some time, experienced contact with their dead spouses. Of that number, 39 percent felt their presence, 14 percent saw and 13 percent heard them, while 12 percent talked to them. In addition, 3 percent of those interviewed were touched by their deceased marital partners (Rees, 1971).

Do people tell of such experiences freely? The answer is a definite "No!" Only 28 percent of those widows and widowers who reported to the interviewers in the British survey that they had had such experiences had disclosed them to someone else. The most common reason for keeping the experience to themselves was fear of ridicule. Furthermore, not a single one of these people talked to his doctor about it (Rees, 1971)! Apparently, the medical profession in Britain is not readily entrusted with such experiences. This, in turn, would tend to reinforce the doctor's dominant opinions of such "nonexistent" phenomena. The patient's distrust is quite likely one of the reasons that many doctors of long years of practice have heard from neither patients nor relatives about phenomena suggestive of an afterlife. It takes such warm, outgoing, and deeply concerned professionals as Dr. Kübler-Ross, Dr. Charles Garfield, and Dr. Michael Sabom (Garfield, 1975, 1982) to fully observe such phenomena.

Later on, George Gallup (director of the Gallup Poll organization) with William Practor (writer) published a major study (1982). Three representative groups of Americans were sampled: the general population of the U.S., elite scientists, and elite medical doctors sampled from *Who's Who In America*. This study provides a wealth of information (and opinions) about how Americans view issues concerning life after death. The tables of poll statistics alone consist of 37 full pages.

One question, "Do you believe in life after death or not?" received 67% affirmative answers; 27% were responses of "No," and 6% of "No opinion." Who are the skeptics? Surprisingly, the largest proportion of "nay sayers" come from non-white, uneducated (grade school), low income groups residing in large cities with populations of one-million or more.

Questions on near-death experiences were also asked by Gallup: 15% of Americans said they had been "on the verge of death or had a close call." Then Gallup states: "The findings suggest that as many as eight million Americans, or about one third of those who have been involved in near-death occurrences, may have felt the presence of some being or otherwise have had a positive other-worldly experience" (p. 14). It is surprising that eight million such experiences could go unrecognized until recently.

CHAPTER 3

Research on Deathbed Visions:
Past and Present

DEATHBED visions have always been with us. They can be found in biographies and literature from all ages. Despite this fact, scientific studies are lacking. Two pioneers of psychical research, British classical scholar Frederic Myers and Columbia University philosopher James H. Hyslop, described deathbed visions in several cases, but they did not undertake a special investigation of them. So deathbed visions remained practically unknown to scientific circles until they intruded into the home of a physics professor at the Royal College of Science in Dublin, Sir William Barrett.

On the night of January 12, 1924, Barrett's wife, a physician specializing in obstetrical surgery, rushed home from the hospital very excited, eager to tell her husband of a case she had been involved with. It seems that Lady Barrett had been called in to deliver the child of Doris (her married name was withheld from the written account), and although her baby was born in a safe condition, Doris herself was dying. As Lady Barrett described it:

Suddenly she looked eagerly towards one part of the room, a radiant smile illuminating her whole countenance. "Oh, lovely, lovely," she said. I asked, "What is lovely?" "What I *see*," she replied in low, intense tones. "What do you see?" "Lovely brightness—wonderful beings." It is difficult to describe the sense of reality conveyed by her intense absorption in the vision. Then—seeming to focus her attention more intently on one place for a moment—she exclaimed, almost with a kind of joyous cry, "Why, it's Father! Oh, he's so glad I'm coming; he *is* so glad. It would be perfect if only W. (her husband) would come too."

Her baby was brought for her to see. She looked at it with interest, and then said, "Do you think I ought to stay for baby's sake?" Then turning towards the vision again, she said, "I can't—I can't stay; if you could see what I do, you would know I can't stay."

Apparently the young woman "saw" something so real to her, so gratifying, so valuable, that she was willing to give up her life and her own baby!

But she turned to her husband, who had come in, and said, "You won't let baby go to anyone who won't love him, will you?" Then she gently pushed him to one side, saying, "Let me see the lovely brightness."[1]

Could all this have merely been wish fulfillment expressed in the form of a hallucination? Barrett considered such an explanation, but he rejected it because among the apparitions of the dead was someone whom Doris had not expected to see. Her sister, Vida, had died three weeks before. However, Doris had been kept uninformed of this because of her precarious health. Therefore, Doris was a bit surprised when the following occurred.

She spoke to her father, saying, "I am coming," turning at the same time to look at me, saying, "Oh, he is so near." On looking at the same place again, she said with a rather puzzled expression, "He has Vida with him," turning again to me saying, "Vida is with him." Then she said, "You do want me, Dad; I am coming."[2]

Barrett was so impressed by the apparition of Vida that he

gathered together all the cases he could and thoughtfully presented them in a small book entitled *Death-bed Visions* (1926).

This was the first systematic study of its kind. Barrett found that in their visions the dying see dead persons who have come to take them away to a heavenly abode. He also found that such visions often occur when the mind of the patient is clear and rational, and that they sometimes portray what the dying do not expect. For example, children were surprised to see "angels" without wings. Moreover, in several of Barrett's cases, the apparitions were received either with exalted feelings or with emotions of serenity and peace. He also reported a few cases where a relative or a nurse who was present seemed to have shared the patient's visions of the dead.

Thirty years later, Barrett's book inspired one of us (Osis) to make a systematic study of deathbed experiences, using modern survey methods only recently available. Osis was struck by the fact that the psychical researchers, except for Barrett, had totally neglected to look at the experiences of the dying themselves, placing great emphasis instead on apparitions of the dead seen by relatives at or after the individual's death. Why not collect the patients' own experiences, he thought, and do so in sufficient number and detail to enable them to be scientifically analyzed?

Osis also noticed that the reports of professional medical personnel in Barrett's book seemed more detached, more objective than accounts given by clergymen or relatives who attended the dying. As in the case of Lady Barrett, Osis thought that this former group would be reliable witnesses. He therefore decided to carry out a mass survey that would ask thousands of doctors and nurses about the deathbed visions of their patients.

A properly conducted survey would require large resources in terms of qualified workers and funding. Fortunately, the circumstances were right for such a survey. At that time, Osis was the director of research at the Parapsychology Foundation in New York, of which Eileen Garrett was president. This remarkable woman was one of the most gifted psychics of her day. She was also a writer and publisher. She literally lived between two worlds, being able to see identifiable images of dead relatives around the visitors to her office while remaining fully functional in the physical world. Nevertheless, Eileen Garrett often questioned the reality of what she saw. She had known Sir William Barrett personally, and so she warmly agreed with Osis's research plan.

The foundation was supported by a prominent congresswoman, Frances P. Bolton, who is a member of the Whitney and Payne families. The planned deathbed observation survey impressed her as a scientific venture into the realm of the spiritual. Friends of the foundation, the eminent writer Aldous Huxley and the well-known research psychiatrist Dr. Humphrey Osmond, were helpful and quite enthusiastic about the project. Some medical advisers, however, were highly skeptical, predicting a total rejection of the questionnaire. And, indeed, the questionnaire did bring in some sarcastic comments. "Why don't you spend your time better—whittling!" "I don't believe in extrasensory conception!" However, other doctors responded enthusiastically and told impressive stories of how deathbed observations had changed their own outlook on life and death.

The pilot survey, carried out in 1959–60, was a success, bringing back 640 questionnaires. The respondents based their answers on observations of 35,000 dying patients. They said that they had seen about 700 cases of a rise in their patients' moods before death, 900 cases of visions, and 1,300 of apparitions. One hundred ninety of the respondents were interviewed in great depth, providing sufficient data for a valid scientific analysis. By 1961, the project had been completed. A report on it was published by the Parapsychology Foundation as a monograph, *Deathbed Observations by Physicians and Nurses.* [3]

In 1962, Osis became director of research of the American Society for Psychical Research. The ASPR, founded in 1885, has over the decades carried out large-scale research in ESP, psychokinesis, mediumship, and other psychic phenomena. In his new position, Osis designed a second survey of deathbed observations in consultation with experts in medicine, psychiatry, and survey design. Its purpose: to confirm or deny the earlier findings. The plan: a systematic survey of 5,000 doctors and nurses, chosen randomly from the five states in the New York area.

The plan was a costly project, and in 1962 the operations of the ASPR were at a low ebb, so low that it looked as if the project would not get funded. Then Chester F. Carlson, the legendary inventor of the Xerox machine, appeared on the scene. He was a physicist and had initially shared the materialistic world view of his colleagues. However, when confronted with facts of a spiritual and parapsychological nature, he changed his outlook. His own experiments with his psychically gifted wife, Doris, convinced Carlson that there is much more to reality than science ordinarily admits.

When Osis first presented his plans for a deathbed observation survey to him, Carlson was well aware that according to the opinion of the scientific community life after death is impossible. However, they had passed the same verdict when he proposed his invention of xerography; twenty major corporations, including IBM and Eastman-Kodak, had turned Carlson down. So, after a careful study of the project, Carlson concluded that the impossible could once again be done.

In a consciously ironic move, he funded this "impossible" project with the income from his invention of the "impossible" machine. Carlson was pleased to see that the medical professions now responded more favorably to the deathbed observation questionnaires. A total of 1,004 responses came back, representing approximately 50,000 observations of dying patients.

Osis now had sufficient data to perform analyses of the medical and psychological variables surrounding deathbed visions. However, the analysis of cultural factors came to a dead stop. The trouble was that Americans are too alike—they all have the same background of biblical religion. It became clear to Osis and his co-workers that American deathbed visions had to be compared to those of a culture where the Bible is not part of the population's religious upbringing. Where else, they wondered, could they determine whether deathbed visions are a reflection of Bible stories, kind of a playback of what Americans learn through acculturation? The president of the ASPR, Gardner Murphy, suggested Japan. Carlson opted for India. After considering all factors, India became the choice.

Unfortunately, before this portion of the study was funded, Chester F. Carlson died. Other major foundations, when approached, proved unready for anything as unconventional as a project on life after death. While research on death-as-destruction was generally supported, no one was ready to even consider the afterlife hypothesis—in spite of the fact that opinion polls showed 70 percent of the American people believing in it. Whatever else may be said about the process of allocating public funds in a democratic country, it can only be described as arrogant to deny the interest of 70 percent of the population.

Thus the deathbed observation project was shelved, and nothing more was done about it until the case of James Kidd arose in 1964. Kidd was a miner in Phoenix, Arizona. To his neighbors, he appeared to be very poor. He even borrowed a prospector's pick when searching for minerals in the Superstition Mountains of Arizona. He lived in the cheapest room he could rent, at four dollars a week.

On the morning of November 9, 1949, Kidd once again went prospecting, but this time he did not come back. He was declared dead a few years later. When a safe-deposit box in a Douglas, Arizona, bank was opened because the rent on it was long overdue, a large number of securities was found. A will, scribbled in pencil on a piece of paper, was also discovered. It read:

> this is my first and only will and is dated the second of January, 1946. I have no heirs and have not been married in my life and after all my funeral expenses have been paid and $100. one hundred dollars to some preacher of the gospel to say fare well at my grave sell all my property which is all in cash and stocks with E. F. Hutton Co Phoenix some in safety deposit box, and have this balance money to go in a research or some scientific proof of a soul of the human body which leaves at death I think in time their can be a Photograph of soul leaving the human at death, James Kidd.

Little is known about James Kidd.[4] Apparently, he lived a very simple, reclusive life. A fellow miner called him a "book-head," saying, "You could learn from Jim, because he always had something to offer. I used to tell the other boys, 'Stop, drink, and listen, fellows, and you'll learn.' "[5]

In July 1971, after a long litigation among 130 contenders, Kidd's $270,000 legacy was granted to the ASPR so that it could test the following hypothesis:

> We present the hypothesis that some part of the human personality indeed is capable of operating outside the living body (becoming ecsomatic) on rare occasions, and that it may continue to exist after the brain processes have ceased and the organism is decayed.

The ASPR used two-thirds of these funds for its own research, while one-third was spent in support of work at the Psychical Research Foundation in Durham, North Carolina, which is devoted to study of the question of life after death.

Although James Kidd had only a grade-school education, he nevertheless stirred up worldwide interest in research on the existence of a soul which might leave the body at death. The news media carried the terse message of his will all over the world. Newspapers gave wide coverage to the 130 claimants' court arguments. *Life*, *Reader's Digest*, and many other publications told Kidd's story.

The week after the court decision was announced in 1969, four television crews from different networks came to the ASPR. The world wanted to know if research could prove the reality of a long-cherished concept, the immortal soul. Scholars of great erudition have written volume after volume about this problem. As mentioned earlier, the list includes the noted historian Arnold Toynbee, such philosophers of world stature as C. J. Ducasse and H. H. Price, such leading writers as Aldous Huxley, and the eminent psychologist Gardner Murphy. But no one has attracted as much international interest as the simple scribblings of the uneducated miner James Kidd.

Thus, the funds for an Indian survey became available. But a survey in India required resources other than money. At that time, one of us (Haraldsson) who was uniquely qualified for the Indian survey joined the ASPR team. He had spent a year in India prior to undertaking psychology studies in U.S. and German universities. He had traveled extensively in the East and had written a book on Kurdistan which was published in Icelandic and German. Haraldsson brought his much-needed firsthand experience of the Orient to the project.

Thus we formed a team which we felt had the necessary training and experience to undertake this major study. In addition, we also had well-qualified psychologist friends in India who knew local conditions and had many contacts in northern India. Dr. Jamuna Prasad, at that time director of the Bureau of Psychology in India's most populous state, Uttar Pradesh, was enthusiastic about the project. However, he clearly saw that our American methods would not work in India and therefore, after considering the possibilities, persuaded us to change the procedures. Several of Dr. Prasad's staff members, especially Parmashwar Dayal, contacted medical authorities throughout the state and provided us with the necessary information. Dr. Ian Stevenson of the University of Virginia was a very valuable consultant. He had traveled widely in India for his own research on reincarnation memories in young children. He traveled with us during our first week there, assisting in many ways. Dr. Prasad also traveled with us at the beginning. He later assigned his staff members—Dayal in particular—to accompany us on our tours.

In Allahabad, after close consultation with Drs. Stevenson and Prasad, our survey methods were adapted to the conditions of India. Surveys by mail and phone were replaced with the new plan of face-to-face interviews with doctors and nurses. Telephones are used differently in India from the way they are in the West. The maximum length of a long-distance call is only nine minutes. Moreover, connections are slow and disorderly. It takes one to six hours—and sometimes days—before a monotonous voice delivers the great news: "Your call to Allahabad has matured." Faced with that situation, we had to conduct our interviews in person.

In India, nothing went as we thought it would, but nevertheless, everything worked out. The Indians could be admirably kind yet not keep appointments. Indian English is a second cousin to American English, and very difficult at first. For example, you would never be able to order a "Coke" in India and get it, but you would be able to quench your thirst if you asked for a "Coca-Cola."

Another difficulty was that Westerners have not developed antibodies as a defense against certain Indian diseases. Regardless of how thirsty you are in India's sweltering heat, we learned, never drink unboiled water or milk and never try to cool off with ice cream. Still, despite all such precautions, we suffered the classic problem of tourists—dysentery.

Traffic in northern India is an unimaginable mixture of twentieth-century vehicles and those of ages past. Cars honk their horns all the time as they wiggle through a variety of highway users who move at the incredible speed of four miles per hour. These include oxcarts, horse-drawn carriages known as *tonga*, innumerable cows, donkeys carrying loads, herds of goats, strings of camels, and, every now and then, an elephant. Nor do these roads lack rickshaws—specially built tricycles for a driver and two passengers.

The rickshaw drivers were eager to be hired by us. After all, they figured, these foreigners don't understand the native currency, so they just might pay twice the normal fare—ten cents more! Moreover, some taxis would not start unless one got out and gave a push.

India has an educated class of about fifty million people, whose culture is highly developed and who have modern Western tastes. They live side by side with a mass of five hundred million poor souls who look as though they stepped out of previous centuries.

Medical schools in India maintain high standards, with most of the faculty trained either in Britain or the United States. The older doctors are well established and live in comfortable apartments or private houses. An intern or resident might be housed in an austere single room with bare concrete walls. When we arrived at a hospital, usually the professor of medicine or professor of surgery would call his staff of twenty to fifty physicians to meet us. On the whole, Indian doctors were kind to us and more generous with their time than the Americans were. Nearly all of them filled in our questionnaires.

Indian nurses are very often Christians; Hindus seem to be prejudiced against nursing. The status of the nurse in India is lower than in American hospitals. For example, nurses listened in apparent disbelief when we told them that doctors frequently marry nurses in America. Most Christian nurses come from the state of Kerala in southwest India. As the legend goes, Christianity was brought to Kerala by a direct disciple of Jesus—the doubting Thomas. Although his mission was very successful in Kerala, he was killed on orders from a maharaja near the present city of Madras.

Often the nurses knew very little English, so many of them were interviewed by our Indian colleague, Dayal. The doctors generally had a good command of the English language and felt offended if they were not interviewed by us personally. Indians are proud of the rapid growth of medical care in the years since they achieved independence, and they have good reason to be. For example, life expectancy has lengthened in that relatively short time from twenty-eight to forty-four years. We are indeed very thankful for the kind cooperation of the Indian medical profession.

During the 1960s and 1970s, we alone were working on the phenomenon of deathbed visions. Then, in the mid-1970s, a new surge of interest in such research occurred, stimulated mainly by the work of Dr. Elisabeth Kübler-Ross and Dr. Raymond A. Moody. Kübler-Ross, who is famous for her distinguished research on death and dying, had interviewed hundreds of terminally ill patients. They revealed to her the same kinds of experiences that had impressed Sir William Barrett fifty years earlier, and us later. While her work along these lines is not yet published, Kübler-Ross has said in a public statement that her data convinced her "beyond the shadow of a doubt" that an afterlife does indeed exist.

Moody published *Life After Life* in 1975. For it he gathered about fifty case histories of patients who were close to death but who were resuscitated and survived. This book has different strengths and weaknesses from ours, and it is highly recommended as valuable supplementary reading. Moody's data, collected mainly after lectures on survival research, came from members of the audience. He thoughtfully presents his findings, which were derived without statistical analyses of the factors involved. However, his cases are richer in detail and include more colorful descriptions of afterlife experiences than ours.

Moody's findings are for the most part in harmony with ours. His patients described to him the experience of a very rapid review of past events—like a film unrolling before their eyes. We encountered very few such experiences in our pilot survey, and we did not ask about them in the cross-cultural surveys. Our reason for this was that such panoramic memory recall also occurs in other situations, not just in patients who are near death.

A different type of study was conducted by Dr. Charles Garfield, a clinical psychologist at the University of California, San Francisco, who specializes in cases of patients facing life-threatening illness. Dr. Garfield's approach is to work for a month or more with terminally ill patients providing emotional support and developing friendship and trust. In the process, they generally share with him what they experience, and they do so much more freely than they would to a doctor with an impersonal bedside manner. In this way, Dr. Garfield has collected very detailed descriptions of what the dying see, and has given a thoughtful interpretation of them (1975).

New approaches to the study of near-death experiences appeared in the 1980s when professionals from different disciplines took an active interest in such phenomena. Dr. Michael Sabom, an assistant professor of cardiology, was able to use his status in the medical profession by interviewing patients in a teaching hospital. During his interviews he thought it important to maintain an unhurried, open-minded attitude, which contrasted dramatically against the depersonalized hospital routine. "Our goal was to create as private and uninterrupted an atmosphere as possible for interviewing and taperecording" (Sabom, 1982, p. 12). Altogether, 116 patients were interviewed, 71 of whom had experiences. Sabom brought to this work both his medical knowledge and the experience he acquired from being present at more than 100 resuscitations. Medical records were examined and patients' statements were carefully checked. Sabom also considered explanations other than those involving the paranormal, e.g., pharmacological causes (narcotics, endorphines), hypoxia (inadequate oxygen level in the brain), hallucinations, dreams, depersonalization, prior expectations, and the possibility that patients' anecdotes were fabrications which occurred at a subconscious level. None of these alternatives sufficed to account for the phenomena. A special control group was formed of patients who also were close to death, but who did not have a near-death experience. Sabom asked this control group to make up near-death stories, and then he compared these fantasy productions with his sample of real near-death experiences; he found the the two sets of data quite different—that made-up stories contained major errors. Thus, knowledge from TV medical shows is not sufficient explanation of near-death experiences. Sabom's book is especially valuable because of his careful study of out-of-body experiences occurring in near-death states. Sabom cautiously concludes that "the out-of-body hypothesis simply seems to fit best with the data at hand" (p. 184).

Psychologist, Kenneth Ring, interviewed 102 patients, 49 of whom had near-death experiences (Ring, 1980). He applied to this small sample psychological assessment methods, such as rating scales, evaluations based on a consensus of "judges" (his students), and grading the experiences from moderate to deep. Ring later published a book subtitled: "In search of the meaning of near-death experiences" (Ring, 1984). In this latter study, Ring included persons he had encountered during his lectures and through the files of the International Association for Near-Death Studies. This was a highly self-selected sample of interested individuals. While Sabom carefully evaluated the authenticity of his patients' reports, Ring included individuals who spoke about their near-death experiences on public lecture circuits and who were propagating their own philosophies. The strength of Ring's study was his wide use of psychological questionnaires and assessment scales. His book sparkles with new ideas and speculative interpretations that are in line with "New Age" philosophies.

Psychiatrists, Glen Gabbard and Stewart Twemlow, published a book (1984) on out-of-body experiences which includes 34 experients who felt that they were out-of-body when near death. This book is relevant to near-death studies, because the authors very carefully compared the ostensible out-of-body phenomena with such mental disorders as depersonalization, autoscopy, and schizophrenic boundary disturbances. The experiential characteristics of each particular disorder are presented side-by-side with the characteristics of out-of-body experiences, including those reported by persons who were near-death. The differences between both groups are very clear: the mental disorders do not explain near-death experiences.

While each of these four books based on empirical studies and published in the 1980s contributes important points about the processes involved, *At The Hour of Death* is the only one which has the afterlife hypothesis as its main focus.

We are very encouraged by this resurgence of research on deathbed visions. We hope that it will be broadened to include all of the basic phenomena suggestive of an afterlife—apparitions collectively seen, out-of-body experiences, reincarnation memories, and mediumistic communications—that are ostensibly coming to us from the dead. If the knowledge acquired from all these phenomena unmistakably points to the same source—an afterlife—then humanity will gain a new realism on the questions of how to live and how to die.

CHAPTER 4

The Pilot Survey:
A Most Encouraging Start

HOW did we go about getting the information reported here?
Three large-scale surveys on the experiences of dying patients
were carried out.

1. *A pilot study*, a national survey, conducted by Osis in the
United States in 1959–60 under the auspices of the Para-
psychology Foundation. We sometimes refer to it as the first
American survey.

2. *A United States survey* conducted by Osis in 1961–64 in five
states, New York, New Jersey, Connecticut, Rhode Island, and
Pennsylvania. We sometimes call this the second American
survey.

3. *An Indian survey* conducted in 1972–73 by both of us in
northern India.

The pilot study, published as a monograph by the Parapsychol-
ogy Foundation in 1961, was entitled *Deathbed Observations by
Physicians and Nurses*. This chapter will summarize it. The United
States and Indian surveys are reported here for the first time at
length, although a technical paper was published in the *Journal of the
American Society for Psychical Research* in 1977.

The United States and Indian surveys were conducted in two stages. In the first stage, our respondents, who were physicians and nurses, were asked to fill out an initial, short questionnaire. If on the questionnaire they reported observations of pertinent cases, they were contacted for individual interviews, which comprised the second stage of our survey. With that overview of the entire research program, we will now describe the pilot study. Later chapters will deal with the second American survey and the Indian survey.

In late 1959, a questionnaire was mailed to a stratified random sample of 5,000 physicians and 5,000 nurses practicing in the United States. This sample included 2,000 general practitioners, 1,000 hospital staff physicians, 1,000 residents, 1,000 interns, 2,500 general-duty nurses, and 2,500 private-duty nurses. The questionnaire asked about the extent of their experience with dying patients. We wanted to know how many they had seen die, as well as their observations of patients' hallucinatory behavior and emotional states shortly before death. These questions were also asked about patients who had had a close brush with death but who had recovered, or "come back." Specific inquiries were made about patients who had reported seeing apparitions, such as of a living brother or a dead mother or of religious figures (for example, Christ). Visions of a primarily environmental context—such as heavenly cities or beautiful gardens immersed in supernal light—were also ascertained. Still another question asked for observations of a dying patient's sudden rise in mood to exaltation. Minor questions were concerned with out-of-body cases, a patient's prediction of his or her own death, and panoramic memory, as if in the form of a "life film" unrolling shortly before death.

In the late 1950s, professional circles held a much stronger bias against paranormal phenomena than they do now. However, in spite of apparent prejudices, 640 medical observers returned their questionnaires. These reported a total of 35,540 observations of dying patients. A surprisingly large number of patients were said to have experienced relevant phenomena: 1,318 of them saw apparitions, 884 reported visions, and 753 experienced mood elevation shortly before death. Apparently the dying do experience much that has some bearing on the question of postmortem survival—for example, having extrasensory glimpses of a possible afterlife.

One hundred ninety cases of interest were followed up with

questionnaires and long-distance telephone interviews. For each type of phenomenon, a special questionnaire was designed to guide the interviewer. We obtained 150 apparition cases, a sample size sufficiently large for detailed statistical analysis. The interview samples of other phenomena were comparatively small—25 visions and 15 mood-elevation cases—thereby justifying the term "pilot study."

The interviews served to explore each case in depth, enabling detailed descriptions of the phenomena to be solicited. For example, the respondents were asked: Who was portrayed by the apparition? Was the patient's perception of hospital surroundings intact during the experience? Why did the "visitor" appear? How did the patient react to the apparition? How long after the hallucination did the patient die? And so on.

We further inquired into such medical conditions as the diagnosis of the main illness, a medical history including a hallucinogenic background, high temperature, sedation, and medication—all of which could possibly cause the patient to hallucinate. Relevant personal information on the patient's name, age, sex, education, religious denomination, attitude toward religion, and belief in a life after death were also collected.

All these factors were statistically analyzed. Equally important were the interactions among them. While some hallucinatory behavior was found to be of pathological origin—just ramblings about this-world concerns—in the greater part of the cases, the visions did not look like ordinary hallucinations. For example, the dying person might be quite rational and well oriented in all respects but still insist that he or she saw apparitions that were "coming to take him away" to another world. Generally such experiences were of a shorter duration, more coherent, and more related to the situation of dying and of an afterlife than the rambling productions of a sick brain. This confirmed the previous findings of the older clinical case observations made by Barrett (1926) and Hyslop (1908)—namely, the majority of the hallucinations of persons were truly apparitional in the sense that only a person was hallucinated or perceived by ESP while the patient's perception of the room and the attending physicians remained intact. In our data of terminal patients, 83 percent of the hallucinated human figures were relatives, and nearly all of those (90 percent) whose relationship to the patient was identified were close ones: mother, father, spouse, siblings, off-spring. This contrasts sharply with the hallucinations of those who were mentally ill, where the majority of hallucinated persons were either strangers or bizarre characters.

As was predicted from early clinical studies, the dying did indeed see more than twice as many apparitions of dead persons (70 percent) than of the living. For individuals in a normal state of health who witnessed apparitions, this trend is reversed. In surveys conducted in Europe and the United States, 10 to 17 percent of persons in the normal population have experienced hallucinations (Sidgwick, 1894; West, 1948; Palmer and Dennis, 1975). Of these hallucinations, two to five times more were of living persons than of dead ones.

What is the reason for such a surprising number of apparitions of the deceased "coming" to the dying? In the majority of cases, patients saw the mission of the apparition as that of taking him away to another world. In other words, the dying are ostensibly visited by dead relatives or religious figures for the expressed purpose of aiding them in their transition to another mode of existence.

Are such apparitions real? That is, are they perceived by ESP, or are they merely hallucinated because of the disturbed brain processes of the dying? Most of the analyses were devoted to scanning for patterns in the data which would give some support either to the "sick brain" hypothesis or the afterlife hypothesis—that is, that the apparitions were real. All patients who had a medical history that might cause hallucinations—for example, brain disease and/or injury—were grouped together and compared to the rest. The hallucinogenic disease group did not see more dead relatives than the others. On the contrary, their hallucinations were more rambling, disjointed, and concerned with this-world purposes, such as reliving past memories or conversing with imaginary visitors in the hospital. While the majority of patients who were not in the hallucinogenic disease group saw apparitions which came to take them away to another world, only one-third of the patients with hallucinogenic maladies attributed such a purpose to the apparitions. High temperature and sedation such as morphine or Demerol (meperidine) did not increase the frequency of seeing otherworldly apparitions. The same applies to the patients' state of consciousness. As Osis reported in his *Deathbed Observations* monograph, "Deathbed patients see apparitions more often when fully conscious and having proper awareness and capability of responding to the environment than when awareness and communication are impaired."[1]

Furthermore, the analyses "clearly indicate that delirium is not the basis of those types of deathbed apparitions, which fit into the concept of the afterlife hypothesis."[2] Basic personality differences between men and women or young and old did not matter. Both sexes had the same share of father and mother apparitions. Moreover, while ordinary hallucinations depend on personality, the visions of the dying were unaffected by this factor. The apparitions seemed to have an external source instead of being mere projections of wishful thoughts or unfulfilled desires.

Of all the apparitions identified as relatives, 90 percent were of the closest kind: father, mother, spouse, siblings, offspring. According to the survival hypothesis, we would expect that the closest relatives would be the ones most interested in the patient and therefore the most likely to visit him. However, close ties might also motivate the patient to hallucinate the person without any paranormal presence. Such hallucinations may, of course, represent the living and the dead equally well. If close relatives were to come with the mission of taking the patient away to another mode of existence, then naturally they would be the dead ones. Indeed, there was a much larger proportion of apparitions of the dead when they were close relatives (83 percent) than with other relatives (50 percent) or people not related to the patient (43 percent).

Did the presence of the apparition, who purportedly came to take the patient away, in any way influence the process of dying? There were some suggestive differences. Of those who died almost instantly (within ten minutes) after seeing the apparition, 76 percent said that the apparition had come to "take them away"; of those who died after a period of one hour or longer, the percentages varied from 44 to 25 percent. Would such a striking difference indicate that apparitions "take away" the patient—that is, hasten the process of dying?

If the apparition is a messenger from another world, would it be experienced with emotions characteristic of all kinds of encounters with the other world, such as the "peace which passes all understanding" that mystics report? The questions were not this sharply formulated, but about half (46 percent) of the patients were calmed by the apparition. This included the "radiant peace" so often reported. Furthermore, a feeling of peace and calm was a far more common occurrence among the fully conscious patients (66 percent) than among the others.

It was concluded that these and other trends found in the pilot study are supportive of the afterlife hypothesis. As this was the first survey of its kind, it was felt that these very interesting results needed further verification. A new survey could indicate whether the phenomena were indeed related to an extrasensory glimpse into the beyond, and not merely unusual coincidences. However, circumstances arose which prevented a second survey from being conducted immediately after the first. Those circumstances included some very colorful ones, including what has been referred to as "the great soul trial." Nevertheless, the second American survey and its cross-cultural check, the Indian survey, were eventually completed. We will devote the next chapter to a general presentation of what the dying see.

CHAPTER 5

What the Dying See

D EATHBED visions are experiential in nature. We therefore invite the reader to look at these experiences as they were told to us, to get a "feel" for what they are about. In this way, our analysis and discussion of the statistical data relating to the cases will be more meaningful. Of course, later it will be absolutely necessary to use clear, theoretical thinking and sharp analysis in order to unscramble the real from the fantasies and waking dreams. But no one can get to the wheat without first threshing away the chaff. Therefore we will first present some cases reported in the second American and Indian surveys.

It would be wrong to think that every time a patient "sees" someone who is invisible to the doctor an apparition is present. There are plenty of rambling, confused hallucinations where the patient mumbles something in his waking dream which does not make any sense to the medical observer. We did not consider such cases in our analyses.

In addition, not all of the visions that were coherent enough for analysis had any relation to the death situation. Some were as this-life oriented as they could be. For example, a thirty-year-old Indian watchmaker was getting even with an enemy who had shot him in the shoulder and chest by hallucinating revenge. He hallucinated burning down his adversary's shops in the bazaar.

Sometimes the hallucination serves simply to compensate the

social deprivation situation of being alone in a secluded hospital
room. An American cancer patient, a woman fifty-eight years old,
had a regular distinguished "visitor."

Every evening when I would come back from dinner she would
tell me the rabbi had been there with her. I thought maybe a
real rabbi was visiting her, but I asked on the floor, and no one
ever came in the room. Almost every evening. It made her feel
better apparently.

Sometimes hallucinations might even serve to excuse a bed-
wetting patient from very mundane routines, as in the following case
of a poor Indian villager who was suffering from heart disease.

He hallucinated either every morning or in the middle of the
night. He used to say that he had seen this or that person in his
village (alive). Sometimes he would urinate in his bed. When
asked about it he would say, "I did not do it; so-and-so came
and pushed me out of my bed, laid in it and did this." He did
not like them. Sometimes he turned his back on them in order
not to see them. He even covered himself with a sheet, saying,
"So-and-so is coming."

In sorting out the cases, we had to beware of hallucinations that
were pathological in nature. There were many such examples in
which the mind seemed to deteriorate as the body's processes were
grinding to a halt. Consider the report of an American woman in her
seventies, a cardiac case.

In the beginning she hallucinated about people who had
recently expired. As time progressed she hallucinated about
people who had been dead for a long time. She regressed in age
with each hallucination until finally she was in her baby
stage—goo-goo, da-da—and expired curled up in a uterine
position. Once the patient had communicated with a person,
she never reverted back to him again. She would go on to the
next one and correspondingly act younger herself.

Cases like these are, of course, easily explicable in terms of the destruction hypothesis, which assumes that the extinction of the personality accompanies the deterioration and final cessation of brain processes. Let us clearly state that there are many facts concerning death and dying which are consistent with the medical view of death as the ultimate destruction. We do not dispute them. However, we are attempting to call attention to a considerable body of previously overlooked phenomena which suggest afterlife. We feel that the data formerly mentioned can be rationally included in a larger picture without denying the possibility of life after death.

Returning to our sorting process, we did not disregard coherent hallucination cases which were obviously this-life oriented. Actually, they furnished us with a very important background for comparison. We carefully sifted and analyzed cases with a this-life orientation in order to see if the ones concerned with afterlife were different in any way. If afterlife-oriented cases were to follow the same patterns as those of this-life concerns, we would expect all hallucinations to spring from the same source: severely disturbed brain processes or schizoid reactions when faced with death. That would be the end of our inquiry. However, as we will discuss in later chapters, striking differences were found between this-life and other-world cases.

About half of our data concerns terminal patients (persons who died) who "saw" persons around them whom the medical observers did not see. We will call such cases "apparitions" or "hallucinations of persons." Many patients who were alert and aware reported hallucinations which appeared to be in some way suggestive of another world. A dying sixteen-year-old American girl had just come out of her coma. Her consciousness was very clear when she said to the respondent:

"I can't get up," and she opened her eyes. I raised her up a little bit and she said, "I see him, I see him. I am coming." She died immediately afterwards with a radiant face, exultant, elated.

What could possibly make a sixteen-year-old girl "exultant" and "radiant" when giving up a life still unfulfilled? The shortened span of years did not seem to matter. We will see this same, inexplicable fascination with an unseen "something" again and again. The same patients who were in pain, who were miserable and scared, seemed to take a peek at the "other-world" reality and become "exultant" and "radiant"—eager to go into it. This young girl did not tell whom she saw. However, in many cases, like the following one of an Indian woman, a diabetes patient, we do know.

> She kept uttering words. I listened because the relatives thought she wanted to tell me something. She told me her mother, who had died many years before, had come, calling her to accompany her to the land of God. When I told this to her relatives, they asked me to tell her not to go. They took this as a bad omen: that she was dying and nothing could be done. The patient said she was going and seemed happy about it. "I am going; mother is calling me. I am going to the land of God." These were her last words. Before this experience, the patient had expected to recover.

This phenomenon was not for women only. A sixty-five-year-old man with cancer of the stomach seemed to be clear and rational when he would

> look into the distance; these things would appear to him and seemed real to him. He would look up to a wall, eyes and face would brighten up as if he saw a person. He'd speak of the light, brightness, saw people who seemed real to him. He would say, "Hello," and "There's my mother." After it was over he closed his eyes and seemed very peaceful. He gestured with out-stretched hands. Before the hallucination he was very ill and nauseous; afterwards he was serene and peaceful.

Here, not only was the patient overcome by the "peace which passeth understanding," but his vision had the otherworldly qual-ities of light and brightness which have often been reported in religious literature.

In some hallucinations the apparition seems so real to the patient that he blends this-world purposes with the otherworldly visitor. Such was the case of a man in his seventies, a cardiovascular patient who died at home. He had a clear consciousness, no fever, and he had been given no drugs.

He looked right past me..and called her [his deceased wife]:
"Mary," he said, "how about going out on the back porch and
getting me one of those fresh tomatoes?" At the conclusion of
his conversation with his wife he turned to me and said, "I
suppose you think I'm insane because I was talking to my wife,
but I saw her."

It all looked so real and convincing to the patient. Only very, very
rarely will a patient doubt the reality of this type of apparition.

Sometimes the apparition is a total surprise.

A man, 50, with coronary disease, saw an old friend who had
been dead for some time. "Why [he named the person] what are
you doing here?" These were the last words he spoke before he
died.

Apparently he "saw" what he did not expect to see.
In our studies we also came across some very interesting cases in
which the patient "saw" an apparition, and although his medical
condition was far from terminal, the patient died, anyway. In the
following case it seems that intimations of death are fulfilled in spite
of the doctor's prognosis. The case, which occurred approximately
three years prior to our interview, was reported by a physician in the
large Ervin Hospital in Delhi. A three- or four-year-old girl was
brought to the hospital by her parents. Three days earlier she had
started to continuously tell her parents that a god was calling her and
that she was going to die soon. The girl exhibited fear and anxiety.
The parents, being upset about her behavior, brought her to the
hospital, though the child did not complain of any sickness. The
physician said he had personally examined her and found her
healthy. She was shouting almost stereotypically, "God is calling
and I am going to die." They tried to divert her attention, but after a
few minutes she would repeat the same thing. In between, she
seemed absolutely normal. She was hearing and, apparently, also
seeing something but did not describe it. Though there did not seem
to be any reason for it, she was kept in the hospital at the insistence
of her parents. The following day, our respondent was very
surprised to learn from the doctor on duty that the girl had died from

a gradual circulatory collapse which had no apparent cause. This case baffled the respondent more than anything else he had experienced in his professional life.

The case is open to two explanations:

1. The child received a death call, via ESP, from some external source.
2. She died as a result of self-suggestion.

In this case, self-suggestion might be a reasonable explanation for the cause of death, but where did the suggestion come from in the first place? Apparently neither the child's parents nor her doctor had the slightest idea why a three-year-old, whose conception of death is still very limited, would chant herself into it. If the "call" did indeed come from an external source, we would be at a loss to identify it. For example, why did the child label this authoritative voice "God" rather than some other male of commanding manners, such as a dead grandfather?

The identity of the religious figure was also quite a problem in adult cases. If a patient sees a radiant man clad in white who induces in him an inexplicable experience of harmony and peace, he might *interpret* the apparition in various ways: as an angel, Jesus, or God; or if he is a Hindu, Krishna, Shiva, or Deva.

Although it occurs very seldom, some patients will restrain themselves from rendering their own interpretations of the religious figure's identity. Such is true in the following case, reported to us by an Indian physician. It occurred only a short time before our interview with him.

The patient [a merchant in his thirties], suffering from acute abdominal perforation, reported seeing some bright light and some new faces, that seemed as if they wanted him to join them, in the hallucination. The patient seemed to think he would die. Before that, he had expected to recover.

Raymond Moody, the University of Virginia psychiatrist who wrote *Life After Life*, calls such apparitions simply "figures of light"—a term that might describe these entities much better than the names of deities assigned to them by our patients.

Moreover, patients seemed to be convinced of the otherworldly nature of such apparitions, even if they did not like their purpose. In one of our cases, a nineteen-year-old girl saw her dead father coming for her, in addition to seeing *bright lights* and other people. In spite of the experience of light, a typical quality of otherworldly visitors, the girl was very scared. She called to the nurse, "Edna, hold me tight," and then died in her arms. Thus, the apparition and the patient seemed to be at cross purposes because she did not want to go. This certainly does not look like any form of self-suggestion or wish fulfillment.

In all of the above cases, the apparitional nature of the hallucination was evident. However, as stated before, we also have instances of "total hallucinations"—cases where the patient is either no longer aware of his surroundings or else speaks as if he were in two worlds at once. In some of these total hallucinations, we found that instead of the apparition's "coming" to the patient in his hospital room, the patient might either experience "going"—spontaneously traveling to the abode of the apparition—or else he might simply find himself there. Such was true of the following case of an Indian patient in his forties, suffering from a liver disease.

He was receiving no sedation, had a light fever, and appeared confused—only able to respond to questions with difficulty, although he seemed aware of his surroundings and the people around him. He described his experience both as it took place and also afterwards. The patient told of how he felt himself to be flying or moving in the air into another world, where he saw gods sitting and calling him. He wanted to go there and asked the people around him to let him go. "Go away from me, I am dying," he said. The patient was very happy to see those gods. He had this hallucination twice, and he insisted it was not a hallucination but a true experience. He was elated after his experience, and said that was the world he wanted to live in. Before the hallucination, he had not wanted to die; he was very much concerned about his illness and that the doctors should help him. After the hallucination, he was not concerned about dying; he looked better and felt very happy about his experience. An hour or two later he went into a deep coma, never regained consciousness. He died two days later.

Total hallucinations are quite different from hallucinations where the apparition is the only thing seen by the patient that the respondent cannot also see. Frequently the nature of this vision is just hinted at. A man in his twenties, who died from multiple gunshot wounds in the abdominal area, saw Jesus. He said, "If this is where I'm going, I am not afraid to die." His mood changed from fear to serenity and acceptance.

It is usually difficult to separate the total-hallucination cases from the out-of-body experiences because our medical observers failed to notice the subtle distinctions that might have differentiated the two phenomena. For example, the other world and its denizens might have appeared to the patient like a flash, as in ESP impressions. In other cases, like the one of the Indian patient with liver disease, they feel as though they are being transported to the other world, as in out-of-body experiences. Whatever the case, the finer details of otherworldly imagery seem to vary with the patient's background. Such major features as bright, saturated colors, peace, harmony, and extraordinary beauty seem, however, to prevail regardless of whether the patient is a Christian, Hindu, Jew, or Muslim.

The imagery might not always be expressed in symbols common to the patient's religion. Occasionally it is depicted in terms of the ancient mythology that the patient learned in school. For example, one man saw his wife standing beside a river, waiting for him. It seemed to be the "River of Forgetfulness" which flows between the two worlds, as related in the Greek myth of Lethe. In our cases from India, the Indian conception of Heaven was seen, rather than the Christian one of pearly gates and streets of gold. In India, the person is usually authoritatively called or even taken away by force. Quite often in the United States, the purpose of the hallucinatory person is expressed by beckoning, leading by the hand, or instructing the patient about where to go. Moreover, interpersonal relationships between the patient and the apparitional figure (deceased relative) are quite frequently so warm that they overshadow everything else, such as the instructing and guiding over. In one case, a patient saw his deceased childhood sweetheart, who had been killed in an accident before they were married. He said to her, "I waited and waited. I knew you were going to come to me."

Sometimes there is quite a conversation. For example, a mother was questioning her dead son about the circumstances in which he was killed in World War II. Such dialogue might also be quite elaborate. One of our respondents related the following story about a woman in her fifties with abdominal cancer.

> When I walked into the room she was carrying on a very vivid conversation with her husband. I looked at her son, who was sitting by her bedside, and he said to me, "She thinks she's conversing with my father who has been dead for seventeen years." The patient's eyes were open but she seemed to be in a trance. She spoke in a monotone: "The children are fine—we have grandchildren." It seemed as though she was bringing him up-to-date on the family events that he had missed since his death. She also answered several questions which her husband asked her.

Cases like this impressed our respondents, but there are also strong, negative reactions to deathbed visions of this sort, which illustrate the realness and warmth of human relations. A woman, sixty-nine, was dying of cancer.

> In a very soft voice, and with a smile on her face, she had an endearing conversation about how much she loved him [her husband], how much she missed him, and how she knew she would join him. She said, "It won't be long now before I'll be with you." Reaching out as if she felt his hand, "You look well and well-cared for."

The nurse told us her feelings in a grim voice.

> It was a frightening experience. One of the most startling things I've ever experienced. It was unnerving. My belief is limited. To see someone, where I'm sure and positive it wasn't drugs, there must have been something. The expression on her face was—I wish I'd had a camera. All wrinkles were gone from her face—smiling, pleasant, comfortable.

Another nurse said, "It was kind of creepy."

Unfortunately, in none of our cases did the patients search for the identity of the apparition, nor did the apparition try to prove itself.

Perhaps it takes a parapsychologist to demand credentials from his own mother.

In their visions, Western patients did not see personifications of death; however, quite a few Indians did. Yama is the god of death in Indian mythology. Yamdoots are his messengers who, according to Indian folklore, come for the dying. They can, some believe, take many forms when they come to take people to the realm of the dead, the form of their appearance depending on the kind of life the person has lived. An unusual characteristic of the following hallucination, in which a Yamdoot is involved, is that it was purely auditory.

An educated lady in her sixties was admitted to the hospital for a checkup, there being no clear diagnosis. I examined her carefully. She had a slight fever but otherwise seemed normal. After the examination, I remember her telling me, "I will recover." I answered, "No doubt you will; you simply have fever and after the investigation you can go home." Some 20 hours later she told visiting relatives that someone was whispering into her ear, "Your time is over; come with me." The relatives asked her who it was. "Yamdoot." The patient told this story two or three times. After that she was quiet and calm, became semi-conscious, and expired two or three hours later.

In this case, the Yamdoot seems to be different only in name from apparitions of religious figures in Western cases.

But a Yamdoot is not always peaceful. An experienced male nurse reported the following case.

The patient, a Hindu policeman in his forties, was suffering from pulmonary tuberculosis. He had, at that time, a low fever and had to be lightly touched or shaken before he would respond to questions. Suddenly he said: "Yamdoot is coming to take me away. Take me down from the bed so that Yamdoot does not find me." He pointed outwards and upwards. "There he is." This hospital room was on a ground floor. Outside, at the wall of the building, there was a large tree with a great number of crows sitting on its branches. Just as the patient had his vision, all the crows suddenly flew away from the tree with much noise, as if someone had fired a gun. We were very surprised by this and ran outside through an open door in the room, but we saw nothing that might have disturbed the crows. They were usually peaceful, so it was very memorable to all of us present when the crows flew away with a great uproar, exactly at the time the patient had his vision. It was as if they, too, had become aware of something terrible. As this happened, the patient fell into a coma and expired a few minutes later.

Another case coinciding with a physical effect was reported to us by a Christian nurse in India. Here, apparitions of this kind were called "angels." The patient was a male in his forties, suffering from tuberculosis of the lungs. The nurse had known him for several years as he was a close friend of her family.

He was unsedated, fully conscious and had a low temperature. He was a rather religious person and believed in life after death. We expected him to die and he probably did too as he was asking us to pray for him. In the room where he was lying, there was a staircase leading to the second floor. Suddenly he exclaimed. "See, the angels are coming down the stairs. The glass has fallen and broken." All of us in the room looked towards the staircase where a drinking glass had been placed on one of the steps. As we looked, we saw the glass break into a thousand pieces without any apparent cause. It did not fall; it simply exploded. The angels, of course, we did not see. A happy and peaceful expression came over the patient's face and the next moment he expired. Even after his death the serene, peaceful expression remained on his face.

The peculiar physical phenomena that coincided with the hallucinations just prior to death in the two cases above left a deep impression on our respondents. Visionary experiences of this kind are common in our sample, but the possible psychokinetic effects are rare. We report them here because they resemble numerous physical phenomena that occur near the time of death, usually at a place distant from the dying person but close to someone dear to him, that have been recorded in psychical research (Rhine, 1961). For example, when Thomas A. Edison died, the clocks belonging to two of his associates stopped at the time of his death; his own grandfather clock stopped only a few minutes later.

Let us now turn to cases in which the apparition seems to follow a will of its own, one that is quite contrary to the inclinations of the patient.

A Catholic woman, sixty-one, had cancer that was in its terminal stages. She saw the apparition of her mother and a vision of God, who, in the vision, seemed to have set a time for her death—the first Friday of the month, an auspicious day in the old Catholic tradition. The patient, however, had mixed up her calendar. Thinking that the *next* day would be the first Friday, she told the priest, "I want you to come tomorrow by ten of eight," when she expected to die. What actually happened was that she died—contrary to her expectations—at seven-fifty a week later, which was *actually* the first Friday of the month, as indicated in her vision.

The next case seems to suggest that bargains can be struck between patient and apparition. This cancer patient (sixty) was the nurse's sister. She saw her dead husband for three nights in a row.

He called her. He wanted her to come. She told him that she wasn't ready to go, not until Agnes [the nurse] was taken care of. It seemed that when she knew that, she was ready: "Now I am ready to go. I can go."

And she did. She died within twenty-four hours. The nurse was impressed. "Some hallucinations are induced by drugs, but some, like my sister's, it was different with her. She could see or forecast things that I never could."

Such experiences might happen to patients who are convinced that they will recover and who are not at all ready to "go." A cardiac patient, a fifty-six-year-old male whose consciousness was clear, saw the apparition of a woman who had come to take him away.

He stared at a bouquet of flowers—he did not seem to be repulsed by it [the apparition], just slightly frightened. He pointed to it and said, "There she is again, she is reaching for me." He described her hand and also the flowers, which were in the room. He did not particularly want to go, but he did not

make a fuss. He became calmer. This experience made him
serene. He died a day later.

At first the patient seemed to be at cross-purposes with the
apparition, but then the "otherworldly" encounter brought him
serenity, peace, and acceptance of his fate. Sometimes, however,
there is a very sharp clash. A college-educated Indian man in his
twenties was recovering from mastoiditis. He was doing very well.

He was going to be discharged that day. Suddenly at 5:00 a.m.
he shouted, "someone is standing here dressed in white clothes.
I will not go with you!" He was dead in ten minutes.

Both the patient and his doctor expected a definite recovery.
The following case is that of a Hindu woman in her thirties
suffering from second-degree burns. At first she interpreted the
apparition's take-away purpose as a cruel abduction. She pleaded
with the nurse:

"Please, sister, save me. There are four men dressed in white
coming toward me. They want me to accompany them." She
felt as if the four men were dragging her away.

The woman was in terror. However, after about ten minutes, she
said to the nurse:

"I then saw a big tree. On each leaf was written: Ram, Ram
[name of the chief Indian deity]."

She was now ready to die. Did she really have an ESP glimpse into
the afterlife, recognizing its value?

CHAPTER 6

To Be or Not to Be:
A Model of Deathbed Visions
and How We Tested It

WE learned much from the pilot survey. All the information
from it, when viewed together with such other sources as
parapsychology, psychology, and medicine, allowed us to formulate
a set of hypotheses about what the experience of dying would be like
if in fact there is an afterlife to be faced. Such sets of hypotheses are
generally called models. Architects build models of buildings prior
to actual construction; scientists formulate theoretical models which
can be "tested"—that is, found to be correct or incorrect through
controlled investigations. Similarly, we developed a model which we
expected to predict patterns of deathbed behavior. The model is
bipolar in the sense that it contrasts two mutually exclusive ideas:
the afterlife hypothesis and the destruction hypothesis. Furthermore, if one hypothesis is indicated by future findings, then the
other hypothesis will be contradicted. Thus, tentative conclusions
about the question of postmortem survival should result from the
research.

The following is an outline of the model of our basic hypothesis. It
presents our fundamental assumptions about deathbed visions as
indicators of survival, and also lists how these arguments could be
refuted by the destruction hypothesis.

CHART 1. MODEL OF THE TWO BASIC HYPOTHESES OF DEATHBED VISIONS

SURVIVAL
Death is the transition to another mode of existence.

DESTRUCTION
Death is the ultimate destruction of human personality.

1. SOURCE OF DEATHBED VISIONS

ESP
There are visions based upon ESP that are not caused by malfunctions of the nervous system and the dying brain.

a. Telepathic impressions from otherworldly visitors—for example, deceased relatives and religious figures.

b. Clairvoyant or precognitive glimpses of that mode of existence where life after death takes place.

Sick Brain and Morbid Reaction

a. Visions of the dying are caused by malfunctions of the nervous system and the dying brain.

b. Visions are schizoid reactions to alleviate severe stress and social deprivation in the hospital through escape into otherworldly imagery.

2. INFLUENCE OF MEDICAL FACTORS ON DEATHBED VISIONS

(Malfunction of the brain, medication such as morphine, uremia poisoning, high temperature, hallucinogenic history)

Relatively Independent
a. The presence of hallucinogenic factors will not increase frequency of phenomena related to postmortem existence.

b. Conditions detrimental to ESP will decrease the frequency of the phenomena.

Dependent on Medical Conditions
The presence of hallucinogenic factors will increase the frequency of the phenomena related to postmortem survival; the more disturbed the brain processes, the more numerous the otherworldly fantasies.

3. CONTENTS OF DEATHBED VISIONS

Perceptions
Contents of the visions will be of two kinds—either hallucinations or true perceptions of external reality via ESP.

Hallucinations
Contents of all visions will be hallucinations and will portray no information that is not already stored in the brain. They will express the

Perceptions

a. Hallucinations will be less coherent, rambling, expressing the
concerns of this life, memories, desires, and conflicts.

b. True perceptions will be more
coherent, oriented to the situation of
dying and the transition to another
world. They will try to portray
otherworldly messengers and an environment of which we have no adequate image or conception.

Hallucinations

memories, expectations, desires,
conflicts, and fears of the individual,
as well as his cultural conditioning
by family, society, and religious institutions.

4. INFLUENCE OF PSYCHOLOGICAL FACTORS ON DEATHBED VISIONS

(Clarity of consciousness, belief in life after death, belief in "another world"
[religion], patient's expectations of whether he will die or recover)

Conditions Related to
Awareness of Another World

a. Clarity of consciousness. Normal or such altered states where contact with reality is intact will facilitate awareness of another world and
its messengers, while states where
contact with external reality is absent will impair such awareness.

b. Openness to, and belief in, life
after death and another world (religion) will facilitate deathbed visions,
especially of the kind that cut across
individual, national, and cultural
differences.

c. Patients' expectancy of recovery from illness will not influence
the occurrence of deathbed visions.

d. Severe stress as indicated by a
patient's mood before hallucination
will not generate ESP and therefore
will not affect the frequency of seeing afterlife-oriented apparitions.

Conditions Related to
Hallucinations of This World
or Other-World Fantasies

a. Clarity of consciousness. Normal or altered states where contact
with reality is intact will be less conducive to all kinds of hallucinations
than states where contact with reality is lost.

b. Openness to, and belief in, life
after death and another world will
facilitate hallucinations of another
world, but they will be specific as to
the beliefs of the individual and of
his culture.

c. Patients' expectancy of recovery will facilitate this-life hallucinations, while expectancy of death will
generate hallucinations of afterlife
fantasies.

d. Severe stress will release schizoid coping reactions and thus increase the frequency of afterlife-
related hallucinations.

5. VARIABILITY OF CONTENTS ACROSS INDIVIDUALS AND CULTURES

Little variability. Perceptions involving basic characteristics of the other world will be essentially similar for men and women, young and old, educated and illiterate, religious and nonreligious, American and Indian, Christian and Hindu. Only modest differences will be expected.

Much variability. Hallucinations, unlike perceptions, have little or no foundation in external reality. They will vary with dispositions, dynamics, and the cultural background of the individual. Hallucinations of an afterlife will portray the belief system of the patient—be it based on the Bible or on the Vedas.

PROCEDURE OF THE TRANSCULTURAL STUDY

Both the second American survey and the Indian survey were done in a reasonably uniform manner so that we would obtain data suitable for close comparison analyses. The same questionnaire was used in both countries, and interview questions were nearly all the same, except for small changes which were made in order to accommodate significant differences in India (for example, religion, tropical diseases, and so on). Data gathering in India had to be different because of the local circumstances. In the United States we could secure a random sample by mailing our questionnaires, but in India we had to personally visit all the doctors and nurses who were available in the hospitals. Postal and telephone services there simply were inadequate for our needs.

Initial Questionnaire

In this questionnaire, our respondents were asked about their experiences with the dying. (For the full text of the questionnaire, see Appendix I). We inquired about how many times they had actually been with a patient at the moment of death and how many patients they had treated during a terminal illness. Furthermore, they were questioned about the hallucinations they had observed in patients who had a terminal illness—hallucinations of persons (whether living, dead, or mythological beings) or hallucinations of surroundings (whether of "another world" or of the natural environment). These same questions were also asked about patients who had recovered from a condition which approached death. A further question concerned observations of a sudden rise of mood in dying patients to happiness or serenity.

In the American survey, the questionnaire was sent to a stratified sample of 2,500 physicians and 2,500 nurses in the states of Connecticut, New Jersey, New York, Pennsylvania, and Rhode Island. Those who did not respond received one more letter asking for a reply. The design of the Indian survey had to be adapted to local customs and circumstances. Because of the severe limitations of communications facilities in India, we were advised not to use mailing techniques. Instead, we relied on face-to-face contact when soliciting answers to questionnaires. The survey was conducted in India's most populous state, Uttar Pradesh in northern India. We worked in the cities of Delhi, Meerut, Agra, Allahabad, Kanpur, Farrukhabad, Aligarh, and Varanasi (Benares), mainly in large university hospitals. Usually the professor of medicine and the professor of surgery arranged meetings with the hospital staff, where we gave a short talk and where questionnaires were distributed and filled out.

In the questionnaire we asked about their observations of the following phenomena, which then were followed up in interviews.

1. Hallucinations of *persons* by
   a. *terminal* patients—those who had died.
   b. *nonterminal* patients—those who were close to death but recovered.
2. Hallucinations of *surroundings* by
   a. *terminal* patients.
   b. *nonterminal* patients.
3. Mood Elevations—sudden rise of mood to happiness or serenity in dying patients.

In the United States, we mailed the questionnaire to 5,000 physicians and nurses; 1,004 of them returned a filled-in questionnaire. In India, practically all of the medical personnel directly approached filled in a questionnaire, totaling 704. Only a few refused. Thus, we netted 1,708 usable questionnaires. Approximately half of the respondents reported cases which we followed up in 877 detailed interviews.

Interviews

American respondents who reported pertinent cases were interviewed by telephone. In India, telephone contact had to be replaced by on-the-spot interviews, mainly in hospitals but also in the homes of the respondents.

We developed three separate questionnaires for the different phenomena: Hallucinations of Persons, Hallucinations of Surroundings, and Mood Elevation. Each consisted of 69 questions to guide the interviews.

We used open-ended questions—for example, "What was the patient's behavior indicating that he or she was experiencing hallucinations?" We also used alternative questions, such as: "Was the patient calmed by the hallucination, did he or she become excited, or was there no apparent effect?" And when inquiring about details of the observations, we used probing techniques.

The questions covered (1) characteristics of the patient, such as sex, age, education, religious belief and degree of involvement in it, and belief in an afterlife; (2) medical factors, such as diagnosis, medical history, medication, and temperature; and (3) such characteristics of the respondent as date of graduation from professional school, degree received, and religious beliefs. The main part of the questionnaire was devoted to details of the phenomena reported, such as how the patient described the hallucinatory person. The data were subsequently coded and recorded on computer cards.

As in the pilot study, most of the cases (471) concerned terminal patients who saw hallucinations of persons: 216 in the United States and 255 in India. There were 120 cases of patients who did not die but were very close to death, and who also described seeing hallucinations of persons: 56 in the United States and 64 in India. Altogether, we had a large sample of 591 cases of apparitions or hallucinations of persons.

Deathbed visions, which were primarily of surroundings, were obtained in 112 interviews: 69 cases (46 United States, 23 India) of terminal and 43 cases (18 United States, 25 India) of nonterminal patients.

A rise of mood to serenity or elation was also reported in a large sample. We conducted interviews of 174 such cases: 106 in the United States and 68 in India.

These 877 cases comprise the data which were submitted for computer evaluation. Besides frequency counts on each question, we analyzed how the factors interacted with one another by cross-tabulating all the relevant data, percentaging, and obtaining chi-square statistics. (For the lay person, chi-square is a statistical test in which obtained frequencies are compared with frequencies that would be obtained by mere chance fluctuations.)

With that broadly sketched picture of our investigation's history and procedures, we can now get on with a presentation of our findings. Along the way, and especially at the conclusion, we will attempt to interpret the findings. We will begin with a report on the results of our most massive sample—the cases where dying patients saw apparitions or hallucinations of persons.

CHAPTER 7

Apparitions:
Hallucinations of Persons
as Seen by Terminal Patients

THE variable encountered most often in each of the three surveys was that dying patients see persons whom others around them cannot see. In the pilot study, Osis found that these hallucinations generally tend to be of three kinds:

1. Rambling, confused, unrelated to the here-and-now.
2. Coherent and preoccupied with themes of this life.
3. Coherent and concerned with the here-and-now situation of dying as a transfer to a postmortem existence.

Hallucinations of the rambling type were found to be of no further value in our study. Coherent hallucinations of persons, the content of which has no relation to the situation of dying, were important for comparison with the afterlife-oriented type of experience. Such hallucinations may be subdivided into two categories:

1. A kind of a waking dream, such as when an Indian villager thought he was being pursued and attacked by his creditor-landlord.

2. Reliving memories of the past, such as when a to .
naval officer was hallucinating the memory of piloting a battle-
ship up the Hudson River.

Reliving memories is certainly not a new creation of imagery, as
other hallucinatory experiences are. They are, therefore, not often
comparable with other hallucinations. For example, obviously there
is no purpose expressed by them which relates to the here-and-now
of the patient. Most of our comparisons will be made between
apparitional experiences with this-world concerns and those with an
other-world orientation, leaving out relived memories.

Many examples were reported in which the hallucinations were
not only consistent and appropriate to the situation of dying but also
exhibited characteristics which seemed to fit into the framework of
the postmortem survival hypothesis. Here is a typical one.

She didn't say a word but I saw her looking at something or
someone who wasn't there, and smiling. She had been so
miserable just before that. She told me [afterwards] she had just
seen her [dead] sister who had come for her. She realized she
would die but did not seem to mind. It [seeing her dead sister]
seemed to relieve her. A pleasant experience.

We call experiences where the patient "sees" a kind of otherworldly messenger "afterlife-related hallucinations." Perhaps *hallucination* is not the right word since there is the possibility that it
was a real perception of a deceased person whose apparition was, in
one sense or another, present. For example, one respondent was
convinced that the following vision of a two-and-a-half-year-old boy
was something more than a hallucination because the child was
apparently too young to have had any conception about death.

He was lying there very quiet. He just sat himself up, and he
put his arms out and said, "Mama," and fell back [dead].

The child's mother had, in fact, died when he was two years old.
Furthermore, he did not engage in any similar behavior before the
time of the incident cited above—that is, moments before death.
Needless to say, a single case does not constitute strong evidence in

ᵥer, such cases do provide us with
ϛϛ ῀rom which greater evidence—either for
ᴧld emerge after careful analysis.

ᴜCINATIONS AND APPARITIONS

ᴧcinations have been separated from experiences of reality
becᴧuse medical observers considered them to be only symptoms
useful for their diagnosis and treatment of patients. In their opinion,
hallucinations indicate malfunctions of the brain and "disorientation"—that is, being out of touch with reality.

This approach is justified in some but not all hallucinations.
Nevertheless, psychologists and psychiatrists have often utilized this
theoretical perspective in an indiscriminate manner by applying it to
all hallucinations. Parapsychological findings squarely contradict
this interpretation. They show clearly that *some* hallucinations can
convey external reality almost as strongly, vividly, and effectively as
sensory perception. In most ESP cases, however, the representation
of reality is only partly true. Like an artist's depiction of landscapes
or people, they show some distortions, displacements, condensa-
tions, transfigurations, and symbolic expressions in a strange mixture with fantasy (L. E. Rhine, 1953; Green and McCreery, 1975).

Our survey netted hundreds of observations where the hallucinations of terminal patients appeared to relate to a world of postmortem existence. Are these images totally subjective, or are they
intimations of "another world" of which we know next to nothing?
This is the central theme of our research. But before proceeding any
further, it might be desirable to determine what exactly is meant by
the term *hallucination*.[1]

Hallucinations are a form of mental imagery involving sensory
qualities similar to perception but not corresponding to sensory
input (which is the normal basis of perceptual imagery). There also
exist many other kinds of imagery which are not called
hallucinations—for example, daydreaming, memory recall, and
dream imagery. However, that which singles out hallucinations
from all other kinds of imagery is the fact that the person is awake
during them and experiences the same sensation of realness regarding the image as he or she does when perceiving real objects. The

experience of realness is a basic component of perceptual processes. It is well known in psychopathology that the perceptual world might feel unreal not only during certain mental disturbances but also during such a severe type of stress as sleep deprivation. On the other hand, nonperceptual images may become very real, as shown by Arthur Deikman in meditation experiences (Deikman, 1963) and Sidney Cohen in imagery during drug-induced states (Cohen, 1964). Therefore, it might be said that *a hallucination is imagery coupled with a misapplied sense of realness.*

However, a sense of realness in ESP-based hallucinations is appropriate because of their correspondence with a kind of external reality that is not within reach of the perceptual organs. As an example, someone has a vision of an accident a thousand miles away which is later found to have actually occurred at the time the person had the vision. Memory images tend to take on a different sense of realness—a kind of recognition or familiarity because it has been seen, heard, or otherwise sensed before. Furthermore, a sense of realness in memory crosses the time barrier and relates to reality as it was, not as it is at present. ESP can reach not only into the past and present but also into the future. For example, precognitive images often feel real, and are real because they match real-life events in the future.

Afterlife-oriented hallucinations of the dying are also images coupled with a definite sense of realness. Only in very rare cases does the patient doubt what he sees. However, the main content of deathbed visions—afterlife and its hallucinatory representative (for example, an apparition of a dead mother)—cannot be directly verified, as can an ESP dream which either does or does not correspond with a real-life event. It would be ridiculous to suggest that someone goes to the "other world" and interrogates witnesses, checks newspaper reports, and so on. The methodology worked out for verification of ESP cases is obviously not applicable. Nor are the usual methods for verifying sensory perceptions or memory images.

Does a lack of *direct* verification preclude research? Should we therefore assume that the subjective experience of realness is as misapplied in cases of deathbed visions as it is in pathological hallucinations? Not necessarily. There are other ways of ascertaining reality aside from the direct-verification technique used in customary research on sensory or extrasensory processes. Courts admit indirect, circumferential evidence. So does science. In astrophysics, information about galaxies that are a million light-years away is based upon the light emanations of a million years ago. Such information is very circumferential, but astronomy has nevertheless made astonishing breakthroughs. For example, odd pieces of information may start to hold together and make sense if we accept the astronomer's assumption that "black holes" of extremely dense matter in the universe is a valid concept.

In any case, over the years we have devoted a great deal of effort to the development of methods for the systematic investigation of the hallucinations of persons seen by the dying. What follows is the result of our labors.

THE ROOTS OF THE APPARITION EXPERIENCE

Our pilot study provided enough data to permit the development of a set of hypotheses, which we organized into a model for postmortem survival as described earlier. This model is like a map in that it assists our orientation and enables us to tentatively state not only how the phenomena would manifest if there is indeed a life after death, but also what different patterns we would expect to emerge if the destruction hypothesis is true. In this section, we attempt to apply this model to the perception of apparitions by terminal patients.

What, then, are the main concepts which hold the bits and pieces of apparition-phenomena together within the model of postmortem survival? In the pilot study, we found the following basic characteristics of apparition experiences in the dying.

1. The majority (two-thirds) of apparitions portray dead rather than living persons. The opposite has been found to be true of hallucinations by persons in normal health.

2. The main ostensible purpose of the apparition is to take the patient away to another mode of existence. This purpose is expressed exclusively by apparitions of the dead and by religious figures. In the pilot study, not a single apparition

involving a phantasm of a living individual was described as coming with the take-away purpose.

3. Upon seeing an apparition with an ostensible take-away mission, the patient's predominant reaction will be that of serenity and peace, religious emotion, and "otherworldly" feelings—like those reported by mystics during their alleged encounters with "transcendental reality."

According to our model, each of these three characteristics would be affected differently by medical, psychological, and cultural factors, depending upon the origin of the hallucination. In the event that they are based upon actual contact with another world, the interactions will be different from mere hallucinations stemming from the malfunction of a sick brain. Therefore, deathbed visions will provide us with a source from which to gather indications either in support or denial of the postmortem survival hypothesis. In other words, our method is designed to identify the roots of the hallucinations as nurtured either by this-world sources or by ESP information transmitted to the patient from hypothetical entities of the postmortem world.

According to our model, the apparition will more frequently portray a dead or religious figure when medical factors which can cause a clouding of consciousness are relatively absent. Conversely, in cases of definite hallucinogenic malfunctions—for example, diseases of the brain, uremic poisoning, oral temperatures over 103°F., or drugs which affect mentality (such as morphine)—the apparition will convey the impression of a living person and engage in pursuing this-world purposes (unrelated to death or dying). If the otherworldly apparitions go with the hallucinogenic factors mentioned above, we will have reason to suspect that they are indeed caused by them. If they do not, the afterlife hypothesis will be supported. To put it bluntly, the sicker the brain processes, the more confused and bizarre the experiences, including otherworldly fantasies of celestial beings and spirits of the dead.

Some psychological factors may also indicate normal explanations for these phenomena. It is well known that hallucinations are often projections of inner conflicts, problems, needs, expectations, fears, desires, and so on (Siegel and West, 1975). If this is so, deathbed visions are projections of what is going on in the patient's inner world and therefore have no basis whatsoever in external reality. According to this counterhypothesis, the hallucinations of the dying are closely related to the expectations, moods, worries, concerns, and desires of the patient before starting to hallucinate. If such relationships are absent, it would speak for the external basis of deathbed visions—in other words, as being messengers of another world. This again is verifiable.

Throughout all cultures we find many instances of phenomena which William James referred to as "varieties of religious experience." Some thinkers in the psychology of religion consider such experiences to be the result of an encounter with the transcendental, the divine, and the supernatural. Others explain these phenomena without resorting to such assumptions. Rudolph Otto and others have tried to track down the emotional components of these experiences (Otto, 1958; Huxley, 1962; Smith, 1958; Tart, 1975; Maslow, 1970; Greeley, 1975). Reports of otherworldly, mystical experiences are frequently characterized by statements referring to a sensing of light, brilliant colors, harmony, serenity, and "the peace which passeth understanding." There have also been reports of feeling the proverbial majesty and fear of God—some force enormously larger and more powerful than we humans are (Otto, 1958). The people who have experienced this insist that such emotions are not a mere extension of the mundane, but a unique response to something extraordinary. A study on meditation experiences by Osis and Bokert (1973) supports the claims about the uniqueness of these feelings.

Although we cannot take a definite stand on metapsychological issues, if there is "another world," such experiences might constitute our awareness of it. We shall assume, for heuristic purposes, that an individual whose health is unimpaired may encounter in such phenomena a level of reality that is somewhat similar to the one found in the "otherworldly" experiences of dying patients. If this is so, then the emotional qualities which go with both situations would be similar. We will carefully examine our data for evidence that such "otherworldly" emotions come with deathbed visions.

Cultural factors could, according to our model, be the origin of some deathbed visions. Visions of the "beyond" could simply be created from materials that the patient has acquired through previous learning, such as religious stories, Scriptures, and societal beliefs—in short, from his cultural background. The hallucinations would then be just fantasies without having any basis whatsoever in immediate external reality. They would vary according to the belief system of the patient's society and individual, national, or racial differences.

On the other hand, if there is another mode of existence, we should expect all patients to see essentially the same thing. Therefore, the same basic otherworldly qualities should appear to patients with different cultural backgrounds. The essential dimensions of postmortem existence should be similarly experienced or mirrored by all people, regardless of whether they are men or women, Americans or Indians, college-educated or illiterate.

This provides us with an opportunity for a test. The differences between deathbed visions in such relatively disconnected cultures as the United States and India will be minimal if another world does exist, and very great if it does not. Allowing for cultural differences to exert some influence, we should expect Indians to see the beyond with somewhat different coloring from the way Americans see it. However, the basic characteristics of the world that they both see should be recognizable over and above the differences in the influences of the cultural milieu, just as we can recognize the same mountain whether it is painted by an American or an Indian artist.

With our model in mind, we will now begin to examine at length the general characteristics of the apparition cases.

CHAPTER 8

General Characteristics of Apparition Cases in Terminal Patients

O F the phenomena we investigated, hallucinations of persons (apparitions) were the most frequently observed in dying patients, and comprised more than half of our interviews. We obtained 471 cases in which terminal patients were reported to have seen hallucinations of persons. Of these cases, 216 were reported by doctors and nurses in the United States, and 255 by the same types of professionals in India. Since each of these 471 cases represents sixteen pages of data that were taken down in detail during the interviews, it is easy to see how this huge amount of material— combined with that from the 135 cases in the pilot study—afforded us a rich opportunity to look into the many facets of the apparition experiences of dying patients.

Once these data were gathered, our first task was to find out how typical each kind of experience was. We wanted to know which experience occurred with the greatest frequency, which were the rare oddities, and which may have been due to a biased or erroneous observation. Careful frequency analyses were performed on all the characteristics found in the cases. (Appendix II provides the exact numerical information. Tables 1 to 7 are for readers accustomed to having statistics in their diet.) Here we shall present an overview of the analyses.

There were basically two lines pursued when gathering our data and analyzing the frequencies of the observed characteristics. They are:

1. *The nature of the apparition experience itself.* How long did it last? How close was it to the time of death? What was "seen"? What was the purpose of the apparition? What were its effects upon the patient?

2. *The characteristics of the patients at the time they had their visions.* What was their type of illness, temperature, sedation, state of consciousness, sex, age, religion, religious involvement, belief in an afterlife, and education?

NATURE OF THE APPARITION EXPERIENCE

How Long Did the Visions Last?

The bulk of these deathbed hallucinations were of short duration, just as ESP apparitions generally are. About half of them lasted only five minutes or less, as is true of the following case.

A female cardiac patient in her fifties knew that she was dying and was in a discouraged, depressed mood. Suddenly, she raised her arms and her eyes opened wide; her face lit up as if she was seeing someone she hadn't seen for a long time. She said, "Oh, Katie, Katie." The patient had been suddenly roused from a comatose state, she seemed happy, and she died immediately after the hallucination. There were several Katies in this woman's family: a half-sister, an aunt, and a friend. *All* were dead.

Seventeen percent of such hallucinations lasted from six to fifteen minutes, and only 17 percent lasted for more than an hour (see Table 1).

How Close to Death Did the Visions Occur?

Another factor which we investigated was the amount of time that passed between the occurrence of the hallucination and the death of the patient. Although most patients did not die immediately after having witnessed the apparition, 27 percent of them died within an hour, and 20 percent died between one and six hours later. In the majority (62 percent) of the cases, the hallucinations heralded death within a day (see Table 1). Moreover, one-third (38 percent) of the patients died after a day had passed. This interval was especially long in patients whose hallucinations were of the rambling type.

Dying is often a gradual process. First, the patient goes into a coma—that is, becomes unconscious. Later, the heart stops and physiological processes come to a halt. The duration of the coma is included in the figures above. For most patients, the time between seeing the apparition and becoming unconscious was considerably shorter than the time between having the hallucinatory experience and clinical death.

Whom Did They See?

The question of the apparition's identity is a critical one. We were able to divide the contents of the hallucinations of persons into three categories: living persons, dead persons, and mythological or historical religious figures (see Table 1). According to our model, hallucinations of the living would indicate experiences which had nothing to do with postmortem survival, while afterlife-related apparitions of the dead and of religious figures would show characteristics indicative of another world. Actually, in all three surveys, there was an overwhelming majority of afterlife-related apparitions in the experiences of the dying: 77 percent in the pilot study, 83 percent in the U.S. survey, and 79 percent in the Indian survey. As illustrated in Figure 1, this contrasts sharply with persons of normal health who hallucinated dead and religious figures in 22–33 percent of all cases of hallucinations of persons (Sidgwick et al., 1894; West, 1948). Apparently, the terminal patients in all of our surveys saw afterlife-oriented apparitions of dead and religious personages three times as often as do individuals in good health. We shall later evaluate such apparition cases together with other factors in order to determine their origins.

In terms of the type of afterlife-related apparitions, the figures for the United States and India differ significantly. In the United States,

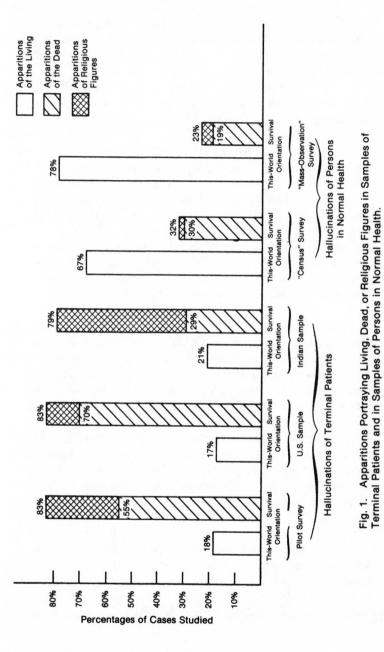

Fig. 1.   Apparitions Portraying Living, Dead, or Religious Figures in Samples of Terminal Patients and in Samples of Persons in Normal Health.

patients hallucinated a greater number of deceased persons (mostly relatives), whereas the hallucinations of Indian patients were primarily involved with religious figures. However, the total numbers of afterlife-related hallucinations were approximately the same for both countries (see Figure 1).

The cases we collected vary from a dramatic appearance of the apparition to experiences where the patient takes the phenomena rather matter-of-factly, as in the following case.

A sixty-five-year-old American (male) cancer patient seemed to be clear and rational in his thinking, but "saw the other world." He looked into the distance, these things would appear to him, seemed real to him. He would look up at the wall, eyes and face would brighten up as if he saw a person—he'd speak of the light and brightness. He saw people who seemed real to him, said "Hello," and "there's my mother." He gestured, stretched out his hands after it was over, closed his eyes and seemed very peaceful. Before the hallucination he was very ill, nauseous; after it he was serene and peaceful.

The dead were most often hallucinated, or in about half (47 percent) of all cases in our combined sample. Furthermore, the great majority (91 percent) of identified persons were relatives of the patient. Ninety percent of the identified relatives were close ones: mother, spouse, offspring, sibling, and father—in that order of frequency. In one-fifth of the cases, the identity of the apparition figure was unknown (see Table 2).

For our combined sample, the second largest category was that of religious figures. On the whole, Christians tended to hallucinate angels, Jesus, or the Virgin Mary, whereas Hindus would most usually see Yama (the god of death), one of his messengers, Krishna, or some other deity. The following case was reported by an Indian physician in a Muslim hospital.

A male patient in his fifties, college educated and a Christian, was going to be discharged on the seventh day after an operation on a fractured hip. The patient was without fever and was not receiving any sedation. Then he developed chest pain and I was called to him. When I came he told me he was going to die. "Why do you say so? Having a little pain in the chest does not mean you are going to die." Then the patient told how immediately after the pain in the chest started he had had a hallucination, but still remained [in] his full consciousness. He said he felt himself for a few seconds to be not in this world but elsewhere. At that time he saw Christ coming down through the air very slowly. Christ called him, rather, waved his hand that he should come to him. Then Christ disappeared and he was fully here. The patient told me he would die within a few minutes. He seemed quite happy and said that the aim of his life had been achieved by Christ calling him to Him. "I am going," he said, and departed a few minutes later.

What Was the Purpose of the Apparition?

Quite often, patients told our respondents why the apparition had visited them. Although the purpose is commonly reported as having been expressed by the apparition itself, in some other cases the patient told of his or her understanding of the reason for such visitations. Our model suggests two kinds of purpose.

1. According to the afterlife hypothesis, the apparition came to assist the patient in making his or her transition to the other world. The purpose would be to "take the patient away."

2. The destruction hypothesis states that, with the exception of fantasies determined by a religious upbringing, the purpose of the apparition involves this-world concerns.

The pilot study showed that 50 percent of the apparitions were of a "take-away" nature. In our later U.S. and Indian surveys, there were even more apparitions with a survival-related purpose: 65 percent of the cases (see Table 1). Actually, this statistic is something of an understatement since included in "this-life" purposes were such ambiguous remarks as the figure "came to comfort"—which could imply otherworldly as well as worldly visitors. Cases of "reliving memories" were included in the group of this-world purposes, though they showed no contemporary purpose what-soever. Excluding cases which are ambiguous in content, we will find that the take-away purpose is expressed in three out of four cases (pilot, 76 percent; U.S., 69 percent; India, 79 percent). These results are presented in Figure 2.

Summing up this aspect, we found that the basic findings of the pilot study were confirmed. The apparitions "seen" by the dying are predominantly experienced as guides assisting them in their transition to another mode of existence. A typical example would be the following case of an 11-year-old girl with a congenital heart malady.

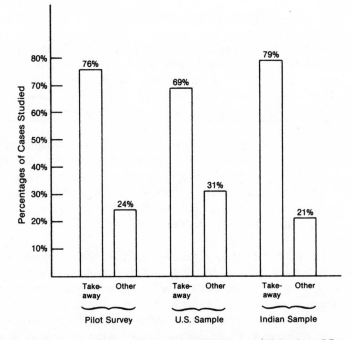

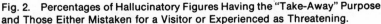

Fig. 2. Percentages of Hallucinatory Figures Having the "Take-Away" Purpose and Those Either Mistaken for a Visitor or Experienced as Threatening.

She was having another bad episode with her
that she saw her mother in a pretty white dress and
mother had one just like it for her [the patient]. She was
happy and smiling, told me to let her get up and go over
there—her mother was ready to take her on a trip.

The vision lasted for half an hour. It left the girl serene and peaceful until her death, four hours later. The unusual part of this case is that the girl never knew her mother, who had died when giving birth to her. She certainly did not have a chance to grow emotionally close to her mother, as most of us do. Yet, when that last hour came, her mother "was there."

The take-away cases were by far the largest category of hallucinations in the United States as well as in India. Furthermore, they showed the same general pattern. Usually it was a deceased close relative who appeared to the patient and told him or her that he was taking the patient away to a heavenly world, although sometimes it was a religious figure.

How Did the Patient React?

What were the patients' reactions to the ostensible visitors from the "great beyond"? Did they want to go with them? We found that three out of four (72 percent) wished to accompany the apparition, while only one-fourth (28 percent) would not go if they could possibly help it.

Although the majority in both countries were ready to go, we found great individual and national differences with regard to the distribution of refusals. While only one American patient did not wish to go when called, one out of every three (34 percent) Indians who experienced the take-away hallucination refused to consent. In a later chapter, we shall analyze this difference in greater detail. Meanwhile, simply bear in mind that most patients were ready to "go."

Not every patient would freely discuss his reactions to the apparition, and there are probably many cases of apparition appearance which have gone unrecorded. A British survey (Rees, 1971) showed quite clearly how very reluctant patients are to confide in

...s. That which the patient is
...an emotional expression, such as
...that much might be obscured by the
...of the dying. The background from
...terminal patients emerge is really quite

...odel, the differences in patients' emotional
...nd upon the origin of the apparition. The
...mortem survival states that otherworldly messen-
ge.   ...eted with positive emotions—especially those of
seren.   ...e, religious feeling, or sudden elation—all bursting out
of an at.. .sphere filled with apathy and gloom. A five-year-old
American girl was suffering from tubercular osteomyelitis of the
right knee. She was in a depressed, listless state prior to the
hallucination, but after seeing the apparition she was "relaxed,
happy, very smiling, elated." She died three hours later.

Although some mood changes are mild, they nevertheless bring
the patients out of their gloom. A thirty-six-year-old man suffering
from internal bleeding suddenly looked up, put his hands up, and
smiled.

> He saw his deceased mother and sister, was surprised but
> pleased to see them. I was surprised to learn that his sister and
> mother were dead. He was so natural with them that I thought
> they were alive at home. "Hello, it's good to see you . . ." he
> would say. Afterwards he was perfectly clear with full memory
> of his relatives' visit. He became more relaxed and content after
> the hallucination.

Forty-one percent of all patients did, in fact, respond to the
apparition with a positive alteration in mood (see Table 1). Of the
remaining cases, 30 percent showed no significant change in emotions, while 29 percent displayed negative feelings. These negative
emotions came largely from the patients in the Indian sample who
did not consent to the invitation to the beyond (one-third). For
example, an Indian woman in her eightieth year was dying from
cancer of the throat.

> She saw people coming to take her away. She wanted to fight

them—to stay, to live. She cried out: "People are coming and they want to take me. I don't want to go. Please hold my hand." She did not let her daughter-in-law leave her by holding her hand tightly, not allowing her to get up.

Here the emotion clearly is fear.

Positive emotional responses seemed to be pretty evenly distributed between elation and that which we describe as serenity and peace. However, one-third (35 percent) of these positive feelings were of a religious nature (in response to religious apparitions), while apparitions of the dead also frequently induced something otherworldly—"the peace which passeth understanding." Understandably enough, to a number of our respondents such reactions were quite incomprehensible. For example, a woman in her sixtieth year was suffering from a very painful cancer that had spread throughout her entire body. She "saw" her dead husband taking charge and preparing her for the transition.

Her husband was giving her instructions—no one was to interrupt—it was so vivid to her. She was like in a semi-sleep, as if talking to herself, having a conversation, e.g., "wait for me." She told me to be quiet. Before she was depressed about conditions getting worse. After the hallucination, she was elated, seemed to have risen above pain, no more moaning.

Negative emotions consisted mostly of depression, fear, and anxiety. This was especially true in Indian cases where the apparition of Yamdoot, the Hindu messenger of death, was encountered. However, displays of negative affect could also be due simply to the gloom of dying. In Indian cases, the patient's negative emotions usually were directly related to the nature of the apparition. The following is an account of a high-school-educated New Delhi salesman who seemed to be recovering from an operation. His consciousness was clear when he said to the physician:

"My [dead] grandfather is just near my bed. He has come to take me with him. I don't want to go! Please don't leave me alone!" Although the patient's physical condition was serious, his consciousness was quite clear; he was able to respond to

questions in a concise, coherent manner. However, the apparition left him scared, with unpleasant emotions. He died within
an hour.

MEDICAL, PSYCHOLOGICAL, AND CULTURAL BACKGROUND

To understand a phenomenon as complex as deathbed visions it is
necessary to evaluate a number of psychological and biological
variables as well as the interactions among them. Before we go into a
detailed analysis of these interactions, we shall first present an
outline of the general characteristics of our patients.

According to our model, afterlife-related apparitions will be
relatively independent of medical and psychological conditions,
while other hallucinations will tend to correlate with such factors
because they are caused by them. Furthermore, the same kind of
relationship is expected between seeing apparitions and such cultural
factors as the patient's degree of education, his religious and national
background, and his personal belief system. Therefore, in this study
we needed detailed information about the patient as a person, and
also about his medical condition and treatment.

Are Deathbed Visions Caused by Medical Conditions?

The origin of deathbed visions is our first basic concern. Are they
merely the result of psychophysiological malfunctions and cultural
influences—causes whose origins can be traced—or do they reveal a
relatively independent and universal characteristic of the human
being? The latter would be consistent with the afterlife hypothesis,
but we must explore the possibility that the alternative explanation is
true.

Some physiological conditions are, in fact, known to greatly
increase the likelihood of hallucinatory behavior. Drug intoxication
or sedation is one such condition. However, of those 425 patients on
whom we have information concerning medication, 61 percent had
received no sedation at all. The distribution of patients who had
received no such treatment is 49 percent for the United States and 71

percent for India, where sedation seems to be used far more sparingly than in America. Furthermore, 19 percent of our patients had received such small doses or such weak drugs that our respondents did not consider them to have been psychologically affected (20 percent in the United States; 17 percent in India). Thus, 80 percent of the terminal patients who had had apparition experiences during their illnesses were not affected by drugs. This means that only one-fifth were considered to have been influenced by the medication. Of these, the largest group were the "mildly affected" patients (11 percent), a category where it is likely that the drug was not the main cause of the hallucination. Only 1 percent of the patients were strongly affected by the sedation, and 8 percent moderately affected. Therefore, it seems safe to conclude that most of our patients' visionary experiences were not caused by drug intoxication.

A second physiological factor which could induce hallucinations is high fever, because elevated temperatures are sometimes known to bring on a delirious state. We received information on the temperatures of 442 of the total 471 patients. Of those, 58 percent had normal temperatures and 34 percent had low-grade fevers of up to 103° (oral readings). Only 8 percent of the patients had high temperatures of 103° or more. Therefore, in only a very minor portion of the patients does it seem possible that the apparitions could have been caused by fever.

We inquired into the state of consciousness at the time the patients had their visionary or hallucinatory experiences. In 86 percent of the cases, definite information was available excluding the uncertain "fluctuating" states, and in that 86 percent, about half of the patients were in a clear state of consciousness and fully aware of their surroundings (59 percent in the United States and 41 percent in India; see Table 3). About one-third were mildly impaired but could still be communicated with, and less than one-fifth of the patients were in a severely impaired state of consciousness where little or no communication was possible with the patient. Therefore, according to the judgment of the physicians and nurses we interviewed, the majority of the patients who had these visionary experiences were in a normal, wakeful state of consciousness.

Sometimes hallucinations are also the aftermath of brain diseases and diseases which affect the brain. The diagnoses of our patients varied widely, and, as was to be expected, there were also considerable differences in the causes of death between our U.S. and Indian patients. While cancer and heart disease caused death in 66 percent of our U.S. sample, they were the agents in only 27 percent of the patients in India, where we found infectious diseases, injuries, and respiratory diseases at the top of the list. In both countries combined, more patients whose diagnoses were known died of cancer (23 percent) than of any other disease. Heart disease was the second most frequent cause of death (22 percent), while the percentages for other groups of diseases were still smaller. For example, hallucinogenic diseases—stroke, brain injury, and uremic diseases—reached only 12 to 13 percent in the United States and 11 percent in India. Thus, only a small portion of patients who had apparition experiences during their terminal illnesses were suffering from diseases which could have been, but were not necessarily, of a hallucinogenic nature.

We were rather puzzled by the marked discrepancy between the two main causes of death in the U.S. sample and those of the U.S. population as a whole. For example, the share of heart patients in our sample was 29 percent while, according to the U.S. Vital Statistics for 1972, it was 38 percent for the entire U.S. population. However, upon closer examination we find that this discrepancy is understandable. The sudden death which is the result of many heart attacks would by its very nature hinder patients from reporting any visionary experiences that might occur. However, with cancer—the slow killer—this discrepancy is even greater; 37 percent in our sample, compared with 18 percent in the general population. Apparently, slow death is more conducive to these experiences, or else it serves to catalyze the patients' tendency to report them. Long-term patients would also know their physicians and nurses better, and would therefore be more likely to entrust unusual experiences to them.

Not only did we obtain the primary diagnoses of our patients, but we also solicited data on secondary illnesses and histories of previous illnesses which in some cases might have been hallucinogenic: mental illness, alcoholism, uremia, and any brain disease (including stroke). The frequencies of those background diagnoses were combined with primary diagnoses which shared the same categories. It is worth noticing that included in the hallucinogenic categories are diagnoses which might have caused hallucinations in some cases but not in others. To illustrate, very few stroke patients actually hallucinate. However, since it is a type of brain disease, we included it in this category. On the basis of the primary diagnosis, respondents frequently only suspected uremia as a secondary illness. Although such diagnostic guesses might often be ill-founded, in order to be on the conservative side, we included them in our tabulations. In cases where pertinent information was available, 25 percent of the patients in the combined U.S. and Indian sample had background diagnoses which could possibly have been hallucinogenic: 33 percent in the United States and considerably less in India (18 percent).

As previously stated, our investigation included looking into the possibilities of drug intoxication, body temperature, and diseases as causal factors for the hallucinations reported. We found that at the time of the visionary or hallucinatory experience, only a small part of the sample was in a hallucinogenic state caused by some known pathology. We formed a statistical "hallucinogenic index" for each patient by pooling available information on medical factors which might (though not necessarily) have induced hallucinations, such as brain diseases or injury, uremic poisoning, medical history suggestive of hallucinogenic causes, temperature of 103° or more, and medication affecting mentality. This index is a somewhat inflated measure in that it includes indices which are only slightly suspect of being hallucinogenic—for example, stroke patients, cases where medication affected mentality only to a small degree, and so on. Nevertheless, such indices are present in only 38 percent of our cases. The majority (62 percent) are free of them. The medical factors are summarized in Table 3 in Appendix II.

From the preceding information, we get the general impression that deathbed visions are relatively unaffected by medical conditions, which is in accordance with the findings of the pilot survey and which supports the survival hypothesis.

Are Deathbed Visions Independent of Sex and Age?

Previous studies with the normal population have shown that women report more hallucinatory and psi experiences than men

(Rhine, 1961; Haraldsson, 1976). This, however, does not appear to be the case in our survey. In the U.S. sample, hallucinatory experiences occurred about equally to both sexes (99 males, 117 females). However, in India, more than twice as many cases were of male patients (175) than female (80). This difference may be due to the fact that in India more males than females are admitted into the hospitals. Unfortunately, we have no exact figures on the distribution of men and women admitted to Indian hospitals.

Apparition experiences occurred throughout all age groups—to children as well as the middle-aged. Naturally, since the population of dying individuals is largely composed of older people, they tended to have greater representation in our sample. The mean age of our American patients was sixty-two; in India, it was forty-four, reflecting the large difference in life expectancy between the two countries. That difference is most evident when we noticed that while 81 percent of our U.S. patients were over fifty, in India only 35 percent of them had reached that age (see Table 4). However, the general impression from our data is that neither sex nor age is a determining factor in deathbed visions. As predicted by the afterlife hypothesis, these phenomena seem to go beyond the gross differences of sex and age.

Do Religion and Beliefs Affect Deathbed Visions?

Religion is a powerful factor, and one to be carefully considered in any study of death and dying. In fact, the very reason that our survey was conducted in two countries with radically different cultures was to determine whether religious beliefs, not postmortem survival, could have been the main cause of deathbed visions. Therefore, we carefully evaluated the *kind* of religion patients belonged to, and the *degree* of their religiousness—that is, involvement in religion.

The religious affiliations of our combined sample fell into two broad groups of about the same size: Hindus 48 percent and Christians 43 percent. In reasonable agreement with the religious distribution of the entire U.S. population, we had 51 percent Protestants, 36 percent Catholics, 6 percent Jewish, and 7 percent unaffiliated or belonging to other religions. Six out of seven (85 percent) of our Indian patients were Hindus, 10 percent were Christians, and 5 percent were Muslims (see Table 4). We did not pool Indian Christians with that U.S. group because of the wide cultural differences between the two countries. They therefore comprised a special group in our analyses. The above-mentioned figures for religious affiliation roughly represent the distribution of these religious groups in the areas where the survey was conducted. Thus it appears that the kind of religious affiliation was not a determining factor in the occurrence of this phenomenon.

Although we tried to solicit data concerning the religious involvement of our patients, respondents remembered and knew patients' involvement in only 58 percent of the cases (68 percent in the United States and 50 percent in India). The patients whose concerns were less in such matters might not bother mentioning it. Some involvement in religion was predominant in patients from the United States as well as India. Only 5 percent of those about whom we had pertinent information were reported as not being at all involved in religion, 14 percent were slightly involved, and 33 percent moderately involved. The largest group (47 percent), however, was deeply involved in religion. Furthermore, this figure was relatively equal in both countries: 44 percent in the United States and 51 percent in India. Unfortunately, we are not aware of any reliable figures on religious involvement in the countries surveyed.

However, it appears that in our sample the degree of involvement in religion exceeds that of the general population not only of the United States, but also of India. This would be the case to a much lesser extent if we assumed that religious involvement was slight or nonexistent in the cases where we have no information about it. It therefore appears that although religious affiliation may not determine the occurrence of deathbed visions, religious involvement—independent of denomination—may slightly enhance them. In a later chapter, we will explore this problem more deeply by scrutinizing the interaction between religion and various other factors. Furthermore, we will search for a reliable answer to the basic question: Do people have these experiences because of their beliefs and expectancies, or does religious involvement—if we accept the hypothesis for a moment—make them more open to otherworldly experiences?

Closely aligned with religious convictions is belief regarding an afterlife. So we asked our respondents about their patients' belief or disbelief in postmortem survival. We learned that most patients did not discuss such beliefs with doctors and nurses; only in 32 percent of the cases was this information available. Out of this number, for both the United States and India, 92 percent of the patients were reported to have believed in afterlife, while 8 percent had not (see Table 4). Apparently, the patients who had talked about an afterlife were nearly all believers.

According to a 1968 Gallup Poll, 73 percent of all Americans hold some belief in a life after death.[1] Although there is a considerable discrepancy between this figure and the 92 percent we obtained from our sample, quite likely it occurs because disbelievers failed to mention the matter to medical personnel. Again, we will explore the issue more closely in the section on interaction analysis.

Do the Less Educated See More?

The educational levels of our patients varied widely; illiterates as well as college-educated persons were represented. Approximately 21 percent of our sample were illiterates (preschool children were included in this category), and the overwhelming majority of them were of Indian birth. Combining figures for the two countries, 27 percent of the sample had attended only primary school, those whose education ceased upon graduation from high school comprised 32 percent, and approximately 20 percent of our patients had attended college. As illustrated in Table 4, the educational levels were much higher in our U.S. sample than they were in our Indian sample, reflecting national differences in education. Our U.S. survey was conducted in 1963, at a time when the average case was about three years old and the mean age for patients was sixty-two. Those persons had attended college around 1920, a year in which only 8 percent of all eighteen-to-twenty-one-year-olds were enrolled in institutions of higher learning. However, in our sample of patients from the United States, the figure is three times higher, with 24 percent having attended college. The preponderance of the college-educated is even stronger in India, where 16 percent were reported as having attended college. The Indian survey was conducted in 1973, the mean age of the patients was forty-four, and the cases were, on the average, between one and two years old. Thus, most of the patients were born in 1928 and attended college around 1948. Although we do not have any figures for that year, evidently these 16 percent far exceed the percentages of persons in India who went to college at that time.

There are two factors which might help to account for this large deviation from the general education level among the Indian population. One such factor is that our survey was conducted mainly in hospitals located in large Indian cities, where the college-educated are more numerous than in rural areas. Second, it seems likely to us that patients with a college education might receive more attention from the hospital personnel than the less educated would. The more time spent with a patient, the more likely physicians and nurses are to observe hallucinatory behavior. However, it should also be remembered that most of the hospitals we visited were government-supported "poor people's hospitals," as one professor of medicine phrased it. This makes it rather improbable that the two above-mentioned factors greatly biased our sample. In any case, it seems safe to conclude that the number of high-school- and college-educated persons in our sample is larger than that of comparable age groups in the general population. Thus, education may be positively related to the frequency of deathbed apparitions. If the assumption is valid that education is inversely related to superstitions and factually unsupported beliefs, then our findings oppose superstition as an explanatory hypothesis for deathbed apparitions.

Data concerning the occupations of terminal patients who had visionary experiences were also solicited. Laborers, farmers, and housewives comprised roughly half of our sample in the United States and India, while the number of professionals, managers, and clergymen totaled 30 percent. It is apparent that among those who had "seen" apparitions, there were many people who had held responsible positions.

SUMMARY

Our frequency analyses were based upon the trends that we discovered in the pilot survey and formalized in our model for postmortem survival. The central findings of the pilot survey were confirmed. The hallucinations of terminal patients portray three times the frequency of "survival-related" apparitions—that is, of dead and religious figures—than do the hallucinations by persons in normal health, as reported in the two British samples mentioned earlier. In 77 percent of the unambiguous cases, the ostensible purpose of the apparition was to "take the patient away" to another mode of existence.

In a sizable portion of the data (41 percent), patients' emotional responses to the apparition were appropriate to having had an encounter with the "other world," while in 29 percent of the cases—predominantly in India—the patient reacted in a negativistic manner. The results concerning emotional reactions call for further analysis before any reasonable interpretations can be made. This will be done in the next chapter.

The frequency analyses clearly indicate that the majority of apparition cases cannot be readily explained by such medical factors as high temperature, hallucinogenic diseases, the administration of drugs that could produce hallucinations—for example, morphine, Demerol—or by hallucinogenic factors in the patient's history. The phenomenon of seeing apparitions shortly before death seems to cut across the gross personal differences of age, sex, education, and religion. However, involvement in religion, regardless of the denomination, seems slightly to facilitate such experiences.

On the whole, these trends confirm the findings of the pilot study. Furthermore, they are consistent with the model for postmortem survival and do not fit in the framework of the destruction hypothesis. However, a closer examination of the *interactions* between various factors is needed before we can come to any final conclusions. The interaction analysis—for example, do patients react more with "otherworldly" feelings if the apparition portrays a dead rather than a living individual?—is the backbone of our study, and in the next chapter we begin our description of it.

CHAPTER 9

Getting at the Roots of the Apparition Experience I

1. THE INTERACTIONS OF VARIOUS FACTORS

O N a nationwide talk show not long ago, Osis was challenged about the findings we are reporting here. "Doctor," Osis was asked, "as a modern man, can you truly believe that these visions are not explainable on other grounds? Perhaps drugs like morphine would make the patient visualize his own religious beliefs as in a dream."

If Osis had had to respond to the question only on the basis of the information we have reported to this point, there would not have been enough for a definitive answer. However, we had a new kind of information derived from complex studies called interaction analyses. These studies showed that drugs and religious beliefs failed to affect the nature of the visions of another world. It was the interaction analyses that permitted Osis to reply definitively to his questioner, "Yes, I can believe that these visions are not explainable on other grounds because we ourselves have already tried to find such explanations—without results."

Let us now look beyond what we have thus far undertaken—an exploration of the various medical, psychological, and cultural factors, one at a time. For example, "In how many cases was the patient's medication a possible cause of the hallucination?" Although these analyses were adequate for helping us relate the raw data to our model, this type of piecemeal approach is not the whole story. The most important questions are not yet answered. It takes the interaction of many factors to form the rich, pulsating tissue of life. This chapter and the one following will attempt to present a picture of these complex interactions. It will be somewhat technical at points, but it is essential to our whole approach to use appropriate scientific methods in order to get at the truth of the matter. The lay reader might find this chapter more difficult than the others. However, we trust that even a light skimming will reward him with some interesting data important for getting to the roots of the experiences at the hour of death.

In the pilot survey, we learned that the experiences of the dying reveal a great deal more information when medical factors are viewed together with the patient's educational and cultural background, beliefs, and attitudes. Thus, questions which could not be answered by examining a single factor could be cleared up by considering factors jointly—for example, the meaning of a patient's emotional reaction to seeing an apparition. For example, we might question whether the feeling of peace came over a patient for the simple reason that he had given up and accepted the inevitability of death instead of having had an encounter with the other world. That, in fact, has been the dominant view of thanatologists. As will be shown later, interaction analyses provided the answer. Peace, serenity, and joy rarely resulted from visions of this-world imagery of living relatives, but it descended upon the patients who saw messengers from another world.

A nurse related this case about an intelligent seventy-six-year-old woman who had suffered a heart attack.

Her consciousness was very, very clear—no sedation, no hallucinogenic history. She was cheerful and confident that she would recover and return to her daughter who badly needed her at home. Suddenly she stretched out her arms and, smiling, called to me. "Can't you see Charlie [her dead husband] there with outstretched arms? I'm wondering why I haven't 'gone home' before." Describing the vision she said, "What a beautiful place with all the flowers and music. Don't you hear it? Oh,

girls, don't you see Charlie?" She said he was waiting for her. I
feel she definitely saw her husband.

The patient became content and peaceful—a kind of religious
peace and serenity came over her. During the vision she was well
oriented, carried on conversations with both the nurse and her
family. Obviously, this case fits in very well with our model of
afterlife-related experiences.

Another case concerns a college-educated woman from a small
upstate New York town who had a broken hip. She was in her late
seventies, somewhat senile, and received Demerol. The clarity of her
consciousness fluctuated. One day a nurse found her talking to her
dead brother and sister.

It was like reliving what had happened a few years ago in a
different setting (than the hospital). She beckoned with her
hand and told them to come to her and talk to her. She did not
seem to know I was there. Her brother had died in Peru.

No purpose as to why the apparition "came" was indicated. There
were no emotional reactions or any change in discomfort and pain.
After having seen the vision, there was no change in the woman's
attitude toward death.

In both the foregoing cases, women in their seventies saw dead
relatives. In that sense, they could be counted as afterlife-related
apparitions, but a closer look at the other variables revealed a striking
difference. The second case had medical explanations. The hallucinations were a replay of this-world memories and had no purpose,
no impact on her personality. The first case, however, was all geared
to an encounter with the beyond.

2. THE ANALYSES

The analyses, though complex, were nevertheless kept as simple
as possible. We cross-tabulated every useful variable with every
other one that could be related to it, found the frequencies and
percentages for each cell, and then compared the distributions by
chi-square statistics. (For the layman, chi-square is a form of
statistical analysis in which obtained frequencies are compared with

frequencies expected by chance fluctuations.) This was done first for each country individually and then for the United States and India jointly, using the combined data.

However, pooling our two national samples often was not advisable, inasmuch as particular aspects of the samples were not homogeneous—for example, many more Indians than Americans die young. Therefore, in cross-cultural comparisons, we frequently found ourselves having to compare the data rather than to pool them. We decided against more elaborate statistical analyses because of some limitations in our survey. Moreover, we tried to keep the analyses free of high-flown abstractions and as close as possible to the ground of the raw data. For convenience, only probability values (p) which are associated with chi-square statistics will be reported. We shall begin the report of our interaction analysis with the phenomenon most central to the survival issue, namely the ostensible purpose of the apparition—whether or not the hallucinatory figure came to take the patient away to another existence. For detailed information, the professional reader is referred to Osis and Haraldsson, 1977.

3. THE PURPOSE OF THE HALLUCINATORY FIGURE: WHY DID THE APPARITION COME?

In two-thirds of the interviews, our respondents reported that patients had told them of the hallucinatory figure's purpose in appearing to them. Most of the apparitions so identified (65 percent) had the ostensible purpose of taking the patient away to a postmortem existence by calling, beckoning, demanding, and so on.

Psychologist friends frequently have asked us, "Could the apparition actually be portraying purposes which the patient himself has generated as a wish fulfillment and then clothed in a ghostly form?" They referred to the well-known tendency in people to project emotions and attitudes into imagery. The pages which follow will show how we found the answer.

The Role of Medical Factors

First, let us consider whether the otherworldly purposes of the apparitions can be explained away by medical factors. In Chapter 8 we found that deathbed visions were relatively unaffected by such medical conditions as medication, high fever, and malfunctioning of the brain. Furthermore, the visions were less frequent when such medical factors were present in terminal patients. According to the afterlife hypothesis of our model, these medical factors will not facilitate but will often decrease the afterlife-related side of the phenomena, such as the take-away purpose of the apparition. Would our data confirm this hypothesis or would they show the death as destruction theory to be true?

In our 1959–60 pilot study, more "otherworldly," peaceful take-away cases were observed in patients who *did not* have brain diseases, nephritis, or hallucinogenic medical histories. Both of the new surveys—American and Indian—again showed that brain disturbances did not generate more peaceful take-away apparitions than experienced by patients who were free of the above hallucinogenic factors. On the contrary, the patients with brain disturbances saw such apparitions less frequently.[1] On the whole, this trend supports the afterlife hypothesis, as predicted by our model.

We further explored the effects of the patient's clarity of consciousness. Patients who had a clear state of consciousness saw slightly more peaceful take-away apparitions than did those with impaired clarity. In the pilot study, this trend was significant. However, in the new surveys it was so slight that it indicated only the absence of a relationship. In other words, the state of consciousness did not matter.

On the whole, the medical variables are rather unimportant except for the truly hallucinogenic ones (brain diseases, nephritis, and, in India, liver disease). These appear not only to throw the patient's mentality out of balance but also to drastically reduce the number of benign apparitions experienced as having come to guide the patient to another realm of existence. The answer to the challenge of the talk-show question becomes clear: *Medical factors do not generate experiences of apparitions which "take the patient away" to another world.*

The Role of Psychological Factors

Now we come back to the crucial question which psychologists often ask us: Do peace and serenity come to patients because they have given up the struggle for life rather than because of an encounter with "another world"? The pilot study revealed that peace and serenity fell more often upon those patients who witnessed apparitions with an explicit take-away purpose than to patients who experienced apparitions with other purposes. Our new surveys fully confirmed that trend. Fifty-one percent of the American patients whose apparitions were of a take-away nature reacted with serenity and peace, while only 7 percent responded so to apparitions with other purposes (p = .00001). The figures for our Indian sample were 33 percent versus 10 percent (p = .009). In both countries, 30 percent of the patients reacted with religious emotions to apparitions that had a peaceful take-away purpose, while only 5 percent in India and none in the United States responded in a like manner to hallucinatory figures with other purposes. The nature of the apparition alone determines the patient's emotional response, leaving little room for other explanations. Patients reacted to the otherworldly messengers with otherworldly feelings—religious emotions or a "peace which passeth all understanding." A coal miner's wife in her sixties was dying from a very painful cancer of the rectum. Her consciousness was clear when she said to the nurse, "Virgin Mary! How beautiful!" She was overcome with religious emotion. "She seemed to be in ecstasy—very happy."

This makes sense if we assume the existence of another world, but it fits poorly with the "sick brain" hypothesis since clear, consistent trends of this kind can hardly be expected to result from a malfunctioning brain. Rather, they suggest an encounter with something external to the patient, something that bears its own specific qualities. Our model stated that apparitions of otherworldly visitors will elicit otherworldly emotional responses, such as those reported by mystics. We feel this aspect of the model is confirmed.

Are apparition experiences just a schizoid reaction to alleviate severe stress?

Hallucinations do sometimes occur in situations of social deprivation and of severe stress (Siegel and West, 1975; West, 1962)—for example, mirages. Not only are visits to terminal patients often restricted, but the patients are going through very stressful situations, including having to cope with acute pain. Could the bases of their visions, therefore, be stress and social deprivation rather than extrasensory perception of visitors from another mode of existence? In order to provide some answers to this question, we analyzed an array of psychological and cultural factors to determine if they have any influence on the phenomena.

We found that neither the patient's age nor sex interacted significantly with the main phenomenological aspects of apparition experiences—these aspects being (1) apparitions portraying living, dead, or religious figures, (2) the purpose of the apparition, and (3) the patients' emotional reactions. Moreover, we have information on indirect indices of stress—the patient's mood the day before the hallucination occurred. We assumed that negative moods, such as anxiety, anger, or depression, would indicate more stress than would positive moods which were called "normal" or "average" by our respondents, such as the following case.

An eighty-nine-year-old Jewish executive of an industrial concern was "a very quiet man, not moody, resigned to being sick." He had not practiced his religion for many years.

> He was quiet and calm when he suddenly said to his daughter, "There is an angel there." She was very surprised at that. I noticed that the patient had a different appearance for about an hour: he was looking far away, he had a very wonderful expression on his face. Then suddenly it disappeared—he was his old self again. Definite change in facial expression and mood.

There were no significant interactions between the patients' moods the day prior to their hallucinations and what the apparitions represented—living, dead, or religious figures. We also found no appreciable interaction involving patients' emotional reactions to the apparitional experience. The purpose of the apparition was not significantly related to the previous day's mood in either the American or Indian samples. However, the relationship was significant in the pooled data of the United States and India ($p = .0015$). This relationship went in a direction opposite from the hypothesis that stress is a determining factor in apparition experiences. More persons who had normal moods experienced apparitions having a peaceful take-away purpose (54 percent) than those who had positive (31 percent) or negative (27 percent) moods. The case of a Pennsylvania housewife in her sixties is typical. She suffered a heart attack but seemed to have every hope of recovering. She was really calm and quiet—cooperative, not apprehensive. Then she looked at the ceiling and said, "I see an angel. He is coming for me." Afterward she was even calmer, more serene. Very soon she became unconscious and died the next day. She had expressed interest neither in religion nor in life after death before this incident. From our data, we may infer that while the stress experienced by terminal patients might have caused other kinds of hallucinations, it is unlikely that it affected apparitions which expressed purposes related to postmortem survival.

A patient's desires, expectations, or "wishful thoughts" can be possible causes of hallucinations. For example, amid desert sands, a thirsty traveler might "see" a mirage of desired water where there is none. To find out if apparitions occur independently of the patient's desires and expectations, we asked our respondents to identify whom the patients had desired to see the day before the visions occurred. Sometimes there had been a very strong desire to see a loved one who lived far away, such as an absent son. Only an insignificant part (3 percent) of our cases were explainable by hallucinations of persons the dying patient desired to see and who had not visited him. There were thirteen cases like that in all. Of those persons who *had* visited the patient, only nine were hallucinated. Apparently such desires did not create the vast majority of apparitions. Furthermore, there was no indication in the data that persons recently seen by patients also appeared frequently in their hallucinations. In addition to this, we also asked about preoccupations and worries experienced by the patient on the day prior to the apparition. As noted above, anxieties and inner conflicts may be projected outwardly in the form of a hallucination. The phenomenon of seeing apparitions, however, was not significantly related to preoccupations or worries of the patient in either the American or Indian samples.

Another powerful factor that might shape hallucinations is the patient's expectation of either dying or recovering from his illness. Those who expect to die, we reasoned, might indulge in otherworldly fantasies in order to assuage their fear of dying. As for those who expect to recover, needless to say, seeing an apparition coming to take them away to the realm of the dead would be contrary to their expectations. We would therefore not expect them to create hallucinations of another world. Nevertheless, both samples showed that these expectancies were not significantly related to the purpose of the apparition. *It seems that apparitions show a purpose of their own, contradicting the intentions of the patients.* This suggests that they are not merely outward projections from the patient's psyche.

Several medical observers expressed amazement and surprise when confronted with cases in which patients died—after seeing apparitions calling them—despite good medical prognoses. For example, a Hindu patient in his sixties was hospitalized because of a bronchial asthmatic condition. His doctor's prognosis predicted a definite recovery. The patient himself expected to live and wished to live. Suddenly he exclaimed, "Somebody is calling me." Afterward he reassured his relatives, saying, "Don't worry, I will be all right," but the "call" seemed to have been more potent than he himself thought. The patient died within ten minutes. We did not anticipate such cases when constructing our questionnaire, and so, except for the time between the appearance of the apparition and death, we do not have appropriate statistics of doctors' prognoses relating to them.

In the pilot study we found that take-away apparitions were reported more frequently (76 percent) by patients who died immediately (within ten minutes) after experiencing them than by those whose deaths came after longer intervals. In fact, one doctor remarked that the apparition really "did the job" and hastened death. This finding was verified in the U.S. data. In America, 87 percent of those who died within sixty minutes, as compared to 46 percent of those who died after longer intervals, reported apparitions with a take-away purpose. In India, this trend was weaker and not significant. It was found to occur only with patients who did not consent to the call of the apparition. We do not claim to have evidence that ghostly visitors in the United States are meddling in medicine without a license, but this trend does make sense within the framework of the survival hypothesis.

Especially dramatic were those cases in which apparitions called a patient for transition to the other world, and the patient, not willing to go, cried out for help or tried to hide. Fifty-four of these "no-consent" cases were observed, nearly all in India. Such cases can hardly be interpreted as projected wish-fulfillment imagery, and they are even more impressive when the apparition's prediction of death was not only correct but contradictory to the medical prognosis of recovery.

Earlier we asked if deathbed visions are merely outward projections from the patient's psyche. In the foregoing, our data have shown that terminal patients did not see in their visions those persons they had expressed a desire to see; nor did their visions seem to be directly related to indices of stress, moods, or worries. Further, we found that deathbed visions also occurred to those who did not expect to die. In many cases the intent of the apparitions seemed to be very different from that of the patients. Such characteristics in deathbed visions support the hypothesis that some apparitions may be independent entities and not merely outward projections from the patient's psyche.

4. THE PURPOSE OF THE APPARITION: A CROSS-CULTURAL COMPARISON BETWEEN INDIA AND THE UNITED STATES

Information concerning the purpose of the hallucinatory figure is much more readily available in the Indian sample than in the American one. Of our 216 American patients who saw apparitions, we have information on the purpose of the apparition in only 98 cases, but we have the same information on 203 cases in our 255-patient Indian sample. Our impression is that American respondents were, on the whole, less at ease with the question concerning the purpose of the hallucinatory person, whereas the Indian culture seemed to provide a context in which the question could more readily be accepted. The purpose of taking the patient away to another existence was expressed in 69 percent of the American cases and in 79 percent of the cases in India, after the exclusion of ambiguous data (see Chapter 8).

Thus we find a remarkable similarity in the frequency of the apparition with a take-away purpose seen by terminal patients in the United States and India. The reactions of the patients to the apparitions, however, were not always the same. While all but one American patient accepted the call, often with serenity and joy, about one-third of the Indian patients (34 percent) resisted. So the real difference between these two countries is found in the cases where the patient did not consent, but was afraid, or even felt that he was being forcibly taken away (53 in India and just 1 in the United States). Nevertheless, the majority of the Indian patients (66 percent) reacted as the Americans did. They wanted to "go" and frequently expressed the same serenity and joy. Is this difference reducible to other characteristics in the samples?

Although there are many more female patients in the American sample than in the Indian one, apparitions with the take-away purpose occurred with about the same frequency in both sexes. Several physicians in India suggested that the reason so many patients there experienced take-away apparitions against their will might be because Indians die at a younger age. In early years, when life is still unfulfilled, one might be more committed or attracted to life than in old age when a lifetime has been lived through, regardless of the prospects of an afterlife. Fortunately, we have data on the ages of patients. In the United States, age made no difference. There was no appreciable interaction between age and purpose. Although in India slightly more older persons saw peaceful take-away apparitions (p = .09), age was not related to seeing aggressive apparitions. Twenty-four young Indians under thirty years of age accepted the take-away purpose of the apparitions. One of these Indian cases involved a young Hindu woman in her twenties, who had been brought to a large hospital in Delhi because of tetanus. She was clearly conscious when she told her nurse that she saw a deity called Murti, who said to her, "I have come to take you." She told her relatives that she was going with him, and refused medicine which might hold her back. The girl was convinced that she would die in a few minutes, and within fifteen minutes she expired. Apparently, age explains only a minor part of the take-away phenomena, but by no means does it explain all cases where patients did not consent to go.

Would the Hindu religion make some Indian patients hesitant to go? We explored the possibility that no-consent reactions might be caused by national and religious backgrounds. No-consent cases were almost absent in the United States, a predominantly Christian culture, and quite common in India, a predominantly Hindu culture. There is, however, a small Christian minority in India, and in that group the frequency of no-consent take-away cases was about half (14 percent) that among Hindus (29 percent). There remains a considerable residue unexplained by religion. Apparently the no-consent cases depend partly on national and partly on religious differences. Indian mythology about the king of death, Yama (or Yamaraj), and his messengers, the Yamdoots, might be one reason Indians are unwilling to accept the call of the take-away apparition. Yamdoots are supposed to appear at the bedside of the dying to take them away to their lord, Yamaraj. The appearance of the Yamdoot depends upon the Karma of the patient. If he has accumulated good deeds, a pleasant Yamdoot appears, but if he has not acquitted himself well in his lifetime, a fearful Yamdoot might come. The Yamdoot in the following case was neutral in appearance. It appeared to a Hindu clerical worker, high-school-educated, who was hospitalized with an infectious disease, septicemia. His temperature was above 103°, he was mildly affected by drugs, but, to his nurse, his consciousness seemed to be clear when he exclaimed:

"Somebody is standing there! He has a cart with him so he must be a yamdoot! He must be taking someone with him. He is teasing me that he is going to take *me!* But, Mamie, I am not going; I want to be with you!" Then he said someone was pulling him out of bed. He pleaded, "Please hold me; I am not going." His pain increased and he died.

Of course, death also has been personified in European mythology as a disagreeable gray figure or a skeleton (McClelland, 1964). But it never appeared in the hallucinations of American patients, while eighteen Indian patients, most of them not ready to "go," saw Yamdoots. Perhaps such death symbols are impotent in the United States but alive in the Indian psyche.

A patient's religious involvement did not significantly affect the purpose of the hallucinatory figure. Both in India and the United States, belief in a life after death was present in nearly all of the take-away cases, where the patient's belief was known. Unfortunately, we do not have much information about patients who did not believe in survival, and therefore comparison is impossible. There was no correlation between the length of the hallucination and its ostensible purpose.

5. THE IDENTITY OF THE APPARITION AS A LIVING, DEAD, OR RELIGIOUS FIGURE

We found that the hallucinatory figure could be that of a living person, someone who is dead, a religious personality, or a mythological being. Hallucinations of the living are not at all related to the afterlife hypothesis. In fact, they are more likely the result of a brain malfunction. Naturally, in our surveys, we came across a few such experiences, and their frequency was quite similar in the United States and in India. However, we found not one case in which the take-away purpose was attributed to an apparition of the living. In both countries, the apparitions of the dead mostly expressed take-away purpose (United States, 82 percent; India, 71 percent). Practically all the apparitions of religious figures, when the purpose was indicated, had come to guide the patient to another mode of existence. For example, a ten-year-old girl was in a hospital in Pennsylvania recovering from pneumonia. Her temperature had subsided, and she seemed to be past the crisis.

> The mother saw that her child seemed to be sinking and called us [nurses]. She said that the child had just told her she had seen an angel who had taken her by the hand—and she was gone, died immediately. That just astounded us because there was no sign of imminent death. She was so calm, serene—and so close to death! We were all concerned.

According to our model, apparitions of dead and religious figures are messengers from another world and are relevant to the hypothesis of postmortem survival. And indeed, they were the kind seen by the vast majority of patients in all three surveys. The number of afterlife-related hallucinations (those of dead and of religious figures) are surprisingly similar on both sides of the globe—78 percent for the United States and 77 percent for India. In this sense, the phenomenon of visits to the dying by otherworldly entities cuts across cultural differences.

Although afterlife-related apparitions are dominant in both samples, the proportions of those portraying dead and religious figures are reversed in the two countries. Americans had five times more hallucinations of the dead than of religious figures (66 percent versus

12 percent). Indians, on the other hand, hallucinated religious figures more often than those of the dead (28 percent versus 48 percent). Apparently nationality and culture do not determine the frequency of afterlife-related apparitions, but they do influence the type. Christian patients in India also experienced a much smaller proportion of hallucinations of the dead than of religious figures. Nationality rather than religion seems to be at the root of the difference.

Perhaps the basic experience of the dying seeing messengers from another world is common in all cultures, but in particular cultures special sensitivities might be developed which would favor one type of apparition over another. Inhibition of one of the two kinds of hallucination also might explain the difference. For example, seeing a female hallucinatory figure seemed to be infrequent—and therefore inhibited—in India. While there were 61 percent apparitions of females in the U.S. sample, India had only 23 percent. Therefore, inhibiting seeing apparitions of female relatives may have reduced the number of apparitions of the dead by 40 percent, leaving only male visitors from the other world. The inhibition of female apparitions in India is present more frequently in men. Therefore, we expected men to see fewer apparitions of the dead in their visions, and indeed they did—13 percent less than Indian women saw. The tendency of Indians to exclude the young from their visions of take-away apparitions could, in turn, further reduce the share of dead persons in their visions.

In addition to the negative bias against female apparitions of the dead, a positive bias in favor of religious figures might also be at work. Indians often seem to experience their deities in an intimate, personal way, and bring offerings of food and flower garlands to the statues of their gods. Americans, especially those of liberal Protestant denominations, often tend to interpret the divine as an abstract, spiritual force.

We conclude that cultural forces appear to be powerful enough to sensitize or inhibit patients' seeing certain kinds of phenomena, but they do not alter the surprisingly high number (three out of four) of those experienced as coming from another world. So here again we have found a remarkable cross-cultural stability of the main phenomena in spite of the obvious shaping done by cultural forces.

In both countries, the take-away purpose with consent was experienced mainly in apparitions of near relatives: mother, father, spouse, sibling, or offspring. In Chapter 8 we discussed in detail why the afterlife hypothesis predicts that, whenever available and suited to the task, close deceased relatives will aid in the patient's transition to the afterlife. However, in the following analysis, let us play the devil's advocate and suppose that the apparition was nothing more than a mere hallucination, a kind of rerun of the cultural programming that was drummed into us during childhood and adolescence. According to cultural programming, we would expect to see the traditional middlemen between us and the other world—people such as ministers, brahmins, and rabbis, who are always around to perform the funeral services and other evocations of the spiritual forces. Yet not a single case occurred in which a dead clergyman acted as an otherworldly envoy to his dying parishioner. Furthermore, of the entire Indian sample, only five patients were "met" by gurus. It would seem that deeply ingrained traditions do not conjure up such apparitions and ascribe to them the take-away purpose.

When probing into another cultural force, we made a discovery. In India, there is a strong respect, even veneration, for elders to an extent that is unusual in the United States. Because of this, would more of the patients in India be received by these esteemed elders than in youth-loving America? Indeed, they would. In the United States, 41 percent of the peaceful take-away apparitions belonged to the previous generation, while this was true in India in 66 percent. Apparitions of members of the same generation as the patient comprised 44 percent of the cases in the United States and 29 percent in India, while the next-generation relatives appeared in 15 percent of the American cases and in only 5 percent of the Indian ones. Although in the United States 14 percent of the apparitions portrayed deceased sons or daughters, no such youngsters seemed to be entrusted with the take-away mission in India.

Do dead relatives come in cases where the patient does not want to go? No, nearly always it is a stranger or a remote acquaintance who performs the mission. Characteristically, there was only one case in which the apparition of a parent "came" to take the patient away against her will. This is quite understandable within the context of postmortem survival. In an analogy of this world, it would be very unlikely for a sheriff to ask a mother or father to take their son into custody by force. Of course, other explanations are possible.

In our analyses we found that the patient's age did not make any difference in determining whether the apparition portrayed a living, dead, or religious figure. This was true despite the fact that most of the relatives of older persons were already dead while those of the younger patients were still living. We also investigated the educational level of the patients as a possible influential variable. This factor did not make the slightest difference in our Indian sample. There was a significant difference in the United States, but it was due to a very small group of illiterate patients who had not attended school. That group saw more hallucinations of the living than of dead or religious figures. We found no marked difference between patients who had either much or little schooling—for example, between those who had attended only grade school and those who had gone to college. If seeing otherworldly messengers was based solely upon superstition, we would expect the opposite trend to occur—that more educated persons would see fewer apparitions of dead or religious figures.

In addition to the patient's age and educational level, we explored the possibility that religious involvement might affect the nature of the apparition. We found no significant relationship between religious involvement and seeing any of the three types of apparitions. Furthermore, benign otherworldly visitors also appeared to patients who had no afterlife or religious concerns. A sixty-two-year-old ex-Marine in New York City was dying from cancer of the prostate. He told his doctor that he was an atheist. To the doctor's surprise, the patient had a vision of Christ—which lasted a few minutes— appear in his room. It seems that the appearance of the apparition is not dependent on the patient's merits or demerits in the overt practice of religion. No apparition asked, for example, "John, why did you stop going to church?" or made an accounting of a patient's sexual transgressions. If these apparitions did, in fact, represent another world, they certainly were far more understanding than hellfire-and-brimstone preachers have imagined. Nor did they seem to be symbolic of the modern-day psychiatric equivalent to hellfire and brimstone—the patient's guilty conscience.

So, on the whole, we again found the same trend as in our pilot survey. *The core phenomena of the dying experience are not much affected by individual, national, or cultural factors.* This is consistent with our model of the afterlife hypothesis, which states that apparitions are perceived by extrasensory perception rather than being hallucinated.

Before turning our attention to a discussion of the emotional effects apparitions have on patients, let us first investigate what part the individual's physiological condition plays in determining the type of apparition he is likely to see.

In the United States, medical diagnoses were not at all related to any of the three types of apparitions that patients saw. There was, however, a significant relationship in India (p = .04). Heart and circulatory diseases on the one hand, and nephritis and brain diseases on the other, are the two groups in which patients have about twice as many apparitions of the dead as patients in other diagnostic categories do (44 percent versus 19 percent). Moreover, the patients in these two categories experienced slightly fewer hallucinations of religious figures. This puzzling trend—more apparitions of the dead in Indian patients whose brains were affected—melts away when we look at afterlife-oriented apparitions with peaceful take-away purposes. We found only three such cases. The rest were not related to afterlife purposes. One of the latter cases follows.

A Hindu woman in her seventies suffered a stroke. She was semicomatose and delirious. She hallucinated only those people she had cheated in her lifetime! For example, she saw her dead sister, who was accusing the patient of having cheated her out of money. The doctor thought she was suffering from a guilt complex abreacted in hallucinations.

Patients with hallucinogenic medical histories, in both the American and Indian samples, had the same proportion of apparitions of living, dead, and religious figures. The same holds true for the patient's state of consciousness. Furthermore, our comprehensive measure of hallucinogenic maladies—the hallucinatory index—did not affect the frequency of the three types of apparition. On the whole, we can say that medical factors appear not to determine the frequency of afterlife-related apparitions, which is in accordance with our previous findings.

6. APPARITIONS OF DIFFERENT GENERATIONS: THE "DEATH QUOTA"

We found rather surprising differences between the younger and older patients in our pilot study. The younger patients saw more apparitions of dead relatives from the previous generation, while the older ones saw mostly apparition figures of their contemporaries. This makes sense according to the survival hypothesis. We quote:[2]

> In the younger group most of the significant persons of the same generation would probably still be living; while in the older group a great many of their contemporaries would be dead. If the living-dead proportion of apparitions is independent of age, the younger group could fill their dead "quota" mainly with persons from the previous generation, while the older group would have many significant persons dead in their own generation. It follows that the younger group would see more persons of the previous generation than the older group. This, indeed, is the case. Taking percentages, the younger group sees about twice as many hallucinations of previous-generation people as does the older group of patients—62.5% : 33.3%. The proportions are exactly the reverse in connection with hallucinations of the same generation—20.8% : 45.4%. Hallucinations of the next generation were equally distributed among the groups of younger and older patients.

We performed the same analysis on our new data, comparing the proportion of apparitions portraying the same and previous generations in the visions of young and old patients. In both countries, the proportions went in the predicted direction, although not to a significant degree. However, 56 percent of the previous generation apparitions were seen by the young Americans in our sample, while 40 percent were seen by the older patients. In India, the difference between the results of these measures is more dramatic: 44 percent versus 22 percent (young and old, respectively). The proportions of apparitions of same-generation relatives were reversed. The elderly patients saw a higher number of same-generation phantasms in both the U.S. (44 percent versus 32 percent) and India (47 percent versus 33 percent). Therefore, we concur with the previous conclusions:[3]

> In our sample the constancy of the proportion relating to hallucinations of living and dead persons in spite of the shift of generations hallucinated is quite remarkable. It indicates that the living-dead proportion in deathbed hallucinations is a real

effect and not an artifact arising from the predominance of older patients in the sample.

The pilot study brought to light even more indices for the postmortem survival hypothesis. Surprisingly, many of the close relatives hallucinated were dead. For example, about 98 percent of fathers, mothers, and siblings were dead, while dead spouses and offspring totaled about 70 percent.

Although one would naturally expect there to be a larger number of deceased relatives of the previous generation than of the next, the proportions of apparitions we obtained from our analyses exceeded that expectation. In our new data, there also seemed to be the same above-expectation preponderance of apparitional figures of the dead. In the United States and India, respectively, the figures ran: dead father, 93 percent, 94 percent; dead mother, 93 percent, 77 percent. There was a surprisingly large number of dead spouses (79 percent) and siblings (85 percent) in the United States, although one would naturally assume the contemporary generation to be evenly divided among the living and the dead because the average dying age would be the same for our patients as for their relatives of the same generation. This was, in fact, the case in India: spouses, 50 percent; siblings, 43 percent. Even more impressive was the unusually high share of dead offspring in the United States (50 percent); this figure was only 19 percent in India. One can say for sure that half of the children in the United States did not die before their parents.

The afterlife hypothesis of our model suggests that many more of those dead close relatives appear because they naturally would have a take-away mission. And indeed we did find a strong predominance of very close deceased relatives among the apparition figures witnessed by terminal patients—mothers and fathers in both countries, as well as spouses, siblings, and offspring in the United States. This may be explained in terms of the afterlife hypothesis which states that close relatives care more and are therefore apt to appear more frequently at the time of death. This trend is less clear in India where apparitions of religious figures rather than of dead relatives dominate the scene. We will discuss some possible reasons, such as the more autocratic family system in India, in the last chapter.

In the deathbed experiences, otherworldly apparitions which portray dead and religious figures appear to be a universal phenomenon that is relatively independent of medical factors and individual idiosyncrasies as well as of national and cultural differences. This phenomenon appears as something objective, like a mountain standing out of the clouds of shifting subjectivity.

7. THE SEX OF THE APPARITION

Although the sex of the hallucinatory figure is not relevant to the afterlife hypothesis, we felt it would be interesting to see the extent to which such images might be shaped by cultural backgrounds and customs. We therefore included this factor in our cross-cultural analysis of the Indian and American surveys. We found that the differences were striking. On the whole, Americans seemed to prefer female apparitions (61 percent), whereas Indians avoided them (23 percent). As stated earlier, India is more of a "man's world" than the United States is, which may explain this finding.

We investigated whether there were any differences between men and women patients regarding the sex of the apparition they saw. We found that significantly more American males than females perceived apparitions of women (71 percent versus 51 percent), while the men of India came very close to excluding them (17 percent). Even Indian women saw twice as many male (64 percent) as female apparitions. Apparently the cultural factors outweigh even sex differences.

Let us now return to cases where the apparition was masculine in practically all of the instances when the patient did not consent to be taken away. In the other world, as in this one, forceful action seems to be more characteristic of men.

In the case of peaceful take-aways, who received whom? Were male patients received or taken away by female apparitions, or vice versa? Women patients in both countries were received by a fairly equal number of male and female apparitions. However, in this respect, there was a striking difference between American and Indian males. American men generally were received by females (83 percent), whereas nearly all of the Indian males had members of their own sex (89 percent) to guide them to the other world.

In the following Indian case, a male experienced being taken away by his mother, possibly because of a strong emotional attachment. A

young Hindu boy who had just started
leukemia. His mother had died when he w
remembered her but was very conscious of

> He often talked about her and of what he had a
> brothers and sisters. He mentioned her and his
> affectionately: The day he died he had no fever be
> "My time has come," to his father. "My mother is calling
> standing there with her arms open." At that moment his st.
> mind was clear. He was conscious of his surroundings a
> talked to his father until the last moment. Then, with one hand
> holding his father's and the other pointing toward where he saw
> his mother, he said, "Don't you see my mother? See! My
> mother is calling." Then he died—stretching forward to his
> mother, almost falling out of bed. He was so happy to see her!

We then looked to see what effect the patient's age would have upon this sex variable. Young Americans saw more female figures than did older American patients (71 percent versus 58 percent), and the youth of India saw slightly more female apparitions than the older patients saw (29 percent versus 20 percent respectively). Whatever the inhibitory factor is in India, it seems to become a little more rigid with age. But would such inhibitions also relax with an increasingly Westernized way of life?

In order to check this possibility, we compared recent cases with those which happened five or more years ago. No change was found to have occurred in the United States, but the degree of female apparitions significantly decreased in India for recent cases. In fact, it cut the percentage in half, from 39 percent to 18 percent. It seems that the psychological process which interferes with Indians' awareness of feminine apparitions has become stronger rather than weaker in recent years.

Apart from the national differences, the patient's religion seemed to play a minor role. Hindus saw 22 percent female apparitions while patients of other religions in India saw 33 percent. The difference between American Protestants and Catholics was insignificant. Moreover, involvement in religion made no appreciable difference in either country. Therefore, it looks as though the Indian inhibition to hallucinate women has nothing to do with religion.

have secular reasons. The
...10 were uninvolved in religion
...reas the deeply involved demon-
...ex.

...have only very slight effects on the
...e. Only Indian patients with brain
...estively more women (37 percent) than
...wonder that the Indian sense of propriety
...vanish in patients with impaired brain

...spect of the apparition experience: American
...ale three times more frequently than are the
...es seen by Indians. Furthermore, although the sex
...figure modifies the experience, it does not affect the
...na. The majority of cases are still of a take-away
nature, and the apparitions are predominantly of close deceased
relatives.

CHAPTER 10

Getting at the Roots of
the Apparition Experience II

1. APPARITIONS—WORLDLY OR
OTHERWORLDLY:
A CRITICAL EVALUATION

WE dug deeper at the roots of the apparition experience, asking critical questions. Which kind of apparition points directly to an otherworldly origin and which to this-world sources? Are transpersonal emotions good indicators of the otherworldly origins of an apparition? Can the preconceived ideas of doctors and nurses explain the ostensible afterlife experiences? In this chapter we will search our interview material for objective answers.

2. APPARITIONAL EXPERIENCES AND
TOTAL HALLUCINATIONS

Hallucinations of persons are not all alike. In our collection of cases we distinguished two types.

1. Apparitional hallucinations—the patient hallucinates only a person, while his perception of his surroundings, such as the hospital room, doctors, and nurses, remains intact.

2. Total hallucinations—the patient hallucinates everything that he sees, and feels himself to be somewhere else—for example, in another world or reliving past memories in a past environment.

Are both types equally important to our study of deathbed visions? There is a difference. In the pilot study we discovered that apparitional hallucinations are like ESP experiences of the veridical hallucinations which convey real information. Hallucinations of ESP cases tend to be lifelike, usually bearing a close resemblance to the real person and often displaying a purpose and conveying a message in one way or another—for example, that a person was hit in a car accident miles away. Deathbed apparitions also were coherent, lifelike, concerned with the death situation, and generally brought a message to the patient of an afterlife which he should enter.

On the other hand, total hallucinations are a "mixed bag." Although they included visions of another world—which are, of course, relevant to our study—many of them were incoherent, rambling events which did not reflect the situation of dying. For example, it was noted in *Deathbed Observations* that some patients had "dropped completely out of the normal orientation system in space and time, living some time and place in the past."[1] The pilot study showed that a large number of these hallucinations were experienced by patients who had hallucinogenic diagnoses, such as uremic poisoning. Nevertheless, in a minority of total hallucination cases, a take-away purpose was expressed, as in the following case.

A man, 86, was suffering from a heart attack; he saw his mother and Jesus coming for him. He kept talking, reaching out. He did not seem to realize I was there. He spoke to his [dead] mother as if he was talking to her while she was right there. He said, "Jesus, don't leave me, I am coming." His eyes closed, it seemed as if he was asleep. Again he said, "I see you, I'm coming." Then he turned, looking at someone, "Mother, I'm here." He then went to sleep. The patient became calm, lost interest in life, and died 24 hours later.

In other total hallucination cases, patients believe that they are in

Heaven and seeing dead relatives there. However, such visions might also feel like an out-of-body experience, where one experiences himself as "flying" to different surroundings.

A Hindu farmer in his fortieth year was suffering from liver disease. He told [his doctor] he felt himself flying through the air and into another world where he saw gods sitting and calling him. He thought that he was going to meet those gods; he wanted to be there, saying to those around him: "Let me go." Relatives tried to talk him out of it. He would be O.K., he should not go. But the patient was very happy to see those gods and he was ready to die. He went into a deep coma a short time later, and died in two days. He was clear and coherent while describing what he "saw."

In this experience, the entire scene was hallucinated. Instead of otherworldly messengers coming to the hospital, the patient felt himself transported to them to the other world, while feeling as though he were out-of-body. We will deal with these experiences in Chapter 12.

Two-thirds of the patients in our combined samples had apparitional experiences; the other third consisted of total hallucinations. There was a difference here between the two countries. Nearly all (83 percent) of the Indian patients were reported to have had apparitional hallucinations, whereas only 47 percent of the American patients had experienced them. In 29 percent of the hallucinations from the U.S. sample, patients were merely reliving memories, and since these hallucinations indicate total disorientation, they are considered to be irrelevant to survival research. We had only one case in India where the patient was reported to have been reliving memories, and twenty-six such cases in America.

The difference might be accounted for by the manner of interviewing. We were able to give more precise instructions in the face-to-face interviews conducted in India than we could in our U.S. telephone interviews. If we subtract the relived-memory cases from the U.S. sample, two-thirds (66 percent) of the remaining cases are apparitional in nature, which comes close to the frequency of apparitional hallucinations in the Indian sample (83 percent). This will then leave us with results that are consistent with findings in the previous study—namely, that the majority of deathbed visions resemble ESP hallucinations of an apparitional nature.

There are rare cases in which apparitional hallucinations appeared to be clearly linked with unusual ESP powers of the dying. A sixty-four-year-old woman, the wife of a barber, was hospitalized with coronary occlusion. The nurse, who was also her daughter, told us:

> She was a very down-to-earth person, calm, not moody, and a strict Lutheran. I married into another faith. At that time, marrying a Catholic caused bad feelings. My parents were opposed. And it [the apparition] came as though she could have her peace of mind.
>
> I was sitting at her bedside. My husband had just brought me from Harrisburg to Reading. She said, "Ted [the nurse's husband] will be back very shortly because there is a host of people gathered at the bed [presumably dead relatives] and they are singing. When he gets back, they are going to pray together and then things will be different." So I said, "Mother, he won't be back—he just left."
>
> In about twenty minutes to a half hour I looked up and Ted was standing in the doorway. It was quite a shock. I exclaimed, "Honey, what brought you back?" "I don't know," he said, "I was going on home and I found myself turning back to Reading. I thought, Oh, well, I am closer to Reading than to Harrisburg. I'll go back and see how things are." He had no other explanation. Then mother, in a reconciliation, asked Ted to pray for her. It was a tremendous relief. It satisfied me too and was meaningful to us all. After that, serenity and peace came over her.

In the next step of our analysis we asked, "Do medical factors influence the apparitional nature of the hallucination?" We discovered that in both countries apparitional hallucinations and total hallucinations were not affected by the type of illness. This was true with only one exception: Patients with brain diseases or nephritis saw significantly fewer apparitional figures (35 percent in the United States, 65 percent in India) than did patients who had other diseases (47 percent in the United States, 80 percent in India). We may, therefore, state that hallucinogenic types of diseases tend to reduce rather than generate the possibility of seeing an apparitional hallucination.

Our composite measure of medical conditions conducive to hallucinations, which we termed the hallucinogenic index, was significantly related to Indian patients' seeing fewer apparitional hallucinations. Such medical conditions did not affect the apparition experiences of American patients. Apparently our model was correct: Medical factors might explain some of the total hallucinations, but they do not enhance the phenomenon when the apparition figure is seen while the patient's perception of his surroundings remains intact.

There is a very interesting relationship between the patient's state of consciousness and the frequency with which he sees an apparition. Figure 3 illustrates that the vast majority of clearly conscious patients (United States, 62 percent; India, 94 percent) saw apparitions in the natural surroundings of their sickrooms. Moreover, patients with a moderately impaired state of consciousness saw a smaller number of such apparitions (United States, 47 percent; India, 83 percent), while those whose consciousness was strongly impaired experienced them only rarely (United States, 17 percent; India, 8 percent).

These effects are highly significant, statistically speaking. Although moderate impairment of consciousness does not prevent patients from seeing an apparitional type of hallucination, strong impairment does. In fact, nearly all of the latter group saw total hallucinations. Therefore, awareness of and responsiveness to the external world appears to be essential to seeing apparitional hallucinations. They certainly cannot be interpreted as having been caused by delirious or comatose states.

In an attempt to find out what other factors might determine whether hallucinations are to be apparitional or total, we analyzed interaction between the frequency with which they were seen and such cultural factors as education. The role of education was not significant. The kind of religion also mattered little in either country. Neither Protestants and Catholics in the United States nor Hindus and other religious groups in India differed very much in this respect. However, while the degree of the patients' religious involvement showed no significant effects in the American sample, it

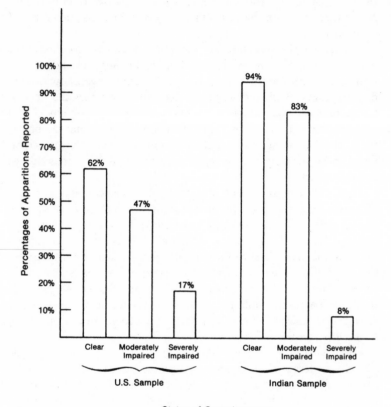

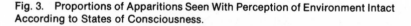

States of Consciousness

Fig. 3.   Proportions of Apparitions Seen With Perception of Environment Intact According to States of Consciousness.

did in India (p = .02). Indians deeply involved in religion saw a greater number of apparitional hallucinations (93 percent) than did the less religiously involved (74 percent). We are at a loss to explain this difference.

Although we thought that belief in an afterlife might also be a factor in seeing apparitions, we were unable to check out this possibility because of limitations in our sample. There were only twelve "registered disbelievers," a grouping not large enough on which to base generalizations. However, we note for the record that of the (twelve) apparition figures reportedly seen, two of the figures were of the deceased, seven were of the living, one was of a religious figure, and two were not identified by the patients who saw them.

It is very interesting to note the effect cultural differences have upon the type of hallucination seen. In our study, we found that although religious figures were seen in both countries, the surroundings in which they appeared varied. Americans seemed to have a propensity for placing such figures in what would stereotypically be considered "heavenly" surroundings (total hallucination) while an overwhelming majority of Indians saw them right in their own sickrooms (apparitional hallucination). One Indian doctor quipped, "Our deities make house calls; yours demand an office visit."

So we asked ourselves whether this difference can be accounted for in terms of the religious or the national distinctions between the two countries. Our analysis showed that the difference is apparently a national one because Christian patients in India had the same share of apparitional hallucinations as did Hindus. Regardless of beliefs, perhaps Indians experience the dimensions of the other world in a way that is more intimately intermingled with their day-to-day, mundane lives than is true of Americans. In any case, the difference here is highly significant ($p = .0002$).

Another point brought out by our interaction analyses was that in both countries more nurses than physicians reported cases of patients whose hallucinations were of an apparitional figure, exclusive of surroundings. Could this in any way be distorting our data? Certainly nurses spend more time with their patients and seem to be more familiar with the details of their experiences. This is especially true of nurses on private duty. However, physicians are supposed to have better judgment, possibly because their training is more sophisticated. Yet, might they not be more apt to share the prevailing skepticism that hallucinations mean nothing? We did encounter cases like this one: "She had seen him and talked with the Savior—we thought she was confused and no one paid much attention to her."

We expected to find less of this kind of skepticism in respondents who were deeply involved in religion—and indeed, such respondents did report more observations of apparitional hallucinations. Of course, the positive bias of believers could also distort observations. We used the information that we had available on cases of deathbed visions of patients who were either friends or relatives of our respondents, and who we could assume had received more attention than regular patients. Our respondents reported a slightly higher frequency of apparitional hallucinations in these better-attended patients. These results, in a sense, verify the higher rate of apparitional hallucinations reported by nurses and physicians involved in religion.

3. EMOTIONAL REACTIONS TO THE HALLUCINATORY FIGURE

Emotional expressions that appear on our faces, the glimmer in our eyes, are often far more revealing than are our words. According to our model (see Chapter 6), the emotions with which patients "receive" apparitions might indicate the true meaning of them: who or what they really are.

If the apparitions are real and represent a true encounter with postmortem existence, we would expect emotions that are consistent with such an awareness of "another world." The patients should exhibit emotional qualities like those described by William James in *Varieties of Religious Experience* (1902). However, if the apparitions are entirely subjective—expressing mundane concerns, inner conflicts and desires, or Freud's "day's residual"—we would expect the accompanying emotions to resemble those experienced in everyday life.

Our expectations were confirmed in the pilot survey. Patients exhibited a greater degree of calmness and peace after witnessing an apparition of the dead rather than one of the living, the latter being indicative of a mere hallucination. Assuming that another mode of reality does exist, such a reality is meaningful only if we can become aware of it. In a healthy person, such ostensible awareness of the transcendental or of the "other world" is commonly known as a "mystical experience"—not necessarily in its highest form. Here we can expect some similarity between religious experiences and the experiences of the dying—if they see something real; namely, the other world. Although our statistical results are in line with this assumption, they do not exclude other explanations—for example, Maslow's (1970) interpretation of these phenomena as "peak experiences."

In the pilot survey, we found many reports of emotions which, although difficult to describe, could be subsumed under the headings "religious emotions" and "serenity and peace." Essentially, reports of these emotions have included such descriptions as peace, harmony, beautiful radiance, or, as several respondents put it, "They light up." These emotions are easy to discern because of their sharp contrast to other emotions so often associated with dying: fear, depression, sadness, resignation, apathy. As an example, we quote a case about a businessman, college-educated and in his sixties, who was afflicted with a very painful and deadly infection. When the apparition came to him, pain changed to serenity.

Well, it was an experience of meeting someone whom he deeply loved. He smiled, reached up, and held out his hands. The expression on his face was one of joy. I asked him what he saw. He said his wife was standing right there and waiting for him. It looked as though there was a river and she was on the other side, waiting for him to come across. He became very quiet and peaceful—serenity of a religious kind. He was no longer afraid. He died a very peaceful death.

As described in Chapter 8, we made a detailed inquiry into the patients' emotional responses. Interactions of various factors with emotional responses were analyzed from two points of view: serenity versus elation, and religious versus nonreligious feelings. The first grouping compared the following: (1) no reactions, (2) negative emotion, (3) elation and excitement, and (4) serenity and peace. The second grouping compared: (1) positive, nonreligious emotions, (2) positive, religious emotions, and (3) no emotions or negative emotions. In order to achieve the most effective comparison possible, we further simplified this scheme by contrasting the assumed otherworldly emotions—serenity and peace in the first grouping, religious emotion in the other—with the most worldly ones: negative or no emotional response.[2]

According to our afterlife hypothesis, reacting with otherworldly feelings (religious emotions, serenity, and peace) to a hallucinatory figure might indicate that the apparition is real. Did our patients react differently to apparitions of the dead than to apparitions of the living? They did. After all, it would seem only appropriate to respond to religious figures with religious emotions and serenity and peace. The percentage of patients who responded with serenity and peace to apparitions of the dead was six times larger in the United States (24 percent) and four times larger in India (24 percent) than when experiencing apparitions of the living. Serenity came twice as often to the patients when the apparition of the dead had a take-away purpose. Of those who saw religious figures, 42 percent in the United States and 24 percent in India responded with serenity and peace. No one displayed religious feelings to apparitions of the living, a few did so to the dead, and many to religious figures (58 percent in the United States, and 35 percent in India). The differences are significant.

Afterlife-related apparitions are much more often met with emotions traditionally associated with religion and another world than are phantasms of the living. If otherworldly apparitions had a basis in external reality, we would expect such reactions.

In our attempt to discern the reason why Indian patients responded to apparitions of religious figures less frequently (35 percent) than did Americans (58 percent), we found a clue. In America, only 10 percent of the patients' reactions to apparitions of religious figures consisted of negative emotions, while in India this figure was 32 percent. The difference is understandable in light of Indian mythology. As explained before, Yama, the god of death, has messengers (Yamdoots) whose appearance may depend upon the moral quality of the dying person's life. They are often portrayed in a rather sinister fashion. When such Yamdoots are encountered, one would not wonder over any display of negative emotion. Hinduism, at its best, is a highly developed religion that propagates love and self-transcendence. But the dark side of the Hindu religion—portrayed by Yama, Yamdoots, and various demons—comprises about one-fifth of the religious figures seen by Indian patients. Positive emotions seem to accompany apparitions of such deities as Krishna, Shiva, or other benevolent celestial beings (for example, the devas).

It is, of course, universal that a certain kind of negative emotion is associated with religion. The Bible speaks about the fear of God quite often in the Old Testament, but Christianity, characteristically enough, has deemphasized these negative aspects. One does not find an expression such as "the fear of Christ" in the New Testament. This Christian emphasis on positive religious emotions might also be the reason for the differences in emotional reactions of American and

Indian patients to religious figures. However, there are more similarities than differences. In spite of very different cultural conditioning, many patients in both countries showed the same emotional reaction. That is, Hindus "light up" as Americans do.

The expressed purpose of the apparitions of dead and religious figures is to receive the patient and guide him or take him away to another world. These visions become more frequent as the patient comes closer to the time of his death. If we assume that most of the apparitions are real—for some may not be—there would be reason to believe that they are in some way aware of how close the patient is to death. Moreover, we would expect the real ones to be greeted with appropriate emotions—serenity and peace and religious feelings—while those which are mere hallucinations would not be received in the same manner. Let us give two examples.

A 68-year-old Polish housewife was afflicted with cancer. Her mind was clear. She was settling some financial matters and asked for her purse. She had not thought of dying. Then she saw her husband who had died twenty years before. She was happy, with a sort of religious feeling and, according to her doctor, she lost all fear of death. Instead of fearing death, she felt it to be the logical, correct thing. She died within 5 or 10 minutes.

Another housewife, whose husband was a butcher, died a whole week after seeing apparitions of her dead daughter and of some friends; the otherworldly emotional experience was absent. Her daughter who was a nurse told us, "She was lying in bed, perfectly calm and talking to my father and me. Then all of a sudden she called these people by name, as if they were standing by the bed. My father finally spoke up and probably spoiled it. There was no reason given [why they "came"]. There was no emotional impact. It didn't upset her, she took it as an ordinary event." And it probably was—a hallucination.

For the purpose of investigating this last assumption, we compared the percentage of patients who died within one hour, the percentage who died within one and twenty-four hours, and those who died more than twenty-four hours after experiencing hallucinations. This was done for both groups of patients who had experienced otherworldly emotions such as serenity and religious feelings, and for those who exhibited either no emotions or negative ones. The middle range (one to twenty-four hours) varied, but the extremes (up to one hour and more than twenty-four hours) showed the expected pattern. When our American patients saw the apparition close to their time of death, they responded to it twice as often with serenity and peace or religious emotions as when the apparition came more than twenty-four hours prior to death. There was no clear trend in our Indian sample.

Can these results be explained by supposing that the intensity of otherworldly emotions overtax the organism, thereby resulting in its death? It seems more likely to us that serenity and peace are less taxing than negative emotions (which proved to be mostly fear), excitement, or elation. However, could these latter emotions possibly hasten death?

If they could, they did not do so in our American sample. In fact, the patterns were exactly reversed. There were far fewer elated or negative emotional reactions than serene ones in the shorter interval, and many more in the longer. This relationship between emotional responses and the interval to death is reinforced by another finding that we described earlier. In cases where the ostensible purpose of the hallucinatory figure was to take the patient away to a postmortem existence, death came more quickly, as compared to cases involving a different purpose. Therefore, these two analyses indicated that the time until death and the presence of otherworldly apparitions are connected events.

Could these emotional reactions be explained by medical factors? In trying to answer this question, we first found that the nature of the disease did not affect patients' emotional responses. However, the hallucinatory index—which combines hallucinogenic illness and history, temperature, and medication—was important. The more hallucinogenic troubles they had, the less dying patients reacted with otherworldly emotions. Patients with no hallucinogenic indices experienced serenity and peace twice as frequently as those who had such indices: 44 percent versus 22 percent in the United States, 24 percent versus 12 percent in India (U.S. p = .005, India p = .07).

Religious emotional responses also were twice as frequent in patients with no hallucinogenic maladies: 29 percent versus 14 percent in the United States, 22 percent versus 11 percent in India

(United States p = .05, India p = .07). *Apparently, serenity and peace predominantly descend on patients whose organisms are relatively free from sickness and medications that can cause hallucinations.* Negative or no emotional responses, on the other hand, occurred in both countries more often with patients who had hallucinatory indices. Therefore, it seems that emotions appropriate for an otherworldly visitor cannot be explained by the above-mentioned medical factors, with the exception of the fear-evoking Yamdoots. Instead, they appear principally in patients who are not afflicted with maladies which we assume to be detrimental to ESP. This is consistent with our hypothesis that such responses are based upon extrasensory awareness of the apparition rather than physiological conditions.

The patient's clarity of consciousness was another point to be considered as possibly having some effect on emotions. In the pilot survey we found that clearly conscious patients experienced peace and serenity twice as often as those with impaired mental functioning. Both of our new samples confirmed that trend. We found that twice as many (46 percent) clearly conscious patients in the United States were serene and peaceful, while only 22 percent of those with impaired consciousness experienced these emotions (p = .01). Clearly conscious Indian patients were serene and peaceful three times more often (33 percent) than those with impaired mental clarity (11 percent, p = .0004).

The quality was lower in the cases where the consciousness was severely impaired and the apparition might be explained by psychological factors, as in the following case. This example concerns an eighty-year-old executive of one of the most powerful U.S. corporations. He handled their overseas operations. During the experience it was impossible to communicate with him. He was

very engrossed. He just sat and stared at the ceiling and talked to someone who was not there—smiling—just like a little kid looking at a Christmas tree. He called a girl's name and said, "I waited and waited—I knew you were going to come to me!"

The nurse knew who she was.

After his wife died—as if out of guilt—he used to tell me, "You know I loved my wife but it was not the same kind of love I had for my girl—my sweetheart." He told me how she had been killed in an accident just before they were to be married. Later he said, "I saw her! I knew she wouldn't go away forever—she will be back." Well, he had been talking about her for several days before the hallucination—it was on his mind. That, plus the guilt he felt about his own wife, probably produced it.

We concur with the nurse's interpretation. The apparition did not exhibit any take-away purpose and did not rouse otherworldly emotions in him—just love in an eighty-year-old heart.

It is generally believed that, for the most part, women are more emotionally responsive than men. However, we found that the patient's sex had no effect on his emotional response in either the United States or India. Age did, though. Older Indians responded twice as often with serenity and religious emotions than younger ones did (p = .05). In the United States, the relationship was reversed in the case of religious emotions (p = .04), but serenity was not affected at all by age. Although we are at a loss to explain these contradictory trends, it is apparent that serenity and religious feelings in the dying cannot be explained as life weariness in old age. Many young patients reacted with these same emotions. Perhaps it should also be mentioned that the patient's educational level seemed to have no effect on the mood phenomena.

Throughout this report, we have been investigating the influence religion might have on various aspects of the deathbed visions. Our analysis showed that Americans' emotional reactions to apparitional experiences were about the same, regardless of whether they were Catholics or Protestants. Hindus, on the other hand, tended to react differently. American Christians who experienced serenity and peace twice as often as Indian Hindus also had a slightly higher frequency of religious emotions.

Is this trend due to the fact that the patients belong to different nations, or is it because they believe in different religions? Our small sample of Indian Christians might be able to help us answer this question. This group not only reacted with serenity and peace much more often (43 percent) than did the Hindus (18 percent) but also outnumbered them when it came to religious emotions: 48 percent versus 15 percent.

Although these figures seem to indicate that religion is responsible for the difference in patients' emotional reactions, we must also note that our data show that Indian Christians even outdid Americans with their otherworldly emotional responses. This leads us to suspect that the difference cannot be due purely to religion, although that factor may have some effect. It is possible that nurses—who, in India, are frequently Christians—biased their reports of religious emotions in Christian patients. Since Christians are a small minority in India, they might be a bit defensive about their religion. However, even if we compare Hindus with American Christians, there are still differences in serene reactions (Hindus 18 percent, American Christians 35 percent) and in religious feelings (Hindus 15 percent, American Christians 26 percent).

On the surface it appears that religion, to some extent, shapes the phenomena. For example, Hinduism might inhibit it, while Christianity might enhance serenity and religious emotional reactions. If this were so, we would expect to find the difference concentrated in patients who were deeply involved in their religion. This was not the case, however. We therefore conclude that involvement in religion had no effect on otherworldly emotional reactions in either India or the United States.

In further explorations of the patients' personal variables, we learned that belief in life after death seemed to affect the phenomena. We have information regarding belief in 139 patients, but disbelief in only 12. This is too small a group for effective comparison. However, a good number of those patients who did not discuss their beliefs might actually have been nonbelievers, and so we contrasted the group of believers with the no-information group. In the United States, reactions of serenity and peace were not appreciably related to belief (p = .48) and only slightly, but not significantly, related in India (p = .08). Apparently, if these emotions are at all influenced by belief, it is only to a very slight extent. Therefore, belief cannot explain these serene and peaceful reactions.

On the other hand, reactions with religious feelings were significantly related to belief (U.S. p = .001, India p = .0004). Among patients who believed in life after death, the effects were extremely similar for both countries: 37 percent of the Americans and 35 percent of the Indians reacted with religious emotions. Of the patients whose beliefs were unknown, 12 percent of the Americans and 13 percent of the Indians reacted in the same way. Consequently, belief in life after death is a very important factor.

Are religious emotional reactions, then, fully explained by belief in an afterlife? Not necessarily. We know from ESP research that belief in ESP phenomena influences performance; believers tend to do better, and disbelievers to block or distort extrasensory awareness (Schmeidler, 1958). Therefore, if deathbed visions involve extrasensory awareness of a postmortem existence, we might expect the same mechanism to be at work.

Would the patient's mood prior to seeing an apparition explain his emotions after the hallucination? Our investigation into this question demonstrated that the correlation between these two variables is not significant. The emotions usually came after appearance of the apparition. Then we attempted to discern whether a patient's expectation of death or recovery would explain the otherworldly emotional responses. We did this by comparing the emotional responses of patients who expected to recover with those of the patients who expected to die. There were no significant differences in either country. The distribution was, for the most part, very even.

We also looked into the distribution of clarity of consciousness in patients who reacted with religious emotions. The majority of these patients fell into the clearly conscious—as opposed to the impaired—group: 35 percent versus 11 percent in the United States, 27 percent versus 13 percent in India (p = .02 in the United States and India). The opposite trend was found to occur in the negative-emotion or no-emotion group. More patients with impaired consciousness responded in such a manner than did those who were clear and coherent to the end. Thus, neither an impaired state of consciousness, nor delirium, nor a comatose state is an adequate enough explanation for responses of serenity, peace, or religious emotions. Quite the contrary, the same impairments which seem to cut down on extrasensory awareness also reduce the likelihood of finding this type of response to otherworldly apparitions. Since the basis for the above emotional reactions seems to be extrasensory awareness of the apparition, we may point out that this trend is in line with the afterlife hypothesis.

To sum up thus far: The interaction patterns of an otherworldly emotional response to seeing apparitions are reasonably consistent with the postmortem hypothesis but fit poorly with either the medical "sick brain" theory, the psychological explanations of stress reactions and wishful seeing, or the explanation based on cultural conditioning or patient characteristics.

4. THE RESPONDENTS

Could our respondents be reading their own philosophies and beliefs into the expressions and behaviors of their terminal patients? This is an important question, one which we tried to answer by appropriate analysis.

We carefully evaluated the possibility that respondent bias might have distorted observations of phenomena relevant to the afterlife hypothesis. For example, could reports of living, dead, and religious apparitional figures have been influenced by some beliefs of the respondents? We found that neither our American nor our Indian respondents' belief or disbelief in life after death related to the kinds of hallucinatory figures they reported to have been seen by their patients. Respondents' involvement in religion did not make any difference, either. We can, therefore, conclude that the observations reported are in good agreement as to the types of apparitional figures—whether living, dead, or religious—seen by patients. Furthermore, it did not matter if the reports on the three kinds of apparitions were made by interns, physicians, or nurses, nor did it make a difference if they personally knew the patient.

We also checked to determine if the purpose of the hallucinatory person seemed to have been observed objectively by our respondents or if there was a difference suggestive of bias. In both countries we found peaceful take-away cases reported rather evenly. Although nurses observed slightly more cases than physicians, the difference was only 7 to 9 percent. However, Indian take-away cases in which the patient did not consent to go were reported twice as frequently by nurses as by interns or staff physicians and general practitioners.

In light of those findings, could there have been a positive bias in nurses or a negative bias in doctors? That is, did Indian nurses read in an aggressive take-away purpose where there was none, or did Indian physicians neglect to note it because of a philosophical bias? We have reason to believe that the cases in which the patient was known to the respondent—a relative or friend—were better observed. Patients generally seemed to have been more open with a relative or a friend, who, in turn, listened more attentively. In both the American and Indian samples, the peaceful take-away was reported more often in patients who were friends or relatives of the respondent. Apparently, if there was a bias, it did not consist of exaggerations by nurses but by understatements of physicians who might have overlooked the take-away nature of some cases. It is also interesting to note that there were slightly fewer aggressive take-away cases in known patients. There is the possibility of some bias in the nurses in India, in terms of their seeing too many cases in which the take-away purpose occurred without the patient's consent. However, if this were true, it would distort only a minor portion of our data, and so would not appreciably affect our findings.

Of course, the respondent's belief in life after death, his involvement in religion, and his age could be factors in biasing his observations of the hallucinatory purpose. Although we did not find in either the American or Indian samples that a respondent's belief, religious involvement, or recency of graduation had any significant effect on his report of the take-away purpose, there was some difference with regard to age. The youngest American respondents reported fewer take-away cases; the middle and older age groups were in agreement among themselves and closer to the rate of patients known to the respondents. Therefore, we can state that the hallucinatory purpose experienced by patients was possibly overlooked by some interns and other younger respondents. No appreciable positive bias or exaggeration of the frequency was detected in any of the groups of respondents.

Observations of patients' emotional reactions to seeing apparitions might easily be biased by overlooking them or exaggerating them. Indeed, we found that the emotion of serenity and peace was observed to a different degree by doctors and nurses. In the American sample, serenity and peace were reported more frequently by nurses (25 percent) than by physicians (14 percent). In India, there was no such discrepancy—25 percent versus 26 percent for nurses and physicians, respectively. The Indian interns saw serenity less often (9 percent).

On the whole, nurses in both countries and physicians in India were remarkably similar in their reports on serenity, while American physicians and Indian interns saw less of it. So we must ask whether nurses have overclaimed or whether physicians have overlooked the emotions in question. We checked to see if the nurses' reports were swayed by their beliefs and religion, and still found no indication of such a bias. Neither the nurses' beliefs in postmortem survival nor their involvement in religion had any effect on their reports of the patients' emotions.

We turned again to the most reliable portion of our data—cases in which the patient was either a relative or a friend of the respondent. In these "known" cases, religious feelings were reported as often as they were by nurses: American nurses, 15 percent, "known" cases 17 percent; Indian nurses, 20 percent, "known" cases 22 percent. We may therefore assume that the nurses' figures are more accurate than those of the doctors. Reports of serenity and peace in Indian "known" cases (26 percent) are also very close to those of the nurses (25 percent), and different from those of the interns (9 percent). In the United States, serenity was not reported differently in known and unknown patients and so there was no indication of bias in that sample. As far as we can see, physicians—especially Indian interns—overlooked some emotions, but there were no signs of overlooking by nurses. It might very well be that women in general are more observant of such subtleties as moods and states of consciousness and therefore report them more accurately.

We also inquired into the possibility of distortions that might be the result of poor memories of old cases. Could cases have grown more "beautiful" with exaggeration as the years passed by? Our analysis showed no such exaggerations. There was no significant difference between the older and the newer cases.

In conclusion, we may say that the interaction analyses—looking at the apparition phenomena along with various other factors—was, indeed, informative. Contrasting apparitions having this-world purposes with those with the take-away purpose yielded, in general, the same result: consistency with, and confirmation of, the postmortem survival hypothesis as stated in our model.

CHAPTER 11

From Depression and Pain
to Peace and Serenity

T HE termination of life is generally experienced as a sad event
in which family, relatives, and friends often weep. Nurses tell
us how hard it is for them to ward off depressing feelings when
caring for the dying, and doctors are used to announcing, "His
condition is desperate." Death anxieties are a common preoccupa-
tion in psychoanalytic literature.

Despite this prevalent morbidity, not all terminal patients are in a
state of fear, depression, or apathy. In our pilot study, we asked a
rather unusual question: "Have you observed a sudden rise of mood
to exaltation in dying patients?" For 753 cases reported by 169
observers, the answer was "Yes." Mood elevation in terminal stages
can rise above the gloom and pain of dying. A common statement
made by medical observers was "They light up."

But why is it that, although the majority do not, some patients
have beautiful emotions as death approaches? Obviously, death
while in an elevated mood is preferable to dying while in a miserable
state—a concept that comes close to the idea of dying a "good
death," and analogous to the one of living a "good life." Perhaps if
we could understand the processes involved, we could help patients
die a good death.

Mood elevation phenomena are also important for our postmortem survival hypothesis. According to our model, mood elevation in terminal stages might be caused by the onset of the patient's extrasensory awareness of oncoming postmortem existence, which, on the basis of the pilot study, we assume to be a good existence. The incoming information, we theorized, might be more or less consciously experienced or kept on a preconscious level. But moods can fluctuate because of many factors. Therefore, we must carefully investigate the known causes as well as the cause postulated by our survival hypothesis in order to get at the truth.

We conducted 174 interviews on cases of mood elevation (106 in the United States, 68 in India). We based our analysis on these cases. It is significant that we obtained a relatively greater number of mood elevation cases in the United States than in India. In a later discussion we will come back to this point.

In the U.S. and Indian surveys, we asked in our initial questionnaire: "Have you ever observed a sudden rise of mood to happiness or serenity in a dying patient?" In lengthy interviews on reported cases of mood elevation, we asked what it was about the patient's behavior that indicated a rise of mood. We also asked whether he expressed it in words, and if so, how. From the responses, we worked out four indices of mood elevation: patient's verbal expression of the mood, increase of activity, social interaction, and religious activities, if any. The phenomena of mood elevation as the patients related it could be placed in two categories: the serene and calm on one hand (49 percent), and the cheerful and elated on the other (27 percent). There was also a third category of lesser importance: those who became full of optimism (20 percent) and started to make plans about work, vacation, or going home from the hospital if they were hospitalized. Moreover, 4 percent of patients had other expressions of mood (see Table 8). Through the rise of mood, many patients became less agitated and more communicative. Some showed evidence of increased physical strength. Many of them became more cooperative toward those treating them and generally more benevolent to persons around them—for example, expressing their gratitude. Of the 174 patients, only 21 were observed praying, singing, reciting religious verses, or talking about religious matters.

As in the case of deathbed visions, most of these mood elevations occurred shortly before the time of death. Forty-one percent of the patients died within ten minutes of the rise of mood, and more than half of them died within an hour of the beginning of their sudden rise of mood to serenity and peace.

In both the United States and India, the rise of mood seemed to be independent of the age of the patients. Although people over fifty years of age naturally form the majority of the cases (about 60 percent), all age groups are found in our sample (see Table 10). Here, great national differences were found. The mean age of our U.S. sample was sixty-one years, whereas in India it was only forty-eight years, reflecting the shorter life expectancy in that country. Furthermore, although the sex of the patients made no difference in the United States, in India considerably fewer women experienced mood elevation. The same was true concerning apparition cases. As we have already stated in our discussion of the apparition cases, this difference might be due to the fact that fewer women than men are hospitalized in India.

In our samples, most (80 percent) of the patients' states of consciousness were clear, and they were fully aware of their surroundings. Of the 174 patients, only 27 had difficulty in communicating with those around them, and 7 were not able to answer or understand questions directed to them. Only 4 percent had brain maladies or uremic poisoning. Furthermore, 85 percent of these patients had nothing in their medical histories or present medical conditions that the respondents thought might explain the sudden rise of mood that they experienced shortly before death and which, in many cases, came at a time of severe pain and stress. About half of the patients were not receiving any sedation, and 21 percent were so lightly sedated that our respondents believed them to be psychologically unaffected by the medication. In only about 11 percent of the cases where pertinent information was available were the patients moderately or strongly affected by their sedation. Less than 3 percent were running a temperature of 104° or more. In short, the majority of our patients were fully conscious, were not running fevers, were not being affected by sedation, and did not suffer from diseases of the brain or other diseases that are considered apt to cause hallucinations or euphoria. This appears to contradict the hypothesis that the medical condition of the patient may be the primary cause of mood elevation.

Our sample contained mainly people of two major religions:

Christianity and Hinduism. In only 10 of our 174 cases was the patient's religious adherence reported as unknown to the respondent. Fifty-six Hindus formed 34 percent of the patients whose religious adherence was known. There were also 39 Protestants (24 percent), 38 Catholics (23 percent), and a few Jews, Indian Christians, Muslims, and persons belonging either to no religion or to other religions.

In those 100 cases where pertinent information was available, 46 percent of the patients were reported to be deeply involved in religion. The figures were similar for the United States and India. Furthermore, 34 percent were reported to be moderately involved in religion. Only 4 percent of these patients were not at all involved in religion. However, most of the 43 percent of the patients who did not talk to our respondents about their religion were, quite probably, involved in religion to a slighter extent. On the whole, it appears that the patient's *religious affiliation* is of little importance to the occurrence of mood elevation. However, the degree of his *involvement in religion* may very well be of some importance.

We asked our respondents if they had known their patients before their illness. Three-fourths of those about whom we have knowledge concerning their religious involvements were either friends or relatives of the respondents. Therefore, we should have more reliable figures for religious involvement for this group than for the whole sample. Of the 46 percent of the entire sample who were deeply involved in religion, 57 percent were "known" patients. Therefore, we have indications that the above figures for religious involvement may, in fact, be too low.

In mood-elevation cases we have scanty information on patients' beliefs in an afterlife. Only one-third of our patients discussed their beliefs in life after death with doctors and nurses; 93 percent of those who did were believers. It is most likely that those who were not interested in an afterlife—those who had no strong belief—did not bother to mention this matter to the medical personnel. Later, we will report our careful analysis of the possible influence of beliefs on mood elevation phenomena.

In our analysis we found that the phenomenon of mood elevation occurred to the noneducated and illiterate as well as to the educated. Because of the differences in education in the two countries, we will deal with them separately. In the United States, 34 percent of the patients attended only grade school, 36 percent went to high school, and 24 percent had a college education. As the mean age of our U.S. patients was sixty-one and the cases were, on the average, three years old, we are dealing here mostly with the generation born around the turn of the century. In 1920, when most of our sample was going to college, the enrollment was only 8 percent of the eighteen- to twenty-one-year-old population. This shows that the percentage of college-educated people in our sample (24 percent) is considerably above the general population of that age bracket. We find the same trend with the high-school-educated. In 1920, the enrollment was 17 percent of the seventeen-year-olds, whereas in our sample 60 percent attended at least high school. This is, again, far above the national percentage for these age groups. Medical care is not evenly distributed among all educational levels, but in spite of that it seems that we can safely conclude that high school and college education brackets are larger in our sample than in the general U.S. population of comparable age groups. Education is supposed to be inversely related to superstitions and factually unsupported beliefs. In our sample, education is positively related to frequency of mood elevation near the time of death. Therefore, the hypothesis that superstitious beliefs may be the cause of these mood elevations is contradicted by the tendencies of our sample.

In India, we obtained our data only from public or university hospitals—as one professor of medicine in Delhi phrased it, "poor people hospitals"—where treatment was, for the most part, free of cost. Professional people, we were told, would go mostly to private hospitals. The Indian figures are: illiterate, 20 percent; grade school, 25 percent; high school, 35 percent; and college, 20 percent. This is, for India, a relatively small number of illiterates and those receiving primary education only, and a relatively large number of educated people. The average age of our patients in India was forty-eight years. The cases were in general only a year old. Hence, most of our Indian patient population was born in the 1920s. It is hard to get even approximate figures of educational levels for that time, but even by using the present-day figures, we find that the number of high-school- and college-educated in our sample is much higher than in the general Indian population. Of course, we obtained our data mostly from hospitals in cities where most of the educated people live. However, that could not adequately explain the disproportionate distribution of education in our sample. So apparently in India also we find the same trend: The less superstitious, better-educated patients experienced a rise of mood more often.

Dawn upon the Black Sea

Suffering precedes dying. One must be blind not to see pain and sorrow in the hospital rooms of terminal patients. Three-quarters of our patients suffered from either cancer, heart attacks, or postoperative conditions which are usually very painful and hard to bear. Metastasized cancer spreading all over the body brings real torture in its final stages, with no relief day or night. Severe heart attacks come with spells of very strong pain radiating from chest to arms. Postoperative or injured patients are usually bound up in bandages, tubes, and splints. Of course, pain and discomfort might affect some patients more strongly than others, depending on the medical conditions and the drugs given to them. Nevertheless, the terminal stages are like a black sea of suffering. This is the bleak background from which, shortly before death, some patients were reported to "light up" in an expression of harmony and serenity. "A dawn upon the black waters," as one doctor put it.

The cases vary widely in their richness of expression and the amount of information in them, depending on the respondent's acquaintance with the patient, the extent of his observation, and the condition of the patient. A nurse in a large hospital in New Delhi reported the following case which impressed her.

A female patient in her forties—who was suffering from cancer and during the last preceding days, had been depressed and drowsy, though always clear—suddenly looked very happy. A joyful expression remained on her face until she died five minutes later.

As in some American cases, the patient never said anything during her apparent rise of mood; only the unusual sudden change of facial expression stuck in the nurse's memory. She was a stranger to the nurse, and so we know nothing about her beliefs, nor of what was going on in her mind.

The same was also true in the following American case, where the facial expression was reminiscent of a description of ecstasy in religious literature.

A woman in her seventies, suffering from pneumonia, was a semi-invalid who spent a painful miserable existence. Her face became so serene, as if she had seen something beautiful. There was a transfixed illumination on her face—a smile beyond description. Her features were almost beautiful on so old a face. Also, her skin had a transparent, waxy quality—almost snow white—so different from the usual yellow discoloration which follows death.

The explanation offered by the respondent was that she might have had a vision which "just transformed her entire being." This serenity lasted until her death an hour later.

The following case is about a man in his sixties suffering from postoperative complications.

I had been out of the room—came back and looked at him. I saw an expression of peace on his whole face—so peaceful. In a few minutes there was no pulse—he had died.

On the whole, our respondents had extensive experience with terminal patients and seemed to be aware that simple changes in the dying organism could be mistaken for serenity and peace. Nevertheless, we also encountered cases which appeared to be mood elevation but actually were not. For example, mere changes in physiological processes and relaxation of muscle tensions might appear to be expressions of peace as illustrated by this case.

My father became more relaxed. His whole being just seemed to slow down. His actions were alert and finally he sank into a comatose condition and died that day.

The whole system's slowing down is a physiological process to be expected in dying and is of no interest for parapsychology.

In addition, a patient sometimes releases acute negative emotions. He ceases being angry or agitated anymore. We had to guard against using such cases, as well as another kind of case in which a patient merely accepted things as they came. "Well, I have had enough of this," is a remark characteristic of a patient tortured by metastasized cancer. It is as though nothing more can be done and one just has to resign oneself. Such sad resignation is certainly not mood elevation in our sense. Since there is a possibility that doctors and nurses could have misinterpreted facial expression—for example, seeing peace where there was actually only a relaxation of muscle tissue at death—we will devote the end of this chapter to a careful analysis of the possible biases in our respondents.

Sometimes the change is sudden and clear, and the otherworldly intimations are not veiled. A male, forty-six, who was suffering from leukemia and who had been rather depressed and lethargic, awoke from a coma, opened his eyes, and said, "How beautiful." He then died within a few minutes.

The following report concerns a fifty-nine-year-old woman who had pneumonia and cardiac involvement.

> The expression on her face was beautiful; her *attitude* seemed to have changed entirely. This was more than a change of the mood I had seen her in many times before. . . . It seemed as if there was something just a little beyond us that was not natural. . . . There was something which made us feel that she was seeing something that we did not see. She was always moody but for the past year she was really depressed. She never had psychiatric help. I feel that she did have some contact with the beyond and it had a happy effect on her.

At other times the clues were more subtle and therefore easily missed. Sometimes we got a hint from the often-expressed suggestion that the strength to die gracefully comes from the feeling that another world exists. In the case of an old man with tuberculosis, it was reported:

> His *serenity* was so sudden. One day he said to me, "Mrs. Jones, will you bring me a tall glass of water with lots of ice?," and I

did. He drank it and said, "Mrs. Jones, this water will see me through the Jordan." I think that by referring to the water of the Jordan, he was telling me that he was going to die. He died in 90 minutes. They, *the doctors*, were very surprised at his sudden death, for there were no visible signs of imminent demise.

Sometimes the patient just seems to be feeling better and is more active or full of desire for activity.

He was confined to bed and wanted to do many things he couldn't do. He wanted to bathe himself, tried to go to the dining room to eat with the family. Appetite good, little pain. It was not an improvement but appeared to be just an expression of a raised mood.

Another respondent reported:

Suddenly one day there was a complete change. He was conscious; his appetite improved. He could do things for himself. He was improved both physically and mentally. The pulse was stronger, the temperature remained the same, and the appetite greatly increased. The gain was not a real improvement; he died within 24 hours.

The respondent, however, was not surprised. He said, "I have often noted that sometimes patients will perk up, take notice of things and, in other cases, eat heartily."

In some cases, there were additional aspects which make sense in the context of our model, such as when patients did not feel pain and discomfort any longer. Could the mind become "loosened up," less tightly connected with the bodily processes when the individual is near death? The following is a typical case where pain and misery suddenly disappeared. The physician who reported it was the director of a city hospital in India.

A male patient in his seventies had been suffering from advanced cancer. He had been in great pain, sleepless and restless. One day after he had managed to get a little sleep, he woke up smiling, seemed suddenly free from all physical pain and agony, detached, calm, and peaceful. For the last six hours the patient had only received a very moderate dose of phenobarbital, a relatively weak sedative. He bade all good-bye, one by one, which he had not done before, and told us that he was going to die. He was fully alert for some 10 minutes. Then he fell into a coma and died peacefully a few minutes later.

This case was about the director's father. He told us that after this experience, his father was prepared to die. He had been a religious Hindu, an educated man, believed in life after death, and had become increasingly involved in religion during the last month of his life. "Detached, calm, and peaceful" seems to be what Indians mean when they speak of a "good death."

According to traditional religious beliefs, something in us called a "soul" leaves the body at the time of death. A few cases seem to suggest that this "leaving" might not be so sudden after all. While still functioning normally, the patient's consciousness might be gradually disengaging itself from the ailing body. That consciousness, or soul, might slowly loosen itself for the transition. If so, we could expect awareness of bodily sensations to gradually decrease, as they did in the following three examples. Of course, other interpretations which do not assume life after death are also possible—for example, the increased dissociation of personality subsystems, the mind falling apart at death.

In our first example, a male patient in his fifties was tortured by metastasized rectal cancer. The respondent noticed that before the patient died, he no longer suffered from excruciating pain.

The thing that brought it to my attention was that he hadn't had any Demerol for 24 hours. This was a departure from his previous pattern. He said he didn't need any drugs because his pain was gone and he was feeling better. He went into a coma and died within a day.

In another case, an eighty-year-old male stroke patient was cooperative but seemed to lose interest in things.

He suddenly didn't want any sedation. He didn't seem to need it. He didn't seem to be in any more pain and was perfectly relaxed; up to this point he had been in severe pain. Blood pressure, pulse stabilized.

Disengagement from pain is very clear in such cases, but they do not pinpoint the reasons for it with sufficient clarity. Fortunately, we do have cases which indicate wholesome changes rather than disintegration—for example, being thoughtful to others.

A 50-year-old male leukemia patient had been previously cranky and apprehensive for two to three weeks. As death was more imminent, he seemed to realize that there was something more to life than just problems. He became more serene and was thoughtful about those he would leave behind.

Quite opposite to the deterioration hypothesis are comments which indicate a broader outlook on life and death and which go well with the hypothesis of a disengagement from symptoms. The following is a typical remark by a respondent.

This leukemia patient was pleasant to his relatives and spoke of death in a matter-of-fact way. He claimed he wasn't physically uncomfortable and didn't want sedation.

In some cases, doctors and nurses mentioned that the patient's consciousness became clear during the mood-elevation period, which of course would not go very well with the deterioration explanation. Does this clarity involve such extrasensory qualities as one might expect from a mind loosening up from the body? In our culture, of course, little attention would be paid in hospitals to an extrasensory perception. However, one of our respondents was surprised about a man, twenty-two, who had been blind since the age of seventeen. "Although he was blind, he seemed to see us."

As strange as it may be, medical observers reported cases where, instead of deterioration of mind and personality, there seemed to be an improvement just prior to death. "Female, 60's, heart disease. She felt wonderful. Started to laugh as she always used to. She was her normal self again." It was then told how much she enjoyed—"as she normally would"—watching her little granddaughter, aged one and a half, playing.

One of us (Osis, in *Deathbed Observations*) had previously reported two cases of chronic psychotics, both completely out of touch with reality, who seemed to the medical observers to be their normal selves again shortly before death (1961). Kübler-Ross told us (in a personal communication) that she had observed chronic schizophrenics as they died. According to her, many of them became lucid and normal shortly before death. This would, of course, go well with the hypothesis of the mind's gradual disengagement from the body and its malfunctions prior to death. Strangely enough, even in diseases which are primarily destructive to the brain, this seemed to happen. We have a case where a meningitis patient, a woman in her thirties, was severely disoriented almost to the end. Then

she cleared up, answered questions, smiled, was slightly elated and just a few minutes before death, came to herself. Before that she was disoriented, drowsy, and talked incoherently.

Accordingly to the model of postmortem survival, it is possible to have a clear mind even though the brain is deadly ill. We might expect the mind to be even clearer without any brain at all if postmortem existence is a reality. In our survey, we did not look especially for cases where severely disturbed patients became lucid and normal before death. However, we recommend to other researchers that such cases should be gathered in large numbers and analyzed with great care in properly designed surveys.

Do Indians "Light Up" Differently?

We found fewer cases of mood elevation in India. That does not necessarily mean that Indian patients die in a gloomier state than American ones. One reason for this discrepancy could be that the observations in India are more hurried because the hospitals are understaffed and do not have enough nurses. There are about twice as many doctors as nurses in India, and there is nothing equivalent to the American private-duty nurse. In the United States, we obtained most of our mood observation from private-duty nurses who apparently had become intimately familiar with the patients and were able to make observations of such subtle factors as moods. However, the mood cases we have from India seemed to run the same gamut as cases in the United States. There was the same serenity, peace, and disengagement from pain and other symptoms. Typical is the case of a woman who, having previously been in severe pain, was "extraordinarily happy, talking with relatives and in a joyous mood." Notice the expression "extraordinarily happy." The Indian patients appeared to be more often happily excited than peaceful, and the respondents did not hesitate to use superlatives in describing them. We saw the same increase in kindness and concern for relatives and doctors as in American patients during mood elevation.

> The condition of one man, suffering from a heart attack, had been serious for the last few days. Suddenly he gained consciousness. He looked better and cheerful. He talked nicely to his relatives and requested them to go home. He also said, "I shall go to my home. Angels have come to take me." He looked relieved and cheerful.

In India, we found that in cases where there were no medical reasons for dying, premonitions of death accompanied the patient's elevation in mood.

> Post-operative female: Suddenly she said she was going to leave this world, although we did not at all expect her to die. She also told this to visitors and attendants, and thanked them with gratitude. She was relaxed and well-oriented. She recognized people. We thought she would come out nicely. At the last round, I found her feeling happy, relaxed. She spoke about dying very soon. The next morning she died.

Does any of the Hindu Yoga training influence the experience of dying? Actually, in spite of our inquiries, we found no cases of dying Yogis or swamis. As one doctor said: "Swamis don't come to die with us. They prefer to die in their ashrams surrounded by disciples, or on some holy ground, like Benares." This hospital (Benares Hindu University Hospital) was located a few hundred yards outside Benares. However, we found some cases concerning lay practitioners of the Hindu teachings. A faculty member of a medical school in Benares described the death of his grandfather, who had practiced Yoga. He was a philanthropist, having helped many persons in his vicinity, and was very religious. People came to him for a general uplift. In his case, the rise in mood started forty-eight hours before death, which the doctor described as perfect consciousness with tranquillity. He seemed to have a premonition of death, for which there were no sufficient medical reasons. He ordered a load of wood for the funeral pyre, sent a telegram to his son, and on the last day at four o'clock, asked the family members to eat something, since he would die at five thirty, and in accordance with Hindu custom, nobody would then be permitted to eat. The premonition came true, and he died at five thirty-five. He had performed Hindu purification procedures in order to prepare for death. He didn't show the slightest anxiety and was seen consoling relatives who were crying. He said to the weeping people, "You should be happy because I am going." He was perfectly controlled, unafraid, and tranquil. He described, step by step, how the body was dying. He told how his legs were becoming stiff and could be pricked without his feeling it, and how limb after limb was becoming numb and no longer a part of "the eternal self."

This case is suggestive of a self-induced detachment of one's self from the body, its afflictions and cares. This kind of detachment from the body was reported to go together with the "onset of tranquil awareness of the transition to a new existence, including a very accurate precognition of death." How would the death of a Yogi compare with the concept of a "good death" in our predominantly Christian culture? We certainly had cases in the United States where patients died in tranquillity and peace, with some ostensible awareness of an afterlife. The difference between the "good death" of a Yogi and that of a saintly Christian might be that the Yogi has more reliance on what he does to prepare for death, while Christians seem to rely more on the grace of such external sources as God or the priest. However, the average Hindu is not a Yogi and seems to rely just as much upon external sources as the Christians do. The ideal "good death" seems to be very rare, present only in exceptional individuals. For the vast majority of patients in both cultures, mood elevation is not worked up, but just happens, or, more frequently, is not there.

Possible Causes of Mood Elevation

Moods are known to be related to physiological processes. For example, when a person produces large percentages of brainwaves in the alpha range, he is usually more tranquil than when he is without them. Tranquilizers and antidepressant drugs obviously influence moods. Certain analgesics, such as morphine and Demerol, frequently used on terminal patients, can also change moods. In our data, it is important to evaluate medical factors in order to see whether the phenomena of mood elevation depend on them or are relatively independent.

Our analyses focused on those moods which are most clearly related to the afterlife hypothesis: serenity and peace, and religious emotions. In our evaluation we not only contrasted serenity and peace with elation, but also religious positive moods with nonreligious positive moods. We again analyzed how these emotions were related to medical variables. The pathology which would be most likely to affect patients' minds are brain injuries and diseases, and uremic poisoning resulting from kidney malfunctioning. Such diseases were practically absent in cases of mood elevation. There were only two such cases with serenity—one with elation—and none at all with religious emotions. We can only say that whatever the impact of brain disorder and uremia on a patient's mentality may be, it is not elevation of mood at the time of death. On the contrary, they seem to suppress mood elevation.

We asked our respondents if there was anything in the patients' medical histories which might effect mood changes—for example, psychiatric history, alcoholism, some senility, and so on. Out of all of our 174 patients with mood elevation, only 23 had such histories. Medical histories of possible psychogenic maladies were mainly in the U.S. sample. There were only 6 cases in the Indian sample. Thus the possibility of performing an interaction analysis was precluded. There was no difference (within the U.S. sample) in emotions of serenity and peace between the cases with and those without such medical histories. However, the difference in religious emotions was striking. Patients with no such histories had a religious rise of mood four times more often (41 percent) than patients with the histories (9 percent): p = .05. Psychogenic pathology did not seem to generate religious emotions. On the contrary, it rather sharply cut the possibility of having them.

Medication that could affect a patient's mentality was not related to the kinds of moods the patients had. The hallucinogenic index (see page 106) was used to analyze combined U.S. and Indian data because the separate samples were small. There was no appreciable difference in frequency of either serene or religious emotions between patients who had hallucinogenic indices and those who had not. Nor did the patient's state of consciousness affect these kinds of emotions in the rise of mood. The analysis of interactions of medical factors and mood data clearly confirmed the findings of the pilot study. There were no indications that medical factors cause afterlife-related mood elevation to serenity and peace, and religious emotions. Some medical factors—for example, brain diseases and uremic poisoning—seem to suppress afterlife-related rise of mood.

Would other characteristics of the patient determine the phenomena of mood elevation at death? The age of the patient did not seem to matter nor did education. The patient's sex did not appreciably influence the moods of serenity and peace. But women in the United States had religious emotions twice as often as men. (The difference is statistically significant.) This pattern makes sense because American women are usually more involved in religion than men. The finding was present neither in the pilot study nor in the Indian survey.

Did the religion of the patients, a strong conditioning factor in any culture, interact with the moods of the dying? There was no difference between Catholics and Protestants. However, there was a significant difference in the U.S. sample when Catholics and Protestants were compared with a combined group of other religions and patients with no religious affiliation. This mixed group of only 20 patients had less serenity and peace and fewer religious emotions (p = .04). However, it is composed of such different subgroups that interpretation is not possible. In the Indian sample, we had too few of other religious persuasions to make a valid comparison.

A comparison between Hindus and Christians would be most

interesting for our purpose because of the radically different indoc-
trination about an afterlife. For example, the differing determinants
of fate are the Last Judgment versus Karma, Heaven and Hell versus
reincarnation. The Indian sample contained too few Christians (7)
for interaction analysis. Therefore, we had to compare American
Protestants and Catholics with Indian Hindus, in spite of the
confounding national, socioeconomic, and other secular differences
which we cannot remove from analysis.

On the surface, the differences are striking. Nearly all of the
Protestants and Catholics taken together had serene moods (85
percent), while half (49 percent) of the Hindu patients were serene.
Elation was observed very seldom in Protestants and Catholics (15
percent), but was slightly predominant in Hindu patients (51
percent).

However, besides religion, the Hindu sample is contaminated by
factors which biased the experiences and the observations away from
serenity and toward elation. First, in the Indian sample, three-
quarters of the patients were male. We saw earlier that male patients
tend to be elated rather than serene. In the American sample—
which, of course, represents the Protestant and Catholic
population—there is a slight predominance of female patients, who
tend to be more serene rather than elated.

There could also be a national difference, apart from religion:
Southerners usually being more excitable than Northerners, who
appeared to be more calm and peaceful. Of course, the bulk of the
American sample came from the immigrant stock of Northern
European countries, while the Indian sample was all from a southern country. We also found that male observers seemed to miss the
more subtle, serene moods of which female observers were aware.
The Protestant and Catholic patients were observed mainly by
nurses (70 percent), which was true of only 34 percent of the Hindus
in India. We have very few (11) non-Hindus in our Indian sample.
There were slightly more serene patients in this group than in the
Hindu one. It is hard to come to a definite conclusion, but it seems
that if there is a difference because of religion, it is slight.

The qualitative differences among Protestants, Catholics, and
Hindus were slight when it came to religious moods. Forty-four
percent of the Protestants and Catholics and 30 percent of the
Hindus experienced religious mood elevation. The difference is well

within the range of sampling variations, especially if we allow for the biases described above. We might assume that if women, who tend to have more religious moods, were equally represented in the Hindu sample, and if nurses had observed as many Hindu as U.S. patients, the distribution would have been the same in both America and India.

Christianity is very different from Hinduism in its rites, beliefs, and doctrines. Apparently these aspects of religion do not have a major effect on deathbed experiences. We have information on the depth of the patients' involvement in religion, regardless of whether they were Catholic, Protestant, or Hindu. Religious involvement was not at all related to emotions in the Indian sample, but it was significantly related in the American sample. Ninety-six percent (p = .008) of those deeply involved in religion experienced serenity and peace, as compared to 69 percent of the others. Religious emotions were present in 59 percent of the deeply involved patients and in only 31 percent of the others (p = .04).

In both countries, a patient's belief in life after death significantly affected his religious emotions (United States, p = .00002; India, p = .02). In the United States, 63 percent of believers had religious emotions, but only 18 percent of those whose beliefs are unknown—that is, who did not discuss their beliefs with our respondents—had such emotions. In India, 53 percent of the believers had religious emotions, compared with 20 percent of those who did not express their beliefs to our respondents. The emotions of serenity and peace were not significantly related to belief in the United States (p = .2), but had a significant relationship in India (p = .012). In the U.S. sample, serenity was experienced by 83 percent of the believers and 71 percent of those whose beliefs we do not know. In India, 76 percent of the believers experienced serenity and peace, as compared with only 40 percent of the patients about whose beliefs we have no information.

We can conclude that a patient's belief in life after death and involvement in religion appear to facilitate—but not necessarily determine—serenity, peace, and religious emotions. A considerable number of patients who were only slightly involved in religion and did not express a belief in an afterlife still had otherworldly emotions. The patient's sex, age, and education seemed to have very little influence.

Why do belief in an afterlife and involvement in religion, but not other factors—for example, education—seem to facilitate such emotions? Could religious beliefs be the sole cause of mood elevation? Patients who at the time of their deaths are deeply involved in religion and believe in survival after death might be comforted by their religious practices (such as prayer) and beliefs—without any extrasensory awareness of a postmortem existence—and therefore became more serene.

However, we found that only 12 percent of the patients were reported to have actually engaged in religious practices of any kind—a rather small and disproportionate share of the whole sample. We assume that there must have been unobserved, silent prayers, and other religious activities of which our respondents know nothing. Therefore, religious activities could explain a good deal of our cases. But why then do the otherworldly emotions mainly occur just before death? Why are the moods of patients with little or no religiosity also raised? We can also interpret these trends within the afterlife framework. According to the assumptions of our survival hypothesis, mood elevation is based upon extrasensory awareness of a postmortem existence. Generally, experimental research has found that belief in ESP facilitates psychic experiences, while disbelief tends to block or distort them (Palmer, 1971). Therefore, if the same ESP mechanisms are at work in the dying, we should expect more clear-cut effects with those who believe in the phenomena. As noted before, such involvement might have cultivated patients' sensitivity to postmortem reality.

The duration of the patients' rise of mood was not related to their emotions. However, the interval until death was significantly related to the survival-oriented emotions in the U.S. sample alone: serenity and elation, $p = .022$; religious and positive emotions, $p = .007$. Of those who died during an interval of up to one hour, 85 percent were serene, and of those who died during a longer interval, 62 percent experienced serenity. Of those who died within an hour, 44 percent had religious emotions, while of those who died after a longer time period, only 16 percent had such emotions.

In analyzing apparition cases, we found that patients died sooner after having seen afterlife-oriented apparitions than they did after having other kinds of hallucinations. According to our afterlife hypothesis, serenity, peace, and religious emotions are the responses to an encounter with postmortem existence and its messengers. If such an encounter is true, the same processes that occur in apparition cases might be at work in the mood cases.

Is ESP the Cause?

Our central hypothesis is that the dying become aware of postmortem existence by means of ESP. We do know a good deal about ESP processes from a century of research. Therefore, if our ESP hypothesis is true, we should find characteristics common to ESP processes in deathbed phenomena. Dr. Louisa Rhine analyzed a large collection of spontaneous ESP cases and found that percipients are sometimes aware of the incoming message. At other times, the message is completely blocked from awareness, but it nevertheless influences the percipient's behavior. For example, he feels uneasy and cancels his flight on a plane which is going to crash. Other percipients react to a distant event only with emotion. Accordingly, the rise of mood at the time of death could also be based upon the patient's unconscious awareness of postmortem survival. If that is true, the patient's awareness of the afterlife should also include the realization that he is dying.

In cases where such awareness does exist, we should expect patients to realize that they are dying more often than in cases without such awareness. Did these mood elevations really change patients' expectancies of death or recovery? We had only the American data for such analysis. Although interesting trends emerged, they were not significant. Of the terminal patients who had serene or peaceful moods, 32 percent switched from thinking they would recover to the realization that they would die. Of those with elated moods, only 7 percent did so. False optimism—switching to a belief that they would recover after thinking they would die—was present in only 7 percent of the serene patients and in about three times as many (20 percent) elated patients. The same pattern was found in relation to religious emotions. Of the patients who had religious emotions, 37 percent changed their opinions from recovery to death; of those with positive and nonreligious emotions, only half that number (19 percent) did so. False optimism was not present in any patient of the religious emotion group, but 17 percent of the patients with positive nonreligious moods experienced it.

Besides patients' expectations of dying or recovering, we had another source of information for false optimism: patients' unrealistic optimistic plans for the near future, such as traveling, vacationing, going home, and so on. We contrasted the cases of such unrealistic optimism with cases where other indices of rise of mood were given. Of American serene patients, only 10 percent exhibited such optimism, but four times as many elated patients (45 percent) did so. The relationship is very significant (p = .002). We do not have comparable data for India because our sample is too small.

The same patterns emerged in another comparison. Of the U.S. patients whose rise of mood was of a religious kind, only 4 percent showed unrealistic optimism. Of the patients with other positive nonreligious moods, eight times as many (26 percent) showed such optimism (p = .015). In the Indian sample, 12 percent of the patients with religious moods and 34 percent of patients with nonreligious positive moods expressed such optimism (p = .10). On the basis of the survival hypothesis, such consistencies as the relationship between the rise of mood and the degree of awareness of postmortem existence is expected. Elated patients who block extrasensory perception of their own approaching postmortem existence also block awareness of approaching death and plan unrealistically.

It was interesting to see if the kinds of emotions present during the rise of mood are related to patients' moods the day before the rise. We found no such relationship in either country. We can, therefore, conclude that the emotions present during the rise of mood were radically new and not simply a continuation of previous moods.

Analyses of Respondent Bias

Moods are sometimes told and sometimes inferred from subtle cues of behavior. Most often, patients described how they felt to our respondents. In other cases, the expressions on patients' faces, their activity, talkativeness, social interactions, and so on also formed the basis of the respondents' judgments. Medical personnel are trained to observe objectively. Therefore, they seldom misjudge physical symptoms. It is much easier to make errors or biased observations on such phenomena as moods. Since medical personnel are mainly preoccupied with patients' symptoms, they can easily overlook moods. It is common sense that some persons are remarkably observant of moods and feelings while others are blind to them. Medical people are no exception; they might even read their own feelings into others—a well-known phenomenon which psychologists call projection. This might seriously affect our data.

Moods are very subtle and intimate states which are usually kept private. They often come and go unobserved. Moods seem to be entrusted to, and observed only by, persons who are intimately known to each other. Mood observation is—to some extent—a two-way street which involves entrusting the mood expression to the observer, and a responsive and understanding reception by the observer. We would expect more accurate observation in situations where trust and openness exist and a sensitive person has time for it. Also, there is some evidence that women generally are more sensitive to moods than men are. Therefore, we expect more adequate observations (1) when the patient is a friend or relative of the respondent, (2) where the patient has been in the care of the respondent for a longer period of time, or (3) when the observer is a woman.

Nearly all our female observers were nurses who spent more time with their patients and were psychologically closer to them. One could expect more accurate observations by respondents whose relationship with the patient is unhurried, such as in private-duty nursing or where the doctor is treating just one relative who lives with him. We carefully cross-examined these variables in our data and found that they do matter.

For detection of possible bias, we compared the observations of physicians and nurses. Serenity and peace were observed to the same extent by physicians and nurses.

Other kinds of moods in which we were interested were moods connected with religious experiences—that is, where the patient's feelings seemed to respond to some transpersonal aspects of reality. Of course, some may feel that religious emotions are out of place in medical settings, so they might not be displayed to an impersonal observer. Would nurses, with their womanly warmth and lesser official authority, pick up more instances of such experiences than doctors? Religious emotions were reported in similar frequencies by Indian physicians and nurses. In the United States, physicians detected religious emotions in only 13 percent of the cases, while nurses saw them in about half of the patients having mood elevations. Apparently there is a definite observer bias in the U.S. data concerning religious emotions. Who is right and who is wrong?

As before, we compared the results with the most reliable part of our data, namely, cases where the patient had been either a friend or relative of the respondent. In such cases, a more intimate rapport was established and the respondent generally spent much more time with the patient. Observations of serenity and peace in "known" patients were not significantly different from the unknown. In both samples, slightly more serenity was reported for "known" patients (United States, 87 percent versus 72 percent; India, 61 percent versus 48 percent). The data of "known" patients are more in agreement with observations of nurses than doctors. The rise of mood based on religious emotions was observed twice as often in the "known" as in the unknown patients (United States, 50 percent versus 26 percent; India, 54 percent versus 23 percent). The proportions are remarkably consistent, and statistically significant, in both countries. The American doctors were way off, reporting just 13 percent religious moods as compared with 50 percent in the "known" patients. On the whole, Indian doctors and nurses also appear to have underreported religious moods. Physicians reported 28 percent and nurses 33 percent, while such moods were seen in 54 percent of personally known patients. American nurses came quite close to the figures in the "known" sample: 45 percent versus 50 percent. Using as our criteria patients personally known to the respondents, we found a strong negative bias in American physicians and a milder one in Indian physicians and nurses—namely, underreporting religious emotions.

Another independent criterion for checking the bias of a respondent was available. This was patient load, the number of patients a respondent attended in an average day. We assumed that if the respondent attended up to 20 patients, he could devote considerable time to each. If he attended a larger number, sometimes 100 or more, he would be less apt to develop rapport and probably would make poorer observations. Serenity and peace were observed in the same way by Indian respondents with both small and large patient loads. However, in the United States, where the difference was significant (p = .003), respondents with smaller loads observed more serenity and peace (81 percent) than respondents who had more crowded schedules (67 percent). By this criterion, there was no indication of respondent bias in observing serenity and peace in Indian cases, but American physicians again seemed to underreport such emotions.

Concerning religious emotions, the difference is much more dramatic and significant in the U.S. sample. American respondents attending fewer patients observed religious moods in 41 percent of the cases, while only 21 percent were observed by respondents with heavier patient loads. In India, the same statistics are almost identical: 40 percent versus 20 percent. Here, too, as in the sample of patients personally known to respondents, is a remarkable similarity between both countries. On the basis of these two criteria—patient load and patient personally known to the respondent—we can definitely infer a negative bias. That is, relevant phenomena were underreported by U.S. physicians and by Indian physicians and nurses, though to a slighter extent by the Indian group. In the U.S. sample, where the bias was more serious, we performed one more analysis: comparing respondents who had been recently graduated (within fifteen years) with middle-aged ones who were graduated sixteen to twenty-five years ago and those who were graduated more than twenty-five years ago. Serenity and peace were observed by the respondent groups in the above order: 55 percent, 86 percent, and 90 percent (p = .003); religious feelings: 19 percent, 34 percent, and 52 percent (p = .05). Apparently the younger group tended to underreport mood phenomena by wide margins.

In addition to the factors discussed above, we wondered whether a respondent's belief or disbelief in life after death would influence his observations. This, if so, might also bias our data. We did not discover a significant bias concerning serenity and peace. However, religious emotions were reported quite differently by the three groups of respondents. Those in the United States who believed life after death to be impossible reported 12 percent religious emotions; those who considered it a possibility, 14 percent; and those who definitely believed, 46 percent. In the U.S. sample, the believers are obviously in agreement with our criterion samples of "known" patients (50 percent) and respondents with smaller patient loads (41 percent). Apparently, respondents who did not have a positive belief in life after death underreported religious emotions.

In the Indian sample, the relationships are quite different. Respondents who did not believe in life after death reported 44 percent of the religious emotion cases; those who considered life after death a possibility, 8 percent; and those who definitely believed, 30 percent. The criterion sample of "known" patients had 54 percent religious emotions. Strangely enough, Indian respondents who considered survival to be either a remote or a fifty-fifty possibility seemed to drastically suppress such observations. Perhaps, being torn between belief and disbelief, they tended to lean over backward.

A respondent's personal involvement in religion might be important. Actually, involvement in religion and belief in life after death are definitely overlapping. The emotions of serenity and peace were not significantly influenced by our respondents' involvement in religion, but the observations of religious emotions were affected (United States, $p = .0015$; India, $p = .016$). Our respondents' involvement in religion was rated as slight or none, moderate, or deep. These three groups of respondents made strikingly different observations of religious emotion. The corresponding percentages of cases were: 13 percent, 25 percent, 61 percent in the United States; 64 percent, 17 percent, 25 percent in India. In the U.S. sample, the deeply involved respondents came closer to the criteria, although perhaps slightly overreporting, while the uninvolved and slightly involved grossly underreported. In India, the uninvolved or slightly involved seemed to overreport to some extent, while the moderately involved respondents greatly underreported religious emotions.

We can conclude that our analysis revealed very little positive bias—that is, overreporting the otherworldly emotions of serenity and peace, and religious feelings. However, in several categories we discovered definite underreporting. What it probably amounted to was muting of the trends supportive of the postmortem survival hypothesis because of the respondents' negative bias. There is no evidence of respondent bias having exaggerated the trends consistent with the survival hypothesis.

We can now sum up our findings on this aspect of our investigation. Mood elevation shortly before death was analyzed in interaction with medical factors, patients' characteristics, and their cultural backgrounds. The afterlife-related moods (serenity and peace, and religious emotions) were found to be remarkably independent of most of the above variables. Traits revealed in the analysis are consistent with the afterlife hypothesis, which assumes that mood elevation near the time of death is based upon extrasensory awareness of oncoming postmortem existence. Negative bias in some respondent groups might have caused underreporting of afterlife-related traits. No significant positive bias, which might exaggerate afterlife-related patterns, was found.

CHAPTER 12

They Came Back:
Reports from Near-Death Patients

NOT all patients who see apparitions die. In 120 cases where patients came back from near-death states, they were able to remember having seen apparitions. About half of these people (47 percent) were so ill at the time that they had given up all hope of recovery and expected to die. Some were resuscitated from their deathlike states by drastic medical procedures. The number of "come-back" cases in which apparitional experiences were recalled is fairly evenly divided between India and the United States. In addition to the 120 patients who saw apparitions, there were 43 who reported having had visions of an afterlife. These vision cases will be discussed in the next chapter.

Before proceeding, it should be made clear that only a small fraction of all the very ill persons our respondents had been caring for reported apparitional experiences. The vast majority reported nothing of that kind to the attending physicians and nurses. However, we believe that the number of near-death patients who did experience apparitional phenomena was great enough to warrant investigation.

Are the phenomena experienced by patients who were near to death the same as those of the dying? Not in all aspects, but many are similar, as in the case of a female 38-year-old teacher who was recovering from a thyroid operation. She first saw a flash of light; then came the apparition.

Her eyes were closed, hands clasped as in prayer. She said that she saw her father and her husband, John, both of whom are deceased. They assured her that she would join them and be very happy. She asked to be alone with them, saying: "I know you don't believe me, doctor, but this makes me so happy and full of well-being that I have to have them here. It will be over in a little while. Let them be here alone with me for a minute." The hallucination left her with a sense of well-being. She became relieved of all worldly cares. She was no longer afraid to die. But she recovered.

A great many of these experiences resembled the apparitions reported by terminal patients. Quite a few of them were of short duration, as in visions of extrasensory origin. However, a closer look into the individual cases reveals that only a minority of them differ from terminal cases. As usual, we traced the medical and psychological elements that might lead us to the roots of the hallucinations. While most of the experiences seem to have typical parapsychological causes, a number of cases in the minority were explainable by medical and psychological factors. For example, the case of a sixty-eight-year-old woman.

[She] saw sentries of the Civil War era standing guard over her bed. They were clad in gray uniforms, held rifles, and watched over her from their stations at her bedposts. Although the patient did not know them, she became very relaxed and calm. She knew she was *protected*, knew that she would be all right. When this patient's condition improved, the sentries disappeared.

This hallucination was prolonged, unlike an ESP experience. This woman was a pneumonia patient and had a fever of over 104°, which may explain why she hallucinated. The sentries may have been bizarre symbols of her need for protection and dignity.

Certainly, cases such as this do not call for otherworldly explanations. Nor does the following case of a woman in her sixties. She had lost her five children in a diphtheria epidemic that had occurred long ago, but during her near-death situation she and her children had a "reunion." "It had a pleasing effect on her," commented her doctor. He believed that the case could be explained by "the toxic effect of the jaundice that had caused her almost comatose condition." The dead children had previously been on her mind, and she had often discussed them with her doctor. This case is easily explainable on medical and psychological grounds. On the whole, there were more cases explainable in this fashion among the come-back patients than among the terminally ill.

We expected to find more apparitions of the living in the comeback cases than apparitions of dead and religious figures. The data proved us wrong. Afterlife related apparitions were as common in patients who came back (80 percent) as in those who died (81 percent). The emotional reactions to these apparitions were also rather similar—serenity, peace, and religious emotions being dominant.

A sharp contrast to the dying patients was found in the moods of some patients, moods which might have stemmed from the message brought to the patient by the apparition. A simple miner said to his nurse:

"I see God." He started to cry and moan that he was going to die. He just stared out into space as if he were really seeing God. When I returned half an hour later, he was a changed man—radiant, a very happy countenance. He said that God told him it was not yet time for him to go.

We saw in previous chapters that the dying seem to become serene and elated because of the apparition's invitation to die rather than to live. Would the apparition in near-death cases, we wondered, be more inclined to engage in this-world purposes because the patient was not going to die? We again compared cases in which the purpose of the apparition was clearly indicated. Come-back patients had apparitions with purposes related to the other world as often (78 percent) as those who died and stayed dead (77 percent).

Although they were not typical, we had such cases of this-world purposes even when the apparition was of the dead. In the following case, an apparition of the dead clearly expressed a this-world purpose. The patient, in critical condition, was a seven-year-old boy with a mastoid infection. He was rebellious, refused to take his medication, and resisted the nurses. Then suddenly he saw his deceased uncle who had worked as a physician on that particular floor in the hospital.

> He [the doctor] had been close to the whole family. The boy insisted that Uncle Charlie came, sat beside him, and told him to take his medicine. He also told the boy that he would get well. The boy was very sure that Uncle Charlie had sat in the chair and told him these things. After this experience, the patient was cooperative. He was not excited, and he took the deceased doctor's "visit" as a matter of course. The next morning, the boy was much better—a dramatic change had occurred in his condition.

In this case the apparition of the deceased physician acted for this-world purposes, as he would have done if he had visited the boy while alive.

In one respect, come-back cases were different from terminal cases. Of the 73 cases in which unambiguous information was available concerning the purpose of the apparition, 78 percent were of take-away purpose. One-third of the take-away purposes were said to have sent the patient back to life in no uncertain terms. No explicit rejection or postponement was expressed in the remaining cases.

We have reason to suspect that the rejection was indeed experienced in more than one-third of the cases. It is possible that it got lost in the process of communicating the experience to professionals busy with resuscitation procedures. This may have been true in the following experience, where we have the reverse of a take-away case. A woman died—apparently following the call to the other-world—but then recovered unexpectedly.

> This woman was in her thirties. She had a badly infected leg injury and no one expected her to recover. She saw her dead mother and seemed to answer her call to the other-world: "I see you Mother. I am coming, Mother. I will be with you."

Up to this point, the case is like that of most dying patients. The outcome, however, was different.

The next morning she began to improve. Her fever went down, her leg began to heal. No one had expected her to get well.

Sometimes apparitions of the dead simply call off a patient's expected departure. An accountant in her fifties had suffered a heart attack, a coronary occlusion.

She said her father and mother [both deceased] were coming to meet her and take her far away. The three of them were going along a hill when her parents suddenly told her to go back. She turned back and left them. The next morning, approximately six to eight hours after the experience, her condition improved. I [her doctor] had expected her to expire that night. I realized how seriously ill she was, how close to leaving.

Religious figures also may "send back" the dying. A Roman Catholic woman in her thirties was critically ill with pneumonia.

She had a picture of the Blessed Mother facing her. She was gazing at the picture. Later she told me that Mary had come out of the picture and said: "Don't be afraid. I don't need you yet. I will come back later." This woman had a new baby to care for. When the experience occurred, she thought that she was dying. She was happy to see Mary—it was so beautiful to see. At first she associated the experience with death, but then she felt relieved—it wasn't her time.

The next case is of an engineer in his fifties, stricken by coronary thrombosis. His doctor reports:

He saw a "bearded man" standing at the opening to a long golden corridor. He was shaking his head and motioning him to go back, said: "Not now, later." This made the patient very happy. He said I [the doctor] need not give him medicine anymore: "I am not wanted up there." It was right after this experience that he started getting better.

Note that the engineer casually described the apparition as a "bearded man," not bothering to name—for example, "God,"

"Jesus," and so on. More emotional patients would have jumped to the conclusion that the man against the golden light was somebody related to his religious beliefs. This is the reason why elaborate analyses are necessary to get beyond the appearances of these cases.

Although an apparition might be characteristically representative of the other world, it might still furnish the wrong information. A pneumonia patient in her eighties saw her dead husband and conversed with him in Yiddish.

> He came to tell her to make plans to join him. The hallucination seemed to calm her and her children believed that she was going to die. Almost immediately afterwards, she went into a deep sleep and awoke very refreshed. She began to improve rapidly, much to her disgust. She was ready to die but she didn't.

(An off-the-record comment made by this patient's nurse was, "Well, you just cannot rely on some husbands, even when they are dead!")

A heart attack patient in her sixties saw Saint Joseph, her patron saint to whom she used to pray.

> Saint Joseph wanted her to come to him, but she was unwilling. She told him that she still had things to do, that she would stay in bed and get better. The apparition calmed her. She was serene and peaceful, in a religious sense, and she began to get better several hours later.

It is interesting that this woman's purpose was contrary to that of the otherworldly messenger, as is true in so many terminal cases. Of course, seeing one's favorite saint at the critical hour could be merely an act of wish fulfillment, having no basis external to the patient's mind. However, sometimes the apparition is the opposite of what the patient wishes to see, as in the following case. This young woman was in her twenties. She came close to death because of complications in childbirth.

> She thought that she saw her patron saint, the one she prayed to. She introduced him to me [the doctor], thinking he was right beside her. I didn't see a thing! It was Saint Gerard—the "saint for the impossible." She was very happy to see him, and

somewhat surprised by his appearance: "Oh, I didn't expect to see you dressed in that clothing!" She said he was dressed in humble attire, like a monk with sandals and a gray gown. "I thought you would be dressed in velvet." She felt he came to help her get well. She still feels that he saved her.

Let us be aware that such apparitions do not wear name tags or speak their names. It is the patient who announces the apparition's name and title. But the factors governing a patient's ability to recognize the apparition and know its name are hard to evaluate. The contradiction noted above between the apparition's actual garb and its expected manner of dress may be due to the patient's having a stereotype in mind. It may also be that the apparition was someone other than the one whom the patient named, and the patient simply applied the name of a favored saint to an unknown apparition.

Come-Back Cases in India

The experiences of Indian patients were basically similar to those of American patients. Four-fifths saw afterlife-related apparitions (dead and religious figures) who exhibited intentions of taking them away to another world. Again, in about one-third of the take-away cases, the patient was "sent back." Emotional responses included serenity and peace, elation and religious emotions, while some 20 patients had negative feelings. The majority of Hindu patients saw visions essentially similar to those of American Christians, but the coloring of these visions was typically Indian in the no-consent cases. The concept of Karma, or accumulative accounts of good and bad deeds, might have been projected in some of the visions. The following is an example of one such case.

The patient seemed to die. After some time, he regained consciousness. He then told us that he was taken away by messengers in white clothing, and brought up to a beautiful place. There he saw a man in white, with an account book, who told the messengers that they had brought the wrong person. He ordered them to take the patient back. The place was so very beautiful that the patient wanted to stay there. Then, according to the nurse, there was another man of the same name in the hospital. When the patient regained consciousness, the other man died, we were told.

We had the opportunity of checking one such case with a nurse who was said to have been present. She disclaimed any knowledge of a case where a patient by the same name was supposed to have died when the other patient gained consciousness. We encountered several cases in which a patient was taken away to another world and it turned out to be a mistake made by the "other-world bureaucracy." Although Indian Christians, a clergyman, and a teacher were among the patients mistakenly taken away, there were no such "error cases" in the United States.

Typical Indian concerns are expressed in the following case of an Indian woman suffering from pneumonia.

She was unconscious and almost died. She later told me, "I felt myself to be in heaven. There were many houses, one was incomplete." She asked the messenger who was with her, "Whose house is it?" He replied, "It is for you, but it is not entirely finished because you have not yet completed your days in the world. You should arrange for your son's marriage. Your day shall come after the birth of your grandson." Years later, she actually died after the birth of her grandson.

Here the information received from a high source was accurate, but this is not always the case. A college-educated woman suffered an allergic reaction to a penicillin injection.

She was unconscious during the crisis. Afterwards she told us that some religious being came to her and asked her to accompany him. She was brought to heaven on a cow; the way was beautifully decorated. She reached a place where many people were gathered. It was there that they discovered she was the wrong person. She was brought back to earth in the same manner. She related this story a few minutes after regaining consciousness. The patient died a week later, not from the allergic reaction to penicillin, but because of a respiratory infection.

In a similar case, the patient was declared dead but regained consciousness.

> He said that he had gone up to heaven. "God sent me back." He had to live more, as he had not completed his life. But he died after two minutes.

These cases suggest that such visions should not be taken literally. First, though they sometimes convey genuine information on the time of death, at times they do not. Second is the implausibility—to our Western minds at least—of events such as riding a cow into eternity. If some of these visions are based on extrasensory glimpses of another world, they certainly are embroidered with religious beliefs and symbolizations, whether it be Yamdoot, the Hindu messenger of death, or the Blessed Mother. We are looking for basic characteristics of afterlife experiences which remain stable across the various imageries of different beliefs. Terminal cases, where patients actually died, showed such fundamental consistencies. We shall now turn toward statistical analyses to decide whether come-back cases also have core phenomena that are relatively independent of medical, psychological, and cultural factors.

The Roots of Visions in Come-Back Cases

Examples of the come-back cases clearly indicate that such visions are not to be taken literally. Therefore, in order to trace the possible roots of these hallucinations, we implemented the same methodology used to assess the various elements found in the experiences of terminal patients. These statistical measures included frequency analyses, cross-tabulation of all relevant items, and testing the differences between items by use of chi-square statistics. Because of the limited size of our sample, the American and Indian data were combined for most analyses.

The proportion of afterlife-related apparitions (dead and religious figures) was the same in terminal and nonterminal cases. The latter group, however, saw more religious figures and fewer apparitions of the dead. Experiences in which apparitions expressed the take-away purpose occurred with equal frequency in both groups. Only in one-third of the come-back cases were patients explicitly rejected from the other world and sent back with such comments as "You have work to do" and "Your time is not up; I will come back later."

The reactions to the apparitional experiences were about the same as in the terminal cases. One-third of the patients did not want to "go," more than half (54 percent) had emotions of serenity or elation, and 29 percent responded with negative feelings. Religious sentiment was reported in 24 percent of the apparition cases. Of the nonterminal group, two-thirds hallucinated only the apparitions; their perception of the actual environment remained intact.

On the whole, the phenomena were similar in both samples of patients. While we were conducting interviews, we got an impression that the come-back patients might have had a greater number of ordinary hallucinations than the terminally ill. The statistical analyses did not substantiate this impression, with the following exception.

The visions of those who recovered were often longer than those of the patients who died. More than half (54 percent) of our come-back patients continued to hallucinate after fifteen minutes, while only one-third (34 percent) of the dying did so. We thought that this might be because a larger proportion of the visions of surviving patients are not based on their extrasensory perceptions of another world (ESP is generally of a short duration). We carefully analyzed the data in order to determine if patients who have relatively short hallucinations will "see" differently from those whose experiences are of a longer duration. Although we found that the latter group did indeed exhibit a lesser amount of afterlife-related phenomena in their hallucinations, they did not do so to a statistically significant degree. They saw slightly fewer apparitions of the dead, only half the number of religious figures, and hallucinated living persons twice as often as did patients who had shorter experiences.

The take-away purpose was expressed twice as often in hallucinations of shorter duration as in longer ones. Furthermore, the prolonged hallucinations were only rarely (5 percent) received with religious emotions. Apparently, afterlife-related phenomena are concentrated in visions of a short duration, as they are in ESP cases. It seems quite probable that the come-back sample experienced more ordinary hallucinations than did the terminally ill.

Could all of their visions have, in fact, been caused by brain malfunctions resulting from their illnesses?

In an attempt to answer that question, we tried to identify any medical factors which might have determined the visions of come-back cases. Brain maladies and nephritis, which could cause hallucinations, were found in proportions similar to the terminal cases. A medical history suggestive of hallucinogenic factors was indicated in 18 percent of the cases and could explain only a small fraction of the phenomena. In the opinion of our respondents, the proportion of patients whose states of consciousness were affected by drugs was also the same as in the terminal group: 10 percent mildly, 5 percent moderately, and 3 percent strongly affected. High fevers (over 103°) were present in 16 percent of our come-back cases, as compared with 8 percent of the terminal patients. This factor might have contributed slightly to the increase in the frequency of long, rambling hallucinations in patients who did not die. Impairments to the patient's clarity of consciousness occurred to the same extent in both terminal and nonterminal groups. Apparently, hallucinogenic medical factors could not explain the phenomena in the majority of cases, although they might have been the cause of visions in some of our cases.

Our interaction analyses showed that drugs that might have caused hallucinations neither significantly affected the main phenomena nor the clarity of consciousness. We combined cases of brain impairment and nephritis with those of hallucinogenic medical histories. Taken together, these hallucinogenic illnesses interacted to a noticeable—though not statistically significant—extent with the take-away purpose of the apparitions and the religious emotions of the patients. The relationships were contrary to the sick-brain hypothesis and in conformity with the afterlife hypothesis: Those patients who had hallucinogenic maladies saw apparitions with a take-away purpose three times less often than did those persons who were free of such impairments. Patients with the above-mentioned hallucinogenic troubles also reacted much less frequently with religious emotions (13 percent) than did the other patients. Therefore, we can conclude that if the medical factors had any influence on seeing apparitions, they tended to suppress rather than generate visions that are suggestive of an afterlife.

We analyzed the data to see what effects demographic factors had on the phenomena. The results showed that neither education nor occupation nor involvement in religion had any significant influence. The proportions of Protestants, Catholics, and Jews in our sample were roughly equal to their proportions in the population of the United States. Hindus naturally dominated the Indian sample (70 percent), but Indian Christians were found to be overrepresented (25 percent). This might have been due to a bias on the part of Christian nurses. They might have listened more carefully to the Indian Christian patients, just as they reported more fully the cases of friends and relatives. Indian Christians comprised 14 percent of our combined U.S. and Indian samples. However, even if half of them contained exaggerations, they would have affected only an insignificant fraction of our data (7 percent). We have no indications that such distortions actually occurred.

Psychological factors are not only very potent in shaping hallucinations; they may also cause them. Severe stress is one such factor known to cause hallucinations, as in the mirage of an oasis seen by a thirsty traveler lost in the vast expanse of the Sahara. As stated before, we found no evidence that stress caused afterlife-related phenomena in terminal patients. Stress was indicated in 22 percent of the come-back cases by such indices as anxiety, depression, restlessness, and so on. However, neither the ostensible purposes of the apparitions nor the patients' emotional reactions to them had the slightest relationship to the patients' moods prior to their hallucinatory experiences. The proportion of the survival-related apparitions was not affected, either.

A patient's expectancies can also act to shape hallucinations. Persons who know they are dying may "see" Heaven as the fulfillment of a wish, while those who expect to recover and go home would certainly not wish themselves dead and in another world. About half (53 percent) of the come-back patients expected to recover; the other portion thought they would die. As mentioned earlier, we found that the apparition experiences of terminal patients were not dependent upon such expectations. In our come-back cases there is a suggestive—though not statistically significant—trend in favor of the wish-fulfillment hypothesis. Patients who expected to die saw apparitions with the take-away purpose twice as often (60 percent) as did those who expected to recover (28 percent). There was no difference between their emotional reactions, but there was a somewhat puzzling trend in the kinds of apparitions they saw. Patients who believed themselves to be dying saw more dead and fewer religious figures; those who expected to recover saw twice as many religious figures as dead ones. We cannot, on statistical grounds, be certain that these differences are real, but if they are, then we assume that the come-back cases are shaped to a larger extent by subjective factors than terminal cases are. We can conclude that most of the psychological factors did not decisively shape the phenomena suggestive of an afterlife. Patients' expectations might have had a hand in the formation of some, but not all, of the phenomena found in come-back cases. However, this trend was not statistically significant.

Let us now consider the basic issue: Are the come-back cases consistent with our model of postmortem survival? We thought that an important test of this problem would come from a comparison between Indian come-back cases and American ones. According to our model, the patients' cultural backgrounds would sway subjective experiences to a much greater extent than would their perceptual experiences. Were the phenomena reported in Indian come-back cases as similar to American ones as found in the terminal cases?

The proportion of afterlife-related apparitions (dead and religious figures) was similar in both countries: the United States, 76 percent; India, 84 percent. As was true of the terminally ill in the United States, American come-back patients saw twice as many dead as religious figures. This proportion was exactly the reverse for our Indian patients. They saw twice the number of religious deities and their messengers as they saw figures of dead relatives. We found the same differences in our sample of dying patients, and were able to explain part of it by the cultural inhibition Indians have to seeing female apparitions. The proportion of afterlife-related apparitions is the same in both countries. The differences were of the same magnitude in both terminal and nonterminal patients.

The purpose of the hallucinatory figure was the main indicator of an afterlife in the data of the terminally ill. They saw apparitions that expressed the take-away purpose in about 80 percent of the cases, excluding ambiguous ones. Similarly, 72 percent of the American and 80 percent of the Indian come-back patients saw apparitions with such afterlife-related purposes. In this respect, Indians were remarkably like Americans, regardless of whether they died or recovered. In both countries, about one-third of the apparitions with a take-away purpose carried out their missions up to a certain point, and then told the patients to go back.

Once again, experiences of this sort are remarkably similar in both cultures. However, the manner in which the ostensible mission was performed showed cultural flavoring. The spirit guides of Americans were experienced as friendly and understanding of the patients' needs and unfinished tasks, as evidenced by one typical comment: "You have work to do." The manners of the Indian apparitions were sometimes more bureaucratic—the messenger of death (Yamdoot) might bring the patient before a desk where his record would be looked up by a man with a white beard (Karma?). It then turned out that the otherworldly messenger had brought up the wrong person.

As in the terminal cases, about one-third of the Indian patients did not want to "go" with the otherworldly caller. Moreover, their emotional reactions were about the same as were those of terminal patients: Indians have more negative and also more religious emotions than Americans, who experience serenity and elation more often.

We conclude that the extent of cultural influences on apparition experiences is about the same for come-back cases as it is for those of no return. This similarity lends support and justification to studies that concentrated on resuscitation cases. We are referring here to studies conducted by Drs. Elisabeth Kübler-Ross (1976) and Raymond Moody (1975), in which patients who were revived and those who were not still told the same tale. The information we obtained from our dying patients is considerably clearer than the data we received from our come-back patients. We therefore suggest that future research should not neglect the non-terminally ill who tell of their glimpses of the beyond. Many questions related to this important category of cases have not yet been adequately answered.

CHAPTER 13

Visions of Another World: Afterlife as Seen Through the Eyes of the Dying

EMERGING from anesthesia, a twenty-six-year-old American was asked the standard orientation question: "Can you tell me where you are?" "Yes, in heaven," he replied and immediately lapsed into a coma. He died half an hour later. Did this man perceive his postmortem destination, or was he simply disoriented?

Whichever the case, he was not unique, and assuming that he truly saw "Heaven," we can say that among terminal patients, hallucinations of environments rather than of persons are far from rare. They range from Gardens of Paradise to earthly factories. Our research brought 112 such cases to light. We will examine them, asking specific questions in order to evaluate the central issue: Did some of these patients glimpse another mode of existence, or were they just hallucinating? If they did discern something real, what do their visions reveal about the nature of this other environment? Can we trust the eyes of the dying?

Our study shows that dying patients hallucinate people five times more often than environments and objects, while drug-induced hallucinations portray things and places more often than people (Siegel and Jarvik, 1975). Including the patients who recovered from a close brush with death, as well as those who died, we compiled 703 cases of hallucinations. Of these, 591 portrayed persons. Visions of places and things were dominant in only 16 percent of the reported hallucinations.

We explored whether such a striking difference in frequency might have its roots in respondent bias. Apparition cases may be more impressive and therefore more easily recalled by our respondents, while hallucinations of environment could easily be dismissed as disorientation and forgotten. In addition, patients may be more reluctant to talk about visions of another world due to fear of ridicule than they would be to mention a visit from Uncle John.

We assume that doctors and nurses would be more attentive if the patient were a relative or friend. Respondent bias can be evaluated by comparing the frequency of cases in which the patient was related or a friend to those in which there were no such relationships. In the same manner we might determine a patient bias, assuming that patients would more easily confide an unusual experience to a relative or friend.

One-third (31 percent) of the vision cases were reported by relatives and friends—certainly a much larger proportion of familiar patients than expected in hospitals. Similarly, 24 percent of apparition cases were experienced by relatives and friends. The difference is too small to explain the discrepancy in terms of respondent bias. We cannot offer an explanation of the difference.

Let us now take a look at the cases themselves. We have 64 American and 48 Indian cases. About two-thirds (69) originate from terminal patients, while one-third (43) come from those who did not die. As in ESP cases, the visions were brief. Half (52 percent) of the cases for which we have information lasted from a few seconds to five minutes. Three-quarters of them (75 percent) were over in fifteen minutes, while only 16 percent continued longer than an hour. Judging from duration only, 25 percent of the cases bear no similarity to ESP experiences, while in 75 percent of the cases ESP might be considered.

What did they see? What was the *subject matter* of their visions? Two-thirds seemed to picture another world, while 32 percent saw places and objects of this world. A characteristic vision of this-world imagery was seen by a man in his fifties who was suffering from a circulatory disease and uremia. He saw "old masted ships" sailing on the ceiling of the hospital room. In his excitement he pointed them out to the nurse, who reported, "He really, really saw them in his mind. You would have to go along with him, saying that you saw them too." In another case, a young Catholic missionary had a high fever. She saw "the boat coming" for her. The nurse thought that this indicated her awareness of oncoming death, but there are many boats which she might have remembered without any death symbolism. After this hallucination, she felt as miserable and nauseous as before.

Not all visions end up like that, however. The wife of a Pennsylvania doctor found herself in

> beautiful surroundings where green grass and flowers grow. She seemed very pleased, happy that she could see these pleasant things. She said that it was like a garden with green grass and flowers. She was fond of flowers and had a garden at home.

She was depressed, dying of a liver disease at the age of eighty. After the vision she became very peaceful and serene. The vision represented a place "like a garden," but not an actual garden, and she died a serene death a few hours later. Was this a glimpse of the beyond? Could an image of earthly grass and flowers cause a woman who had been depressed to be happy at the time of death?

A rather matter-of-fact, unemotional buyer for a department store was dying of cancer. She was in her fifties, her mind was very clear, her judgment was good.

> She saw open gates and felt she was going to a place with flowers, lights, colors, and a lot of beauty. A voice said, "Come to my garden." She was annoyed with me for disturbing her and accused me of not permitting her to get into this place. She was aware of the hospital room after I disturbed her. She was calmed by the vision. She was thrilled with it and angry at me.

This patient did not talk about God or religion, but peace came over her and she became "more quiet, less complaining, not so restless." She never identified the voice, but the expression sounds biblical.

A college-educated woman in her eighties was suffering from a cardiac failure.

> She was an unusual patient, very alert and intellectual, keen sense of humor. She was a down to earth person. That morning she was listless, but her temperature and pulse were normal. She told me that a taxi driver had taken her to a beautiful garden where she saw beautiful, endless gardens, all kinds of flowers. She said that she had never seen anything like it, it was gorgeous. She did not want to return, but the taxi driver was impatient to get started. He took too long to get home, taking all the wrong streets. She would go back there any day—beautifully done garden. It sounded like a dream to me, but it seemed real to her. Four days later she died peacefully.

A taxi to Heaven? That seems too urbanized to accept as "otherworldly." However, we must realize that all visions which are translated into the language of this world must necessarily be filtered through the imagery of this world. "Gates," "flowers," and "grass" are no less material than a yellow cab or a cow (the vehicle for an Indian woman's transition to the other world). The connecting link is that peculiar beauty beyond reality which the respondent identified in this vision. We must rely in our analysis on *experiential qualities, rather than imagery.*

In the previously cited cases, something otherworldly was hinted at but not designated as such. The patient in the following case said it more directly. She was a miner's widow in her fifties suffering from a cardiac disease.

> She saw a beautiful garden with a gate. God was standing there and an angel was nearby. She insisted that God had appeared to her. She would get well if she stayed with me [the doctor]. She had just been transferred to my care. The vision gave her serenity and confidence in her recovery. She followed church doctrines, but wasn't a regular churchgoer.

She recovered.

A registered nurse in her twenties was suffering from malignant hypertension which led to a stroke.

> She said that she saw gates leading into a vast country, vast space. She felt utter peace, no fear, no worries. As the gates

were opening she began to improve. Her speech, which had been affected, cleared up. The experience was very reassuring to her, completely eliminating her fear of death.

She was healed. Psychologically speaking, the "gates" were real; the vision resulted in serenity and peace.

Another patient did not want to come back when Saint Peter told her that he was not ready for her. The place was so beautiful that she wanted to stay. How can the visions be so gratifying that they even outweigh the wish to live? The patient was unable to say.

A seventy-eight-year-old woman was reported as

always nasty, a very mean person. One night she called me to see how lovely and beautiful heaven is. Then she looked at me and seemed surprised: "Oh, but you can't see it, you aren't here [in heaven], you are over there." She became very peaceful and happy. She felt at ease, pleased, and she permitted her meanness to die. She became so much better. I don't think these are hallucinations, they are visions—very real.

And then there are visions with a ring of technological grandeur. One nurse reported on an Irish milkman in his seventies who was suffering from "cerebral spasms."

All of a sudden he had a sort of glow about his face and he said, "You know these wonderful things they are doing today, all the Sputniks and all those rocket things up there," and he looked at me and said, "I was up there and they did not let me in." He seemed to be happy. That glow—it was almost like a trance. It was very strange.

The nurse mused and described another unusual incident at the end of this patient's life.

He died on a Tuesday in Connecticut—the day after his sister's death in Ohio. He mentioned seeing his sister Mary in the hospital, but he did not know that she was dead. He and Mary were very close.

Often such "seeing" changes the patient's attitude toward dying. A fifty-year-old Philadelphia housewife

> felt that she had visited heaven. She said that she had been in that beautiful place. "If heaven is like that, then I'm ready." She was very happy about it and calm.

These cases present the spectrum of dying patients' visions of Heaven. We find no indication of a unique locality in the manner which would be expected if several individuals described Grand Canyon or New York City. The ostensibly nonmaterial reality is pictured in very material terms: a garden where the grass is very, very green and the flowers are very, very beautiful. Of course, no one said that the grass grew so well because it was fertilized and sprinkled or that the flowers were made of carbohydrates like earthly ones. "Seeing Heaven" did not arouse such questions in any patient, regardless of education or occupation. Whether trees, buildings, or space rockets, the visions all used images of earthly things to fashion their heaven. Yet these experiences seemed to be very meaningful to the patients, often changing their outlook on life and death.

Heaven is sometimes pictured as a secluded, well-organized place, complete with someone like an immigration officer. The patient is "called to the gates," but entry may be postponed by the pronouncement of Saint Peter, saying, "I am not ready for you." A nurse arriving at the patient's side to revive him with an injection was said to be "interrupting the appointment which will never come again." Such talk does not sound reasonable from our worldly point of view. Nevertheless, these dying patients felt that they had something great to tell.

Here is the experience, reported by a nurse, of a rather unemotional woman in her sixties whose job was assisting in buying food for the hospital.

> The patient said, "It looked like a great sunset, very large, you know, and beautiful. The clouds suddenly appeared to be gates." She felt that somebody was calling her to them, that she had to go through there. "It was very pretty."

The interviewer asked: "Did she see through the clouds?"

No, no, she just saw what *appeared* to be gates formed from the beautiful clouds of the sunset. She was not exactly called, she had the idea that she was drawn to the gates, I suppose. After this vision the patient became very serene. She said that she was now prepared to die. Before she had qualms whether she wanted to go.

And the message got through to the nurse:

I must have had some feelings about it because I kept calling her daughter-in-law. It was something that was very interesting to me. It had strong religious overtones. These are things you feel, but you can't talk about them.

The same experiential qualities seem to be hidden behind the "gates" seen by this seventy-year-old woman:

She felt that she died and was going to the gates. They began to open for her. They were bright and very beautiful.

Likewise, the same expression of extraordinary "brightness" appeared in the following case.

She said that the gates of heaven were opening. There were shining tall portals and there was shining light, much brighter than here. Everything looked so bright.

"Light" here seems to sum up the symbolic message which mystics have tried to convey over the centuries.

How frequently do patients "see Heaven"? We have specific information concerning this question in 100 cases. One-third (32 percent) are clearly hallucinations of this-world places and objects, while two-thirds are concerned with otherworldly matters. Images of Heaven were reported most frequently (41 percent). Gardens and landscapes with intense colors, brilliant lights, and beauty were reported in 16 percent of the cases, and symbolic architectural structures comprise 5 percent. Nearly all of the otherworldly environments are expressed through visual imagery. In sharp contrast to hallucinations of the mentally ill, who mainly "hear" rather than "see," sacred music or heavenly choruses are heard in only 6 percent of our cases. Because ESP impressions are also mostly visual, we find here another similarity between deathbed visions and ESP.

We found only one case in all the American and Indian data where a patient saw "Hell." If these visions stem from programming imparted by religious upbringing, should we not expect more of such cases? The unfortunate person was an Italian-born housewife from Rhode Island. Her vision occurred after a gallbladder operation.

> When she came to she said, "I thought I was dead, I was in hell." Her eyes were popping out of fear. "My God, I thought I was in hell." After I reassured her, she told about her experience in hell and said that the devil will take her. This was interspersed with descriptions of her sins and what people think about her. As fear increased, nurses had difficulty holding her down. She almost became psychotic and her mother had to be called in to quiet her. She had long standing guilt feelings, possibly stemming from marriage to a man who was 25 years older than her and an extramarital relationship which resulted in illegitimate children. Her sister's death from the same illness scared her. She believed that God was punishing her for her sins.

One does not need to be a psychiatrist to trace the worldly origins of her "Hell"—the conflict between the "ought" and the "is" of her lovelife.

Ethereal music was heard by a Connecticut plumber. In spite of severe pain following a cancer operation, he was "very serene, it was pleasant to him. He wanted to know if we heard it and told us that it was beautiful." Apparently, his serenity was contagious: "It was a pleasure to be with him—deep satisfaction in helping even if you don't pull them through."

For the wife of a department store owner, the hallucinated music was simply "something wonderful that happened."

In another case the music seemed to intimate a foretaste of the other world: "She heard music like a huge choir and saw pleasant surroundings like she was near heaven."

In all cases, hearing music seems to express a harmonious experience. Serenity and harmony is surprising in suffering patients, as in the following case of the sixty-two-year-old wife of an actor, who was tortured by advanced cancer.

> She had a very peculiar look on her face. I rearranged her pillows, slightly elevating her back. She was very lucid. I stepped out of the room. When I came back, her eyes were open, then she had this look on her face, not aware of me, smile, raised right arm as if reaching for something, resting quietly. She seemed to be somewhere else, I can't explain, transposed to another world. I spoke to her, she did not answer. Later she told me that she had heard organ music, saw angels in brilliant white. She was smiling more broadly—very pleased at the whole thing.

Here we can ask the parapsychological question: Where was her consciousness—in her body or really "transposed" via an out-of-body experience?

A sixty-nine-year-old stroke patient was partially paralyzed and depressed.

> Suddenly his face lit up, pain gone, smiling—he hadn't been cheerful until then. He said, "How beautiful," as if he could see something we couldn't see. And then, "No body, no world, flowers, light and my Mary [deceased wife]." He was released and peaceful, went into a coma and died shortly after.

A nineteen-year-old college student, dying of leukemia, had sensations which are typical in out-of-body experiences.

> He had heard the angels singing and music. He felt like he was floating. Peace followed the hallucination—he seemed to be restless before.

A typical out-of-body experience was described by a sixty-eight-year-old salesman who

> felt he had gone through the window to the outside. He felt suspended in air, floating, as though lifted out of bed. He had no pain or any other sensation during the floating.

A college-educated pharmaceutical salesman in his late thirties suffered a severe heart attack.

He thought he was flying deep in space. He thought he was riding in a space capsule. Objects, people went floating past him. He was struggling to get out of there.

Here the same sensations seem to be interpreted in technological images of the space age.

A pneumonia patient in her fifties felt that she had died.

She found herself up in the sky. It looked like clouds. She was walking on clouds. She saw many castles there. They were in bright light, very beautiful. She was so impressed with their beauty. Afterwards she became quiet—real acceptance of death.

When we consider that an afterlife might be nothing other than a permanent out-of-body experience, then the experiential qualities in some of the cases cited are consistent with the postmortem survival hypothesis.

Visions of extraordinary, intense light and color are not uncommon. In 17 cases they are specifically mentioned, but they might be inferred in many more.

Experiential qualities with emotional overtones were identified in 50 cases. Experiences of great beauty were reported in 72 percent of the cases of which we have information. Peace was an outstanding characteristic in 14 percent of the patients. The visions were threatening or otherwise negatively toned in 14 percent of the cases, and most of these were located in this world—for example, a vicious dog attacking a patient who had been severely injured in an accident.

Peace was the core experience in the following cases. A seventy-eight-year-old German-born mill foreman suffered very severe angina pain.

When he had visions the pain would disappear and all you could see was a smile on his face. "It was so beautiful, you just can't tell anyone. It was a breathtaking scene, more so than anything in real life." That was all he could say.

A nurse told of a Pennsylvania Dutch patient in her fifties:

When she was sick, she was there in heaven. "Oh, it was so peaceful," she exclaimed. But she continued to have pain just like before.

A young woman nearly bled to death during childbirth.

She thought that she had come into this other world, "It was so beautiful, quiet, peaceful, serene." She repeated, "It was so beautiful." The patient was gone for a little while, not dead, but it was touch and go.

Sometimes we found textbook examples of symbolic imagery as in this case. "A lonely veteran became very excited and said he saw a beautiful room and all the people there were waiting to greet him." A terminally ill bank teller remarked that "he had seen across the river a golden light." Then he said to the relatives present that he would "see them on the other side." Bridges and the other shore are common symbols of transition.

Experiences beyond description were explicitly mentioned in only three cases, although ineffability is said to be one of the main characteristics of mystical experience and psychedelic trips (Clark, 1969; Pahnke, 1966; Stace, 1960).

Symbolism of death was discernible in 43 vision cases. Nearly all (84 percent) pictured death as a transition to another state of existence that was deeply gratifying.

As previously stated, two-thirds of the visions depicted other-worldly environments while one-third dealt with this-world surroundings. We took another look at the data by asking how the surroundings appeared to the patients. Again, mundane appearances were relatively infrequent: threatening, 10 percent; everyday environment, 14 percent. Beautiful but natural environments were seen in 21 percent of the cases, while extraordinary beauty beyond reality was the most frequent appearance (37 percent). Conventional Christian, Hindu, or Muslim ideas of the other world were expressed in surprisingly few (17 percent) of the cases. Apparently neither the Bible, the Gita nor the Koran had etched the majority of the visions of the dying. The imprint of conventional images—such as "the Pearly Gates"—was clearly discernible in only one out of every six cases.

We have indicated throughout this chapter the main features of visions of another world as seen through the eyes of the dying. There are seven main characteristics indicated by our data. We can summarize them as follows.

1. Subject matter of the vision
2. Appearance of surroundings
3. Emotional qualities of the visionary imagery (seeing great beauty and peace)
4. Death symbolism
5. Ostensible location of the patient's consciousness
6. Emotional effects
7. Religious emotional reaction

Having identified them, what can we now say about these characteristics? Are they really indicative of another world in which humans enjoy an afterlife?

So far, our analysis has revealed that about one-fourth to one-third of the vision cases are rooted in this-world matters while two-thirds to three-fourths of the cases were judged to have content and subject matter suggestive of another world. According to the afterlife hypothesis, the visions which contain otherworldly subject matter would include some ESP glimpses of a postmortem existence, while the remaining third (visions with mundane concerns) would be entirely subjective—a kind of waking dream. Our model indicates that mundane hallucinations would be fully dependent upon hallucinogenic medical factors, psychological variables, and cultural forces, while the otherworldly visions would be relatively independent of such factors because of their ostensible external origin. We tested this hypothesis by examining the extent to which the main phenomena are swayed by the above-mentioned factors.

First question: Could brain disturbances be the cause? Brain disease, injury, stroke, and uremia accounted only for 10 percent of the cases. Therefore, they could explain only a small part of the data. Did diseases affecting the brain generate more of the phenomena which are suggestive of another world than patients who were free of brain disturbances? One out of seven characteristics of the visions—seeing great beauty and peace—was significantly ($p = .01$) affected; 80 percent of the brain-disturbed patients experienced beauty, while only 32 percent of the patients with other diagnoses saw scenes of great beauty and peace. None of the remaining characteristics interacted significantly, but four of the six tended to be the same way. That is, otherworldly characteristics were reported slightly more often among brain-disturbed patients. Likewise, these patients reacted with positive emotions and with religious feelings less often than the other patients. This is the same trend that was found in apparition cases. These results are certainly not expected according to our hypothesis of postmortem survival. They suggest that the experience of beauty and peace might be generated by brain disturbance. However, our sample of just 10 patients with brain maladies is too small to reach firm conclusions. We need to consider these results in conjunction with analysis of the rest of the medical factors.

Narcotic and psychedelic substances acting on the brain can generate beautiful visions. Could visions of the dying be considered just another "drug trip" caused by a chemically or otherwise disturbed brain? We had data on medication for 94 patients. In the judgment of respondents, consciousness was affected by drugs in 18 percent of the cases. However, the effect was too slight to cause hallucinations in half of them, leaving only 9 percent with moderate or strong impairments. We analyzed the interactions of medication and the seven main characteristics of the visions. There was no relationship whatsoever between medication and experiential characteristics suggestive of an afterlife.

Medical history and background diagnoses which might cause hallucinations were present in 21 percent of the cases. As previously explained, this is an inflated measure often based upon respondents' vague suspicions rather than facts. It did not interact significantly with any of the seven characteristics.

Body temperature higher than 103° was practically absent (7 percent) and therefore could not have shaped the experiences. Clarity of consciousness at the time of the vision was clearly indicated in 96 cases. Clarity was normal in 35 percent of the cases, mildly impaired though communication was still possible in 27 percent of the cases, and strongly impaired in 37 percent of the cases. In sharp contrast to the apparition cases, the clarity of consciousness was drastically reduced during the visions of environment.

Were visions with characteristics suggestive of another world generated mainly by those whose consciousness was impaired? This was not the case. There were no significant interactions with the seven main characteristics of the phenomena, with one exception: 77 percent of the impaired felt as though they were "elsewhere," while 50 percent of the clearly conscious patients felt transported—for example, to a beautiful garden. The clearly conscious experienced another world, beauty and peace, death symbolism, and appropriate emotions with approximately the same frequency as those with impairments of consciousness. Apparently, impairment of consciousness does not shape the phenomena to a substantial extent.

Our findings indicate that the characteristics of visions of environment may to a considerable extent be independent of medical conditions, although in cases of brain maladies visions could be caused by them.

Patients' sex does not significantly shape any of the characteristics of vision phenomena, either, although a definite difference exists. Women experienced more otherworldly subject matter and saw surroundings as more otherworldly. Age does not interact significantly with any of the vision characteristics.

Patients' education interacted significantly ($p = .01$) with only one variable. High-school-educated patients saw more otherworldly visions (89 percent) than the less-educated (57 percent) or college-educated patients (61 percent). We have no interpretation to offer on this point.

Patients' belief in life after death doubled the frequency of visions symbolizing death as a gratifying transition ($p = .003$) and responses with religious emotions ($p = .006$). Belief did not significantly change the frequency of experiences of beauty and peace and the frequency of images of another world. Apparently, the belief in life after death changes very little of the afterlife images themselves, but rules the religious emotions and sharply increases positive valuation of death.

Patients' personal involvement in religion did not affect the subject matter of visions at all. Deeply involved patients saw gardens, gates, and Heaven no more often than those of lesser or no involvement. Experiences of great beauty and peace were also independent of the degree of patients' involvement in religion. However, deep involvement in religion sharply increased the symbolization of death as a transition to a gratifying existence, from 27 percent to 53 percent (p = .06). It more than doubled the frequency of responses with religious emotions, from 23 percent to 62 percent (p = .006). Apparently, visionary imagery suggestive of another world does not depend on deep involvement in religion, but positive emotional reactions to death are more evident among deeply religious patients.

Patients who thought they would recover and those who expected to die saw visions of another world with the same frequency. Their expectations or wishful thinking apparently did not shape the visions.

Evidence of stress such as anxiety, restlessness and depression had no influence on the frequency of otherworldly visions. Patients who showed no such signs of stress experienced images of another world as often as patients who had these indices. Apparently, the visions of another world are not generated in order to cope with unbearable stress by conjuring up cheerful images of Heaven.

On the whole, we found that those characteristics of visions which are suggestive of afterlife seem reasonably independent of psychological factors discussed above. Belief in life after death and involvement in religion do not change the content of visions but significantly increase the positive symbolization of death and reactions with religious emotions.

Indian and American Experiences of Heaven

Do Indians and Americans see Heaven in the same way, or are their visions as different as the Bible is from the Vedas? Do we get only a playback of Scriptures and traditions, or do patients of both cultures see basically the same? If the other world does not exist, a playback is the main content to be expected. If the dying really perceive a postmortem reality—however poorly—then some more similarity should emerge from their observations.

Interaction of the phenomena with patients' religion were evaluated in the U.S. sample. No significant relationships were found. Unfortunately, we had too few non-Hindu patients in India for a meaningful comparison. All we can do is compare the Indian visions with the American.

Otherworldly matters were portrayed slightly more often in Indian visions (77 percent) than in American visions (62 percent).

Both cultures were more alike than different in this respect. Another analysis concerning the appearance of surroundings also showed similarity. Conventional images of Heaven combined with "places of extraordinary beauty beyond reality" were as common in India (52 percent) as in the United States (58 percent). While 17 percent of the American patients saw threatening environments (mainly of this world), none of the Indian patients reported such surroundings. Let us remember that Indians did see threatening apparitions much more frequently than American patients. Perhaps Americans project their fears on places, while Indians project them on persons.

Indians considered their visions to be religious (67 percent) slightly more often than Americans (55 percent). Symbolizations of death, where they could be ascertained, mainly depicted death as a transition to a gratifying reality in both countries (United States, 77 percent; India, 90 percent). Great beauty and peace dominated visions in both cultures (United States, 82 percent; India, 94 percent). Experiences in both countries are basically similar. The slight differences observed are well within the range of sampling errors and respondents' biases.

Emotional effects from the experiences, however, are not significantly different. Indians are more emotionally responsive, and experienced more positive emotions (India, 66 percent; United States, 57 percent) and less negative feelings (India, 9 percent; United States, 19 percent).

Another look at emotional reactions showed that Indians reacted with religious emotions twice as often as Americans, 47 percent and 24 percent, respectively. The difference is not statistically significant $(p = .10)$.

Indian and American patients saw the same kinds of visions, but Indian emotional reactions were more lively, more positive, and more religious. From these statistics it seems that Indians see the heavenly abode while in a happier mood than American patients.

Let us now take a critical look at the visions themselves in Indian reports. We again see two kinds of experiences—those of the mundane world and those of another world.

A young man from Agra dying from a bullet wound in his chest told about a very worldly celebration.

"I am in a village fair, lots of people are present." He was describing it vividly as if aware of actual showroom things.

Visions beyond this life again had the perceptual quality of intense "light." An engineer in his forties suffered a heart attack.

He described things lit in very bright light coming toward him just before his death. He said, "Now I am going to die. Please don't disturb me—no medicine."

His mood changed to serenity and peace, and he died in ten minutes.

A Hindu farm laborer, after gaining consciousness, told that he had been to a place which was very beautiful, a nice place. It looked as if it was *Swarag*—Heaven.

But what does *Swarag* look like? A Hindu housewife of Allahabad told a bit more: "Look, I am seeing heaven. There are beautiful gardens with flowers." So far, it sounds like the American cases, but then she added some Indian warmth to it: "Children are playing and singing there. Many people, high houses. There I also saw God. It looks very beautiful." The respondent said, "She feels very happy, even now when she describes it years after her recovery."

A Hindu student in his twenties was dying of smallpox in Aligarh. His experience seems to give an academic twist to the imagery of Heaven.

Twenty minutes after the hallucination the patient told me, "I have seen beautiful buildings and gardens surrounded by hills. I saw noble persons, learned persons. All were very happy and cheerful." Then he realized, "I am going to die," and after that he started to cry.

Apparently the Hindu Heaven was as beautiful and serene as the Christian Paradise, but the student was not ready to go.

A young nurse, who was a Christian converted to Islam through marriage, was bleeding to death from a ruptured uterus.

She saw all the comforts of the next life, beautifully furnished interiors with sofas, etc. No sorrow, nothing disgusting— everything is gay and happy there. [Then the doctor added dryly,] She wanted to attain more worldly comfort there than a well placed doctor can get in this world.

(Apparently, there is nothing stingy about being "up there.")
A forty-year-old man with a gastric infection told his nurse:

"I see a temple with closed doors. Open the doors for me, I have
to go to God." Later he saw messengers of death in black
clothes: "They are coming to take me."

He became serene. Apparently this was the Hindu counterpart of
Christian "gates" and their way of entry.
A Hindu from Bihar in his forties was suffering from gangrene
and came very close to death.

He said the next morning: "Yesterday I was in a beautiful place.
There were beautiful gardens and a temple with many gods
residing in it." From his description it seemed that he was
seeing heaven.

His mood was miserable before and became serene and peaceful
after the vision. He recovered. Like the sight of the Christian
Heaven, this vision left him in serene acceptance of death.
    The vision of an Indian Christian, a nurse, was similar to Hindu
experiences, except that she saw her Lord:

I felt myself going up. There was a beautiful garden full of
flowers. I was sitting there. Suddenly I felt beaming light and
Jesus Christ came to me. He sat and talked to me. Light was all
around.

She became very peaceful and gradually recovered from typhoid
fever.
    A young Hindu housewife was in a coma for two days because of
infection during pregnancy. Her heaven was different. "She saw big
boxes full of fine clothes and attractive jewelry. She put on the best
of them and then danced." But she did not quite dance her way into
Heaven—she recovered.
    A seventeen-year-old Hindu girl was badly hurt in an accident,
unconscious for twelve hours. She saw a beautiful garden with girls
playing there, good-looking girls. "Let me go and play in the garden,
it's a very nice garden, let me go." Instead of letting her go, the

medical personnel decided that she was violent and gave her a shot of morphine.

We didn't find American cases of dancing and playing. Perhaps our Heaven is too solemn for that. But why did they all come back from such lovely places? Here are those who didn't want to return.

A college-educated patient in his thirties suffering from a liver disease thought that he was dead and told the nurse later:

> After death I went to heaven. It looked beautiful. There were beautiful gardens full of flowers. I saw Yamdoots [messengers of death], of black complexion. I also saw Yamaraj [king of death], all black, tall, and in robust health.

This patient didn't want to come back; he wanted to remain there. Here he made his choice in favor of dying—a choice which he dreaded before the vision.

A college-educated man in his twenties chose to end his life in suicide by barbiturate poisoning. He felt himself to be in Heaven, but the doctor thought otherwise.

> The patient was calling irrelevantly, saying, "I am in heaven. There are so many houses around me, so many streets with big trees bearing sweet fruit and small birds singing in the trees."

In the United States, some cases resembled out-of-body experiences of floating and flying. Some Indians also report floating in empty space. A Hindu business proprietor told his doctor, "I was going in circles in the sky—smooth journey." The doctor asked him what vehicle, but he was not sure about that.

A Christian nurse was undergoing a cesarean section. "I was put on the operating table. I prayed. I felt myself going higher and higher, I was very peaceful. I felt dying is a very peaceful experience."

A Farrukhabad housewife in her forties seemed to have died of pneumonia.

> The patient was taken for dead. Resuscitation methods were applied. No response for 10–15 minutes. She was unconscious. Then she recovered, opened her eyes. She said that she had

died. "I was going in space. There was nothing but space." She
did not want to go back there in space.

A college-educated member of the Indian Communist party
adhered to a materialistic philosophy. During cardiac arrest

he felt himself flying among clouds. He thought it was a
beautiful place, but not of this earth. He felt himself very light,
riding on the clouds. He heard music and also some singing in
the background. When he recognized that he was alive, he was
sorry that he had to leave this beautiful place. When he told
about this he seemed to have enjoyed the experience. He was a
jolly college graduate, joked a lot. He was not a sentimental
person, not religious, very independent of his family, and liked
to see a lot of movies. He said: "That was the bright spot of my
illness, to be out of the misery and suffering of humanity."

A strange trip for a nonbeliever.

A myocardial infarction case: "She went to a place where she saw
high mountains covered with snow. All white. There were no signs
of life. She was pleased to be there." No American saw a snow-
covered Paradise, but in India, snow is associated with the grandeur
of the Himalayas.

A fifty-year-old patient was afflicted with cancer of the rectum.
"The patient said that he was feeling as though he was in Benares,
Allahabad, Mathava and other holy places. After that, he meant, he
would go to heaven." In other cases, the holy places "visited" were
Varanasi and the Taj Mahal. We found no "astral pilgrimage" cases
in the United States.

We had many American cases in which patients resented the gates
of Paradise remaining closed—the doctors revived the patient, who
then responded with resentment. The Indian data showed similar
cases of resentment toward doctors for saving the patient's life.

A Hindu constable's lung was removed because of advanced
tuberculosis: One day we thought he was dead and we administered heart massage—no heartbeat for 1–2 minutes. He was
unconscious for 2–3 minutes. Then his heart started to beat
again and he reproached the nurses: "Why did you call me

back? I have been to a beautiful garden, very good garden which I cannot describe." For two hours he was alive, then he died. He was happy about the experience, but feeling very sorry that he was brought back from that beautiful place.

Again there was the same overwhelming experience of beauty and resentment for being revived as found in some American cases.

A Hindu farmer in his sixties underwent a cardiac arrest. He was revived within a few minutes by the medical team. The patient told that he was taken to a palace made of silver, furniture was made of silver with silk cushions. A few ladies wearing beautiful ornaments were sitting in a pool as if they were only waiting for him. All five village leaders (judges) were seated in the middle of the palace to welcome him. The palace was filled with perfume. The patient was very happy about this experience of a lovely palace. He became rather angry at the doctor: "Why have you saved me?"

This poor farmer's vision was sensuous rather than spiritual, but great beauty was there nevertheless. We described several American cases in which the patient was rejected from the other world. Numerous Indian patients also were "sent back," but in a more dramatic way.

A young Hindu girl was considered to be dead, but regained consciousness. This is how a doctor reported her story.

Two messengers tied her with ropes on a stretcher and carried her up to God. There she saw beautiful people—women. They were cooking meals. She was tempted to eat. On a high place she saw a very influential person sitting in a decorated chair. He said to the messengers, "Why did you bring her?" and then gave specifications of someone else who was to be brought. Those messengers then sent her back. She did not want to come back—the place was so beautiful. Afterwards, signs of tying with ropes could be seen on her legs.

Indians have a custom of tying the corpse to a stretcher to be carried to the funeral pyre.

A high-school-educated Muslim housewife was in critical condition after an operation on her uterus.

"I saw four persons in black clothes who asked me to go with them. I was afraid of them. They took me up. In the sky there was an open space which was green. God was sitting there. He asked me my name. He said that I shouldn't have been brought up. They sent me back." Upon coming to, she complained bitterly to the nurse, "Sister, why did you save me? I liked this place. I wish to go back there."

Indian Christians also experienced this "you-are-the-wrong-person" type of rejection. Even a Swedish missionary was tangled up in the error and "brought up" mistakenly.

A West Bengali clerical worker was a Christian.

The patient was dead and all preparations for the funeral were being made. Suddenly he regained consciousness. He complained of pain in his body. When asked about it he told that he was pushed down and got hurt. He remembered that he was taken up through a long staircase. Then he saw a beautiful scene, lovely flowers. In there he saw a man dressed in white sitting with an open book. He looked into the book and told the men who had taken him there that they have brought the wrong person. And then the messengers pushed him down.

He did not explain how his soul was actually manhandled, but when he came to, his body was in pain.

Characteristically for India, an authoritarian manner is attributed only to the lower echelon of heavenly personnel, the messengers. The man with the "book of accounts" is always pictured as a benign ruler. An aura of sacredness rests upon him regardless of whether he is called "the man in a white robe" or "God." The same aura of sacredness appears in the visions of religious figures seen by patients in the United States. When they appear, the patient "lights up."

Is this air of sacredness attributed to any of the visionary environments? All heavenly abodes are fashioned after this-world reality: flowers, trees, gardens, streams, gates, tall buildings, castles, silver palaces, temples, and even staircases. The common denominator is not any special kind of heavenly form or "spiritual stuff" from which forms emerge. However, the earthly appearances are often illuminated in visionary intensity and perfection. The only unity which transcends the bewildering variety of imagery is experiential rather than perceptual. Common to most is the experience of "great beauty beyond reality," joy, peace, and serenity. Most of the dying seem to experience something completely gratifying, a value fulfillment—they don't want to "come back." Sometimes these experiential qualities seem to irradiate the visitors with lightened brightness and intensified colors.

The images themselves, if they indeed depict reality, seem to be symbolizations—signs pointing to an existence beyond our perceptual capabilities but not congruent with that reality. If the dying indeed tell about another world, then terms of beauty, harmony, peace, and value fulfillment are the closest ways they are able to describe it.

CHAPTER 14

The Meaning of Death:
What We Learned from This Study

W E are now at the end of a long journey, having looked into more than 1,000 death or near-death experiences of patients on two continents. Each experience was presented either directly in words spoken by doctors and nurses or in statistical averages which we calculated. The statistics are, of course, only abstractions of these experiences—abstractions of the anguish, the flickering hopes, and sudden bursts of joyful insight which real people had. Like dried-up flowers, statistics are pale representations of reality. However, statistical data based on large numbers of experiences undergone by patients with different illnesses, upbringings, cultural inheritances, and beliefs helped us to gain new insight into the mystery and meaning of death. We could not have gained this knowledge any other way. Our journey was the first of its kind and, by necessity, a crude scouting of unknown territory. As in the time when the wagons of American settlers were first rolling into the "Wild West," there were no roads in this study for a Cadillac of elegant design. Thus, we hope it is understandable that the knowledge we brought back is only a crude approximation of what subsequent explorers will find when they apply new ingenuity, more rigor, and more resources than we pioneers could.

We have reported that knowledge in earlier chapters. Here we will summarize it and attempt to draw conclusions—highlighted markings on our map intended to benefit those coming after us.

The Core Phenomena

What are the basic characteristics of deathbed visions? In general, we found that phenomena suggestive of postmortem existence are of a shorter duration than those which are concerned with this life. This situation is analogous to a forked road. Brief experiences lead mostly to otherworldly phenomena, while longer ones usually wind up in worldly imagery and feelings. We know from parapsychological investigations outside the field of survival research that ESP experiences are usually of short duration. According to our afterlife hypothesis, deathbed visions involve extrasensory perceptions of an afterlife state and its messengers. We reasoned that the visions, therefore, should be brief. They were.

When afterlife-oriented experiences occur, death approaches sooner than when the same kind of phenomena are related to worldly concerns. According to the afterlife hypothesis, these phenomena are by-products of transition and should accompany it. We found a significant number of cases where patients died in accordance with the "call" of the apparition, even when the medical prognosis was recovery. Of course, the interval between the experience and death does not apply to cases where patients did not die after seeing an apparition or vision of an otherworldly environment.

Osis pointed out in his *Deathbed Observations* monograph that hallucinations of persons in deathbed visions mainly portray otherworldly messengers—that is, apparitions of dead and religious figures. On the other hand, only a small minority of hallucinations in the general population are concerned with such otherworldly apparitions. The new surveys clearly show that this is, indeed, the case. In both the United States and India, the visions of the dying and of near-death patients were overwhelmingly dominated (four to one) by apparitions of dead and religious figures. This finding is loud and clear: *When the dying see apparitions, they are nearly always experienced as messengers from a postmortem mode of existence.* Of the human figures seen in visions of the dying, the vast majority were deceased close relatives. This is in agreement with our hypothesis that close relatives would be the natural guides in transitions to an afterlife. Hallucinations of mental patients and drug-induced visions seldom portrayed close relatives.

The pilot survey revealed the most dramatic characteristic of deathbed apparitions: the ostensible intent to take the patient away to the other world. *This was again found to be the dominantly stated purpose of the apparitions of the dying, as well as of come-back cases, in both American and Indian cultures.* The apparitions seem to show a will of their own, instead of expressing the desires and inner dynamics of the patients. Needless to say, such a dominance of the take-away purpose in apparitions seen by patients near death is in close conformity to our model. If there is a postmortem world of survival, it seems likely that the dead would give us a hand during our transition to their kind of existence.

In the pilot survey, it was noted that patients responded to the otherworldly apparitions in a most surprising manner. They wanted to "go"—that is, to die. Some even bitterly reproached those who successfully resuscitated them. Again, we encountered cases of such resentment in both countries. Nearly all the American patients, and two-thirds of the Indian patients, were ready to go after having seen otherworldly apparitions with a take-away purpose. *Encounters with ostensible messengers from the other world seemed to be so gratifying that the value of this life was easily outweighed.* However, on the basis of the pilot survey, we did not expect that one-third of our Indian patients would not consent to go. Part of the difference was traced to the influence of religion, part to national origins.

Emotional responses to seeing an apparition were the same in dying patients as they were in those who recovered from a close brush with death. In view of the general misery and pain experienced by very sick patients, the response is surprising. An absence of emotion was observed in only one-fourth of our patients. Most of those who did respond had positive emotions: serenity, peace, elation. Serenity and peace could be regarded as appropriate responses to a transcendental reality. Of these positive emotions, one-third were said to be of a religious nature—for example, those experienced when "seeing God." Negative emotions were not infrequent, but they mainly came either from patients who saw hallucinations concerned with this-world purposes or from Indian patients who did not want to go.

Patients who saw apparitions concerned with this-world purposes seldom experienced serenity, peace, or religious feelings. Reactions with the appropriate emotions to "otherworldly visitors" are in accordance with the hypothesis of postmortem survival.

When patients had visions which were predominantly environmental (Heaven, beautiful gardens, and so on), the positive emotional response was even more dominant: mainly serenity, peace, elation, or religious feelings. This leaves only a small portion of patients with negative emotions. They were, to a great extent, those who hallucinated mundane, this-life scenery.

While most visions of surroundings depicted another world, a considerable number—one-third—were mere hallucinations of this-world places and objects. Although otherworldly images were fashioned after this-world scenery, they were greatly heightened and refined. Brightness and intensity of colors were mentioned. In the U.S. sample, about half of the otherworldly images were of a conventional nature, in accordance with religious Scriptures. We could not safely determine what is conventional in India. Nearly all visions of another world expressed beauty, peace, and harmony— great beauty being the most outstanding experiential quality. Furthermore, of those reports which supplied enough information for interpretation, visions seemed to portray death as the transition to a gratifying existence in five out of six cases.

Some patients who saw no visions whatsoever became as serene and elated as those patients who encountered otherworldly messengers. Serenity and peace were dominant in more than half of the mood-elevation cases, while a third of the patients experienced elation, and the rest had miscellaneous moods. Serenity, peace, and religious emotions did not correlate with moods of the day before. Instead, they seemed to be experienced as something new breaking through the gloom of the dying. According to our postmortem survival hypothesis, serenity, peace, and religious emotions came in response to extrasensory contact with transcendental reality.

We found that mood elevation near death resembles those ESP cases where a person will respond with emotions appropriate to a distant event, even though he is not consciously aware of what happened there. For example, a mother suddenly undergoes severe depression at the time her son is killed in action, and *before* the telegram informing her about it arrives. Dying patients felt serene without apparent reason. Many tried to rationalize it by way of false optimism about their situation: thinking it was an indication of recovery, and so planning vacations, and so on. These characteristics closely resemble ESP cases.

There were some cases where patients ceased to feel pain. According to our afterlife hypothesis, the mind or soul may disengage itself from awareness of bodily pain and discomfort, as if gradually separating from its physical frame. In rare cases, incoherent patients suffering from brain diseases or schizophrenia were said to become their lucid, normal selves shortly before death.

Mood elevation, like other near-death phenomena, may be open to interpretations other than an afterlife. We evaluated alternative explanations by analyzing the extent to which medical, psychological, and cultural factors influenced the cases. Here is a summary of our findings in this area.

Explanations Other Than Afterlife: A Critical Evaluation

From the very start of our research, we were aware of radically different explanations of the core phenomena of deathbed visions. Our research methods were aimed at systematically gathering data which might support the usual medical, psychological, and anthropological explanations. We will critically consider these factors first, then scrutinize other factors to see whether they have biased our data—factors such as respondents, patient's response bias, our sampling methods, and possible biases of our own.

In any critical evaluation of deathbed experiences, *medical factors* have to be considered. Possible similarities to visions induced by hallucinogenic drugs were suggested. Morphine, Demerol, and other potent hallucinogenics are frequently administered to the dying in order to make their pain more bearable. Only a small minority of the patients who had deathbed visions had received such drugs. Those who had received medication had no greater frequency of afterlife visions than the other patients. Whatever these drugs did, *they apparently did not generate deathbed phenomena suggestive of an afterlife.*

Brain disturbances caused by disease, injury, or uremic poisoning were not always significantly related to seeing apparitions. The trend was clear: They either decreased the afterlife-related phenomena or did not affect them at all. Therefore, *there is no acceptable evidence for the notion that brain disturbances generate such phenomena.* One possible exception should be mentioned. In a minor fraction of our data on visions of environments, we had ten patients with brain disturbances or nephritis, and eight of them chiefly experienced visions characterized by beauty. We have no explanation to offer for this.

It has been suggested that lack of oxygen (anoxia) may cause hallucinations in dying patients. Extensive experimental and anecdotal research has been made in aviation medicine on the effects of reduced supply of oxygen. A thorough search made for us at the Aeromedical Library of the U.S. Air Force School of Aerospace Medicine in San Antonio, Texas failed to find any support for this conjecture.

The presence of a medical history suggestive of hallucinogenic factors also did not increase the frequency of afterlife-related experiences.

On the whole, we found some evidence that medical factors which cripple communication with the external world also cut down phenomena related to an afterlife. These findings are in close agreement with the afterlife hypothesis of our model.

Psychological factors—such as severe stress and intense expectancy—might cause hallucinations. For instance, a thirsty desert traveler might envision water. We clearly found that phenomena suggestive of postmortem survival are not related to indices of stress, expectations to die or to recover, or the patient's desire to see a person dear to him. No evidence was found in our sample to suggest that psychological factors known to facilitate hallucinations also cause afterlife-related deathbed visions.

Cultural background has enormous shaping power over human experiences and behavior. According to our model, cultural forces should sway the phenomena greatly if the destruction hypothesis is true. It should influence it only moderately if there is an afterlife, since people agree more about what they perceive than about what they imagine. Cultural sway can be observed in two ways:

1. The extent to which the visions follow one's cultural conditioning—for example, the Bible, in the case of American patients.

2. How much the phenomena differ between the U.S. and Indian samples.

Actually, cultural influences were much harder to judge than were interactions involving medical and psychological factors. For example, the determination of an influence as "moderate" is a matter of judgment rather than measurement. This is further complicated by the fact that extrasensory perception is even more beset with subjective embroidery, symbolizations, and distortions than sense perceptions are. The composition of subjective vignettes pertaining to the phenomena will, of course, depend on cultural factors and personal idiosyncrasies. We assumed the general core phenomena would, however, be more stable than specific details which, even if they did include extrasensory glimpses of the other world, could be mixed up in a subjective jumble. We described these core phenomena in the preceding pages, and have summarized them in Chart 2.

CHART 2.
COMPARISON OF CORE PHENOMENA SUGGESTIVE OF AFTERLIFE IN U.S. AND INDIAN PATIENTS*

Phenomena Expected According to Our Model	Phenomena Present In Patients	
	U.S.	India
1. Duration of experiences suggestive of afterlife are short, as in ESP.	X	X
2. Apparitions are mainly seen as coming from another world.	X	X
3. Most apparitions portray religious figures.		X
4. Most apparitions portray the dead.	X	
5. Most human apparitions are close relatives.	X	X
6. Majority of apparitions "came to take the patient away."	X	X
7. Most patients respond to apparition with readiness to "go"—that is, to die.	X	X
8. A considerable minority of patients refused to "go."		X

Phenomena Expected According to Our Model	Phenomena Present In Patients	
	U.S.	India
9. Patient sent back by the apparition in some nonterminal cases.	X	X
10. The most frequent emotional responses to apparitions are serenity, peace, elation, and religious emotions.	X	X
11. Mood elevation occurs shortly before death in some patients.	X	X
12. Visions mainly portray otherworldly environments.	X	X
13. Visions of environment mostly express beauty, peace, harmony.	X	X
14. Environmental visions symbolize death as transition to a gratifying existence.	X	X

* X = phenomenon confirmed in survey.

One can easily see the similarities outweighed the differences by a wide margin. Some of those characteristics which presumably had nothing to do with the ideas of another world were also different across cultures, but were not included in the chart. For example, Indians see a predominance of elderly male apparitions, while Americans favor female apparitions who often portray younger persons. We interpreted these differences on purely secular grounds.

In our judgment, the similarities between the core phenomena found in the deathbed visions of both countries are clear enough to be considered as supportive of the postmortem survival hypothesis.

We found another source of evidence: The phenomena within each culture often do not conform with *religious afterlife beliefs.* The patients see something new, unexpected, and contrary to their beliefs. Christian ideas of "judgment," "salvation," and "redemption" were not mirrored in the visions of our American patients. Furthermore, while we had many reports about visions of Heaven, visions of Hell and Devils were almost totally absent. The afterlife figures and environments experienced by Christians were entirely of a benign and pleasing nature.

Several basic Hindu ideas of an afterlife were never portrayed in the visions of Indian patients. The various Vedic "loci" of an afterlife—Hindu Heaven—were never mentioned. Nor were reincarnation and dissolution in Brahma, the formless aspect of God which is the goal of Indian spiritual striving. The concept of Karma—accumulation of merits and demerits—may have been vaguely suggested by reports of a "white-robed man with a book of accounts." In both cultures, the visionary contact with deities and other religious figures seemed to be gratifying and value-fulfilling. With the exception of some Indian Yamdoots, the white-robed figures seem to have had an aura of numinous qualities around them.

We reached the impression that cultural conditioning by Christian and Hindu teaching is, in part, contradicted in the visionary experiences of the dying. It seems to us that besides symbolizations based on inculcated beliefs, terminal patients do "see" something that is unexpected, untaught, and a complete surprise to them.

The Other World: How Certain Are We About It?

The time has now come to ask the critical questions. The reader has seen for himself the stories told by dying and near-death patients—stories which repeatedly relate encounters with otherworldly messengers, and visions of beautiful and peaceful surroundings. Although we tried to explain these experiences in terms of the known medical and psychological causes of hallucinations, the data would not support such arguments. Nor could the influences of religion or other cultural factors be used to explain away the phenomena. Could these observed trends be considered as statistical artifacts stemming from unusual fluctuations in our random sampling procedure? Or are they the result of the ways in which we grouped our data together?

Since the patterns found in the pilot survey emerged from a large array of possibilities, we were unable to regard them as real effects with definite certainty. Because of the pioneering nature of our work, we could hypothesize trends to be expected. However, on the basis of the findings in the pilot survey, we were able to predict the probable patterns that the phenomena in the new surveys would assume. The trends found in the pilot survey and those suggested by our model allowed us to narrow down the range of the patterns expected to emerge from statistical analyses. Throughout this book, we have indicated the two major consistencies found in the phenomena.

1. *Consistency between the surveys*—for example, the greatly predominant take-away purpose exhibited by apparitions in the pilot, the U.S., and the Indian surveys.

2. *Consistency of the basic findings among the various phenomena investigated*—apparitions seen by terminal patients, apparitions seen in near-death cases, environmental visions, and mood-elevation cases.

Not every phenomenon discovered in the United States was also found in India. For example, Indians who encountered apparitions with a take-away purpose did not die much sooner after their experiences than those who saw other kinds of apparitions—that is, except in cases where the patient did not consent to "go." But on the whole, all three surveys were dominated by similar patterns. Our confidence was greatly increased by such consistencies. They demonstrated that we were dealing with real effects in our data and were not being deluded by capricious sampling variations.

The consistencies among the various groups of phenomena in our findings were also not without exceptions. However, the common ground was much more visible than the variations were. Consistencies among the classes of phenomena—in addition to similarities among the findings of the three surveys—diminish the probability that chance fluctuations could account for our results.

Could our research methods hold hidden biases which would tend to accentuate the data favorable to the afterlife hypothesis? Because we opted for gathering large numbers of observations for statistical analyses, we had to rely on the reports of doctors and nurses instead of checking with the patients themselves. Our medical observers could not provide the descriptive richness of the experiences which the direct approach—firsthand reports from patients such as Moody (1975) presents—seems to supply. The reports of our medical respondents were usually crisp and short. Of course, medical personnel are trained to be accurate observers and to avoid mere opinions and fleeting impressions in their medical records. We hoped that such trained observers would provide data that would be more objective than information which would be supplied by the patients, who might embellish their stories as they tell them over and over again.

Our survey had built-in checks and balances on such possible sources of respondent biases as religious beliefs, attitudes toward hallucinations, length of contact with the patient, patient load, and relationship to the patient (i.e., as a professional, friend, or relative). After an extensive analysis of the data, we found no serious respondent bias that exaggerated the afterlife-related phenomena. However, some respondent groups showed quite a strong tendency to underreport these phenomena. This bias was prevalent among young doctors, especially in America. More experienced physicians and nurses seemed to provide the most reliable data. We found no indication that any of our respondent groups biased the data by a gross exaggeration of the afterlife phenomena. We therefore concluded that our data show a *lesser* proportion of afterlife-related experiences than there actually were.

Another possible source of distortion is the fact that our cases were recorded sometime after they happened. We checked for the presence of such errors by comparing new cases with older ones. There was little difference within the same age group of respondents. For example, more respondents who reported older cases could not remember the patient's mood a day before the event occurred. However, no major distortions of the phenomena themselves were found.

We used the customary methods of random sampling in our American survey—for example, selecting every seventh intern from an alphabetized list. In India, however, we had to use a different method. We were able to solicit responses from practically all the medical personnel in selected units, such as the departments of medicine, surgery, and obstetrics in a teaching hospital. We believe that both methods yielded reasonably random samples. The American sample was, however, more questionable since only 20 percent returned questionnaires. At first we suspected that only those who were in favor of the afterlife hypothesis had responded. We reasoned that the real enthusiasts would jump at the opportunity and answer sooner than those who sent in questionnaires late or only after repeated requests. However, we did not find any relationship between speed in responding and the phenomena reported. Spot checks of nonresponders via telephone indicated that their attitudes toward the phenomena were not substantially different from those of the responders.

The patients' own response biases were also analyzed. Again, we failed to find exaggerations of afterlife-related experiences. In fact, our analyses showed something quite to the contrary. Patients seemed to be hesitant to entrust their otherworldly experiences to skeptical physicians and nurses, except when they happened to be relatives or friends. This kind of response bias would tend to suppress communication rather than provoke exaggeration of experiences related to postmortem survival.

We can conclude that *our surveys might have detected less phenomena supportive of the postmortem survival hypothesis than patients had actually experienced*. This, again, increases our confidence in the findings from the transcultural survey. In our judgment, these surveys have provided reasonably realistic data. We believe that new information of some importance has arisen from our pioneering work.

In any study there is always the possibility that the researchers themselves might be a biasing factor. However, we are fully aware that biases are counterproductive to elucidating the full truth, and so we did our best to be objective. As a further precaution, we have endeavored to clearly state our personal philosophies so that the critical reader may also take them into account. When Osis started the pilot survey, he was quite critical. However, after having encountered many consistent doctors' reports supporting the theory of postmortem survival, he slowly changed his attitude toward the positive. Haraldsson also began with a reserved but searching attitude. Gradually he became impressed by the data from the many interviews he conducted. The outcome of long labors on statistical evaluations moved him further toward acceptance of the afterlife hypothesis as the most tenable explanation of our data. Osis concurs with this interpretation. We tried to conduct our investigation from a neutral, middle-of-the-road position. Moreover, we have tried to present our data objectively without adherence to the two belief systems (materialistic and theological) dominant in our society.

Science, of course, is a group endeavor where many researchers work with different methods and varied theoretical outlooks in such a way that the shortcomings of some works are eventually balanced out by the efforts of others. Afterlife-related phenomena are still in a relatively early stage of research, so it would be misguided to proclaim final answers. However, in order to gain a proper perspective on the matter, the relevant work of others must be related to our own. It is this task to which we now turn.

Have Other Researchers Found Similar Phenomena?

How do our research and findings relate to other such efforts involving the experiences of dying or near-death patients? Kübler-Ross told us privately in 1976 that she has frequently observed the phenomena we studied and found the same main characteristics: a predominance of survival-related apparitions, the take-away purpose, and the striking emotional responses of mood elevation and of serenity and peace. Likewise, Moody reports experiences of many people who almost died but were resuscitated. Many of those patients in the near-death state ". . . became aware of the presence of other spiritual beings in their vicinity, beings who apparently were there to ease them through their transition into death, or, in two cases, to tell them that their time to die had not yet come and that they must return to their physical bodies."[1] Moody also reports that resuscitated patients frequently experience "a being of light," which, according to him, is given a name in accordance with the patient's religious orientation. This being may be identified as Christ by a Christian, or as an "angel" by those of the Jewish faith. In addition, Moody states that encounters with "beings of light" also occur among patients with no religious belief or training. This encounter is "certainly the element which has the most profound effect upon the individual."[2] This finding is strikingly similar to many patients' reports of what we have termed "apparitions of religious figures."[3]

Certain other researchers into the question of postmortem survival, such as Noyes and Kletti, hold a traditional psychiatric view of the various deathbed experiences, however. They interpret them in terms of depersonalization (Noyes and Kletti, 1976). They define the *depersonalization syndrome* broadly as consisting of altered awareness of the self, feelings of strangeness and unreality, loss of emotions, detachment, slowing of time, receding of space, and blunting of sensations. Their respondents were very different from ours—mainly survivors of accidents such as falls, drownings, or auto accidents— and excluded terminal patients. They had to answer yes or no questions which precluded expression of more detailed nuances of the experiences. As evidenced in their Example 1, experiences of another world were said to be a sense of unreality. Nevertheless, they found self-transcending mystical experiences—joy, a sense of harmony or unity, a loss of fear of death—in these so-called depersonalization experiences. Such experiences are interpreted in accordance with the older psychiatric conceptions of Heim and Schilder. No effort is made by Noyes and Kletti to relate these research findings to those of parapsychology which suggest an afterlife. According to this view, which is close to the destruction hypothesis, the phenomena we have discussed here are psychological defenses against recognition of the imminent extinction of life. Noyes makes a useful distinction between dying and death. We fear dying, he says, but not death. It is the pain and suffering and depersonalization of dying that engender these deathbed phenomena as elaborate devices to evade the brutal truth of ultimate destruction. Death itself, however, is simply a state of nonexistence. As such, it provides no cause for the sensations and emotions of pain and suffering. With all due respect to the useful research of Noyes, Kletti, and others in this "camp," we must point out that our findings concerning the experiences of the dying do not fit into the psychiatric explanations when they are analyzed in more detail, including medical, psychological, and cultural factors.

In a later publication, Noyes and Slyman (1984) appear to have had second thoughts. They found their accident cases—the vast majority of their sample—so different from cases of "serious illness" that they excluded the latter from their main analyses. They rightly urge us to distinguish between the two groups of respondents: those who were close to death physically, and those who only approached it psychologically. At The Hour Of Death is exclusively based on the reports of persons who either died or were physically close to death, that is, individuals who faced the ultimate mystery itself, not just the danger of a close brush with death. This may explain part of the differences between our findings and those of Noyes et al.

The out-of-body experience might be like a prelude to the

irreversible separation of self from the body at death. In Chapters 4, 10, and 13, we gave examples of how this might be so, but we did not concentrate on them. Our data consist of reports by outside observers (physicians and nurses) who lacked the details which would be known by first-hand experients, details which are necessary for an assessment of the out-of-body phenomena. It is in this way that the later research of Drs. Ring, Gabbard, Twemlow, and especially Sabom fills the gap.

Cardiologist, Michael Sabom (1982), concentrated his research effort on the out-of-body experiences of resuscitated patients. He was fascinated by patients' detailed observations of the resuscitation process that took place when they were unconscious. He carefully explored the possibility that patients gathered such information by normal means, such as hearing what was going on while they were in an unconscious state, staff members telling patients about the resuscitation procedure, knowledge gathered by watching television medical shows, etc. After painstaking investigations. Sabom concluded that:

"During the autoscopic portion of the NDE [near-death experience], near-death survivors claimed to have seen and heard events in the vicinity of their own unconscious physical bodies from a detached elevated position. The details of these perceptions were found to be accurate in all instances where collaborating evidence was available. Moreover, there appeared to be no plausible explanation for the accuracy of these observations involving the usual physical senses. An out-of-body (extrasensory?) mechanism would explain both the personal interpretation afforded these experiences by those who had them (i.e., 'the spirit left the body') and the visual accuracy of the autoscopic observations. My own beliefs on this matter are leaning in this direction. The out-of-body hypothesis simply seems to fit best the data at hand" (p. 184).

Ring also quotes cases in accord with Sabom's views and states: "On the basis of the separation hypothesis, however, I do endorse the proposition that consciousness (with or without second body) may function independently of the physical body" (Ring, 1980, p. 233).

Out-of-body experiences were often misconstrued in medical circles as signs of mental disorder. Two psychiatrists, Gabbard and Twemlow (1984), dealt with this problem. They gathered questionnaire data from 339 cases and used their expertise in comparing them with such mental pathology as depersonalization, autoscopy, and schizophrenic distortions of body images. In every category they found out-of-body experiences radically different from syndromes of mental disorders. For example, depersonalization was emphasized by Noyes and his collaborators, while Gabbard and Twemlow find dissimilarities, as can be seen from the following table we reproduced.

Table 3.1
COMPARISON OF DEPERSONALIZATION AND OBE

Depersonalization	OBE
Observing self watches functioning self	Observing self and functioning self are experienced as one (physical body is inactive)
Usually does not feel "out-of-body"	Must feel "out-of-body" by definition
Experienced as dreamlike	Not experienced as dreamlike
Typically unpleasant	Typically pleasant
Affects: anxiety, panic, emptiness	Affects: joy, ecstasy, feelings of calm, peace and quiet
Often stress-induced (sympathetic)	Usually relaxation-induced (parasympathetic)
Experienced as pathological and strange	Experienced as religious, spiritual and noetic
Age distribution 15–30; rarely over 40	No characteristic age group
Sex distribution 2:1 female	Even sex distribution

Gabbard and Twemlow also encountered 34 near-death experiences, of which 14 cases were either drug-affected or under anesthesia, while the remaining 20 were not affected. We consider that sample too small for reliable interpretations.

There is more to out-of-body experiences than meets the medical eye. Questionnaire surveys, anthropological studies of out-of-body phenomena in different cultures, and laboratory experiments are reported in parapsychological literature. Nevertheless, interpretations are still widely divergent. While reductionists try to reduce out-of-body experiences to pathological or psychological factors, and the out-of-body perception to ordinary ESP (Blackmore, 1982), positive contributions which delineate the uniqueness of these experiences have also emerged.

Psychologist, Charles Tart, who is an expert in altered states of consciousness and parapsychology, pioneered modern research. He was the first to find brainwave (EEG) patterns during out-of-body states and provided original system theory to interpret the data (1974, 1977). One of us was able to verify some of the EEG patterns (Osis and Mitchell, 1977). Osis developed special equipment and methods for laboratory testing of out-of-body projections. He found indications that out-of-body perception of distant objects has some characteristics different from ordinary ESP. He and McCormick (1980) obtained strain-gauge registration of out-of-body presence. The physical effects which occur at the place where an out-of-body projection was "sent" are a strong indication of the realness of such phenomena.

British clinical psychologist, Morgot Grey, collected 38 near-death experiences and was impressed by patients' reports of leaving their bodies. She concludes her report on out-of-body phenomena by saying: "Having duly reviewed the accounts that contained resuscitation events, and wherever possible, sought to confirm the information with members of the medical team, or alternatively to obtain testimonies from others who were present at the time of the near-death event, I am obliged to conclude from the evidence I found that somehow it would seem that conscious awareness survives physical death" (Grey, 1985, pp. 40–41).

We were able to show clearly that patients' experiences at the hour of death are not explainable as "drug trips" caused by medication which affects consciousness (see Appendix Tables 3, 6, 9).

Then it was discovered that very potent substances somewhat like morphine—"endogenous opiates"—are manufactured by the human organism and released in the brain, which, in certain regions, has specific receptors for these substances. Soon it was questioned: could near-death experiences be caused by the release of endorphines in the dying brain, like dreams of opium takers?

Cardiologist, Michael Sabom (1982), p. 172), compared the reactions of patients who were injected with B-endorphine to near-death experiences of his patients. Reactions were different: endorphines provided pain relief which lasted longer and was not complete, as it is in near-death experiences. While endorphine suppresses alertness and often induces sleep, near-death patients reported hyper-alertness during their experiences. Psychiatrists Gabbard and Twemlow also rejected the endorphine hypothesis.

By far the most thorough, informed, and dispassionate discussion of the probable role of endorphines in near-death experiences comes from endocrinologist, Carr (1984), of the Harvard Medical School. He says that the key to the problem is that endogenous peptide hormones are released at time of physical stress and lists the following: "infection, hypoxemia (low oxygen supply), hypoglycemia (low blood sugar), psychological stress (e.g., restraint or pain), electroshock therapy, exercise and ether anesthesia" (p. 128). He concludes: "In other words, I am proposing to assign to certain behaviorally active peptides an operational role as 'endogenous halucinogens' in agonal states" (p. 131). A modest and cautious conclusion far from saying that endorphine release is the sole cause of near-death experiences. Carr sees the enormous complexities involved and leaves the doors wide open: "Lastly, even if careful scientific studies established beyond any doubt the physiological substrata of dying, they would still have no relevance to the philosophical meaning of death or its religious aspects" (p. 133).

We found no positive correlations between indices of stress (as observed by our medical respondents) and the frequency of the core phenomena investigated (pp. 84–85). However, that does not exclude the possibility that some influence of endorphines was undetected by our simple measures. Some patients in our sample received injections of morphine and other substances closely resembling endorphines, yet afterlife-related experiences were not increased in that group. If these medically administered substances did not induce the phenomena, why should they be the cause when internally secreted by the body?

Taking a position more in line with our own, Garfield emphasizes the transcendental qualities of deathbed experiences in which patients make references to such Eastern concepts as detachment, loosening of self-boundaries, and even ego dissolution beyond the limitations of space and time. Although these Eastern concepts were absent in our interviews, we did find a rich abundance of transcendental qualities in the deathbed visions. Garfield suggests an "increased likelihood of enlightenment experience immediately prior to death."[4]

We also found similarities between experiences of the other world by the dying and by mystics. The same touch of the sacred was there. Maslow describes genuine, religious "peak experiences" as being the culmination and self-actualization of one's life (1971). We also found that patients' encounters with visions of another world and its messengers often outshine everything else for which they care. They may be so gratifying and value-fulfilling that the patient does not want to come back to life, and so angrily scolds the resuscitation team.

In visions of the supernal light, everything appears beautiful and harmonious. The harsh qualities of human existence are no longer in sight. Deathbed visions seem to be sweetened by a kind of fairytale unreality: "and they lived happily ever after." Writers such as Aldous Huxley (1955) remind us that a mere touch of another world could not possibly change the human race beyond recognition so that there would be no more conflict and fights, no neurotic entanglements. C. S. Lewis, in a charming little book about the Christian Heaven and Hell, *The Great Divorce* (1946), describes how a smothering, tyrannical mother comes to claim her son, and a nagging wife, who drove her husband crazy, demands domain over him. We certainly did not encounter any quarrelsome relatives or sadistic neighborhood bullies in the descriptions of take-away figures. However, what would happen if the dead family members of the patients really were cruel? Perhaps this is when an experienced professional is needed, and so religious figures appear instead of those "not-so-loved ones." Perhaps that is one of the reasons why so many religious personages appear in Indian visions. There, the old family structure is more autocratic: Parents arrange marriages, and the head of the clan demands obedience. Certainly this possibility is worthy of follow-up research.

Even at their best, our deathbed vision cases provide only short glimpses into a presumed other world. We have no reports of prolonged excursions. We have many descriptions of the initial stages of postmortem existence, but nothing of what happens the next day, or the next year, or of what the "life" after death is really like—its activities, purposes, joys and sorrows, customs, social structure. What is going on behind that "curtain of silence"?

There is extensive literature purporting to give information of those who have been on the other side for some time. Although such sources are beyond the scope of this book, ignoring them completely would make for a lopsided view of the postmortem survival issue. Each of the world religions tells a story: the Bible, the Upanishads, the Tibetan *Book of the Dead*. Their empirical foundations are, however, very difficult to trace. Communications with the dead are widely claimed. According to a national opinion poll conducted by Greeley (1975), every fourth American says that he or she has had contact with the dead. Haraldsson (1976) obtained similar results in Iceland, and some even say that they have talked with them (Rees, 1971). Legitimate, scientific studies of such communications are rather scarce, though.

Those who have ostensibly witnessed the other world beyond its initial superficialities are individuals who claim to be able to "see" it or meet its inhabitants. Mystics such as Saint Paul and Saint Theresa claim to have been "transported" there. Persons capable of out-of-body experiences—such as the Swedish philosopher Emanuel Swedenborg or such contemporary personalities as J. H. M. Whiteman, a mathematician (1961), and Robert Monroe, an engineer (1971)—give elaborate descriptions of their "travels." A psychologist of the University of California at Davis, Dr. Charles Tart, provides realistic interpretations of out-of-body experiences (1974, 1975).

Mediums reverse the process and claim that the other world comes to them—that is, spirits of the deceased visit them, talk to or through them, show them scenes, write scripts by controlling the medium's hands (that is, automatic writing), or even possess them (Hart, 1959; Heywood, 1961; Cummins, 1965). Descriptions of the afterlife vary considerably, depending on the subculture of the seer (Pearce-

Higgins, 1973; Roll, 1974). Many American and British mediums talk of a "Summerland," where life seems to go on as usual, only in a more idealistic manner. These "spirit messengers" essentially talk about the same kind of life as they enjoyed when they were alive. However, the philosophical and educational levels of the communications are often, though not always, that of the medium and not of the deceased, who purportedly does the talking.

The souls of the deceased are said to spend an enormous amount of time benevolently intervening in the earthly lives of their loved ones. They are said to be "watching over you and helping you all the time." They never seem to tire or become bored with the everyday, nitty-gritty events in the lives of their relatives.

It is unfortunate that in addition to the foregoing people, the mediumistic field is infested with unscrupulous exploiters, whom Keene and Spraggett have dubbed the "Psychic Mafia" (1976). For example, in their book these authors tell how the late Bishop James Pike was apparently taken in by Arthur Ford. This, of course, does not decrease the value of genuine achievements recorded in rigorous research settings. The elite among the community of mediums have produced information of such high quality that the best minds of their time—for example, William James—were impressed (Murphy and Ballou, 1969). A former prime minister of Britain, Lord Balfour, spent years studying mediumistic communications (Salter, 1961).

Some communications exhibit an astonishing amount of evidential information about the lives of deceased persons. They will often include very private events, which no one present at the sitting knows. The eminent American psychologist Gardner Murphy (1961) describes celebrated cases of "cross correspondences"—that is, messages received independently by mediums in Britain, America, and India who did not know each other. These separate statements are like the pieces of a jigsaw puzzle: The full meaning of the message is revealed only after the puzzle has been pieced together by the researchers. Some of the statements reported by Murphy contained old Greek and Latin phrases, indicating acquaintance with very obscure sources of classical literature. Such information was far above the heads of the mediums, but quite consistent with the interests and knowledge of the supposed deceased communicators, two classical scholars named Myers and Butcher (Saltmarsh, 1939).

With admirable diligence and skill, British Victorian scholars tried to track down possible this-world sources of mediumistic messages. Evaluating the evidential value of single cases became their passion. They found a great deal of data that were much more consistent with the postmortem survival hypothesis than with the destruction hypothesis. Hart (1959), Jacobson (1973), and Salter (1961) provide thoughtful overviews of the early research. However, we know of no comprehensive statistical surveys performed on mediumistic data from different cultures. Such an investigation would delineate the general characteristics of mediums and their communications in a way similar to our study of deathbed experiences. But since no such work has been done, it is difficult to judge the nature of mediumistic communications. We have no way of determining whether the elements found in these messages are attributable to the medium's personal philosophy, national and/or international trends, or whether they are genuine core characteristics—beyond the influence of the psychic's idiosyncrasies and cultural background. Yet we can say with confidence that the best of the research with mediums has provided cases of postmortem communications that are very hard to explain with this-world sources of information (Hart, 1959; K. Richmond, 1939; Z. Richmond, 1938; Saltmarsh, 1939, Gauld, 1966–72). Although a great deal of evidence suggesting the existence of an afterlife has accumulated, there is little information about how it functions (Pearce-Higgins, 1973).

We both have had extensive firsthand experience with mediums. Their messages show some similarity to the data that we have obtained in our surveys. For example, mediums tell about spirits of dead relatives, and special "spirit guides," who receive the dying in the same manner as our take-away figures. Their descriptions of Heaven also seem to be fashioned from the images of this world. However, there is a glaring discrepancy between the reports of mediums and those of our respondents. According to most mediums, life goes on as usual, only more happily, in "other dimensions" or "Summerland." The dead are said to pursue essentially the same interests, keep the same habits and attachments as they had when living. According to our patients, even a brief encounter with the "great beyond" changes these considerably. It elicits an increase in benevolence and drastically changes their interests, values, and emotions. Whatever might characterize "life after life," it certainly does not seem to be "more of the same old thing." Instead of a continuation of the mundane sort of life, postmortem survival appears to plunge into a radically new mode of existence and way of experiencing.

According to the Oxford philosopher H. H. Price (Toynbee, 1968), there are basically two ways of thinking about the other world:

1. *As a semiphysical reality*—created from some sort of "higher matter," or ethereal stuff, where the inhabitants have "astral bodies." Fashioned out of this "higher matter" is a real, external environment that one can look at, move about in, and adjust to.

2. *As a kind of dream world*—the "environment" would consist of entirely subjective images which, as in dreams, cannot be shared with others. This personally manufactured "world" would change according to our wishes, desires, and fears, in the same way we are able to change our daydreams. Each soul would be bottled up in its own totally private environment, which no one else could see. Telepathy would be the only line of communication between these disembodied entities.

Nils O. Jacobson (1973), a Swedish psychiatrist, intricately describes a dream-world theory developed by a Danish writer, Martinus, who claimed to have had out-of-body visits to another world. This theory is quite comprehensive in its explanation of different spheres or locales in the other world (such as Purgatory), several hierarchical loci of Heaven—which one has to evolve through by personal development—and such concepts as Karma, reincarnation, hauntings, and so on.

The visionary experiences of dying patients seem to contradict the essential features of the dream-world theory. First, apparitions often exhibit a will of their own, contrary to the patient's wishes and expectations. Second, the environments seem to exist independently of the patient's motivations. Scenes do not change according to his wishes or fears, as predicted by the dream-world theory. Martinus's theory assumes that only like-minded persons of the same level of spiritual development will be able to perceive each other; communication with the rest would be impossible. This was not so in the visions of the dying. Close relatives, rather than like-minded individuals, are the dominant take-away figures. Therefore, deathbed observations are more consistent with the view that the dying do indeed encounter something "out there." Furthermore, we have reason to believe that the take-away figures are independent entities rather than thought projections. As such, they seem to share the patient's visual space, instead of coming with their own.

The only common ground between the dream-world hypothesis and our data is the close likeness between otherworldly images and this-world scenery. Dreams are built by recombining elements of the sensuous, perceptual world; so are the visions of Heaven. However, there is a way to reconcile this discrepancy. Suppose that the other world is a true, external reality, independent of the patient's mind. Suppose it is formed from something other than the physical energies and matter we are familiar with through science and sense. If this is true, then the perceptual process involved in seeing it should give us difficulties. Nearly all perception is learned. As babies, we see little more than a fuzzy blur. We learn how to perceive by developing our perceptual equipment, and this is accomplished by interacting with the physical world. These sources of perceptual images and categories (schemata) might, therefore, be useless in a world organized by rules of another kind. All we could initially do in such a predicament would be to apply our old perceptual equipment and images—however inadequate—to the new environment. It would work better than nothing until we had a chance to develop new categories through perceptual learning. Until death, the only training we have in perceiving incorporeal things would have come through telepathy—provided that the thoughts and feelings of others are nonmaterial. In this case we would be able to "see" nonmaterial persons rather than things. This might be the reason why many more dying patients report seeing persons than environments. It also might be that there are individual factors involved in one's ESP ability. If so, this would affect a patient's capacity for "seeing" the other world. Some would be better disposed by nature to have deathbed experiences based on psychic perception, thus explaining why not every dying person has awareness of the other world.

In conclusion, our surveys on the experiences of the dying, as well as of resuscitated patients, agree reasonably well with what was found by other researchers—specifically Elisabeth Kübler-Ross,

Raymond A. Moody, and Charles Garfield. Reports of mediumistic phenomena also suggest the same type of experiences at death as those described by our patients. However, the descriptions of the nature of the other world and the continuation of "life" in it vary widely and are hard to evaluate.

After Deathbed Visions: A New Look

"I've got quite a lot of changing to do before I leave here," said a resuscitated patient to Moody.[5] The few resuscitated patients interviewed by one of the authors (Osis) also said that the experience meant a great deal to them. The old, customary ideas of life and death no longer fitted. Revision and expansion were needed—and were being attempted by them. Still, we did not find a single patient who, like a butterfly out of a cocoon, was immediately transformed into a saint. Though the metamorphosis was not that complete, it pointed in the direction of future humanness.

Just as individuals are spurred into transformation, so, too, we feel, might different fields of science and society undergo radical change in light of a truer understanding of the meaning of death. However, the deeper part of the message—the dying insist—is experiential and hard to get across to those who have nothing similar in their memories to which they can relate. The famed psychologist Maslow (1970) called such life-changing occurrences "peak experiences." He remarked that the founders of religions, having had an abundance of peak experiences, are "peakers," while theologians are often "nonpeakers"—that is, thinkers who never had such experiences. According to Maslow, their writings often amount to the "nonpeakers" telling the "peakers" what their experiences really should have been! Jesus was equally pessimistic when saying that if. Lazarus were sent from the world of the dead to the rich man's house, "they would not believe him."

But what if a hundred Lazaruses kept coming and coming, or a thousand witnesses like those in this book? We hope they would be noticed by some of the scientific community and would stimulate them to enlarge their theories of what we humans are and how the universe is structured. Omitting the basic meaning of death and the large body of facts concerning it from scientific investigation is certainly not realistic or in keeping with the spirit of science. More adequate knowledge of ourselves and the human condition surely would lead to many applications of that knowledge, not only in practical, everyday life but in science, education, and religion as well.

For example, what if some of the leading psychologists and psychiatrists were to experience, say, cardiac arrest and awaken from resuscitation after otherworldly experiences such as we have reported here? The great Swiss psychologist Carl G. Jung did just that. He described his near-death experience as the greatest event of his life until then—his late sixties—and it marked a major turning point in his work. Perhaps those in the helping professions would, like the resuscitated patient, have quite a lot of changing to do in their own disciplines. Physicists, physiologists, and biologists likewise would find themselves in a position of having ignored parapsychology—a major body of knowledge germane to their own. If the afterworld and a soul which can "go" there exist, a new set of dimensions interpenetrating our own space-time continuum needs to be traced and new concepts developed.

A thousand experiences of the other world certainly should have something to say to religion. It takes time for research findings to be read and to be assimilated into theological thought; for example, the famous German theologian, Hans Kung, made strong negative statements with out referring to any relevant research publications in English (Kung, 1981). We enjoy religious freedom in pluralistic denominations composed of uncountable ideological groups as well as in totally new religious expressions. What particular experience of the dying would be useful to each group is difficult to say. If nothing more, to those ministers who are obsessed with this-world concerns and political actions, it might serve as a reminder that the sacred, the transcendent—"the other world"—seem to be real after all and, in another dimension, as active as ever. Everyone has the right to experience "the breath of the eternal" in his own good way.

The main message of our work, however, concerns us simply as men and women living in the human community. We all have faced the death of a relative or friend and, try as we might to evade it, we, too will die someday. What can we say to a friend whose prognosis is death? How should we react to his family? Some knowledge of the deathbed visions of persons who died "the good death" certainly would be helpful. We hope that the professionals who interact with terminal patients and their families will utilize the new information about the otherworldly side of death experiences to make their work more meaningful and effective. As implied by Kübler-Ross (1974), it is, after all, more rewarding and emotionally more bearable to help terminal patients to *transition* rather than to impending *ultimate destruction*. There is plenty of room for creative thought and action here. And above all, we need more research.

Epilogue

SUPPOSE a modern Lazarus, with a hearing aid and dentures, were to rise up and talk to us over a public-address system or on a talk show. What would he say? His advice might go like this.

"When your heart stops and the hour of death comes, you will not break up and disintegrate like ice in the rapids of a river. Instead, it will be like diving into a new kind of reality. You will feel well and be happy in a very special way—'the peace which passeth all understanding.' The weariness, the pain, and the sadness all will be left with the sheets on the hospital bed. You will 'light up from within,' and then you will see someone warm and caring waiting to receive you. If your own close relatives are suitable for the task—and you for them—one will 'pop in' as lifelike and loving as when you last saw him. But there will be a strange air of serenity around him. If the situation calls for professional help, a religious figure will come in brilliant light. Whoever they are, the visitors will 'turn you on.' Something mild but powerful will envelop you. It will feel like the best moments of your life—when on a mountaintop, in a church or temple—and much more. You might have to grope for words—*sacred, light, love.* No, none will really do, but you will feel it in the core of your being.

"Wherever you look, your perspective on everything will be changed. The feverish resuscitation efforts of the doctors and nurses to save your life will seem totally out of place, as though they were working on someone else's body. The heartrending anguish of weeping relatives will appear to be childish and beside the point. Your own grand concerns—the unfulfilled dreams of the future, duties to loved ones, work, everything you ever looked forward to—will become small and unimportant, fading like dried flowers. With a sudden wave of joy, you will be ready to go.

"If you are a Hindu, you will most likely experience the same things, but you may be received by a Yamdoot rather than by the 'professional' himself. But don't despair; you will be brought to the man in the white robe, and he is always a benign ruler with an aura of sacredness around him.

"You may be reminded of your earthly travels—the arrival terminal of an international airport where you have to pass through customs. Actually, the terminal might look more like a wonderful garden with beautiful gates and temples, and the desks might look more like a throne. Don't worry about that. All your ideas are inadequate approximations, something like the dry leaves of yesteryear in your earthly garden. Soon you will see more clearly, for now it is still 'through the glass darkly,' but 'then your eyes will be opened.' You will learn more than you did in any school. It will taste good, look beautiful. You will feel at peace and fulfilled until the next—"

Hands will go up in the audience. "What are the next stages of afterlife?"

The modern Lazarus will hesitate before the broadcasting system.

"What comes next? Well, that cannot be made clear to you now. Each one of you has a personal passport that will allow you to experience it eventually, but the knowledge is not yet declassified for this state of existence."

Lazarus and a thousand others have spoken. In our judgment, it would be prudent to pay attention to the central message whispered by them at the hour of death.

Evidence for Life After Death

Karlis Osis

SINCE the time of writing *At the Hour of Death*, some marked changes in our culture have emerged which affected, more or less, the basic thinking and methods in some domains of scientific investigations. Calls for rethinking research approaches are not rare, especially related to the most complex areas of life, such as personality, selfhood, deeper unconscious processes, parapsychology and religion. At the time we wrote the first edition of this book, I myself had a stronger belief in the invincible power of facts which appropriate research can establish: do it right and the truth will convince! I am still a firm believer in the value of scientific research on phenomena suggestive of afterlife—very valuable knowledge is accumulated. I no longer believe so strongly in the commanding power of facts to convince. The roadblock which hinders most acceptance of research findings concerning afterlife is a basic world orientation, a fundamental belief that there is nothing spiritual, nothing non-physical in us or in our universe. This framework automatically excludes afterlife. However, a careful and discerning review of the information may lead us closer to what is true and useful, as I will try to show in the following pages.

This is a personal view, a panorama over decades of participation in research and interactions with colleagues and experiments. It is not meant to be a scholarly survey where each step is documented and referenced. At my age, the passionate involvement in research and debate is gone, but not the fascination with the basic phenomena

This chapter is adopted from a talk I gave at the Annual Conference of the Academy of Religion and Psychical Research in 1995.

indicative of life after death. The mystery of death still looks so grand and so far beyond what the scaffolding of scientific methods can fully reach. The psychic phenomena surrounding it are still awe-inspiring to me. The paranormal remains my window to that side of our being which transcends our mundane limitations, obsessions and self-centeredness. But don't misunderstand me: these are not my only windows to something more. I love the stained glass windows, too—symbols emerging from immensity. Poetry, art, music—I concede there are so many magnificent windows, but my real engagement has been in the scientific, the scholarly work.

What are the main things most apparent in my panorama? Three characteristics stick out. First, survival research in the second half of the twentieth century was a success story—modest, slow growth of information in spite of the hostile zeitgeist which surrounded it. The scope of phenomena researched was widened. Emphasis shifted from mediumistic communications and apparition experiences to hitherto little worked areas: reincarnation phenomena, out-of-body experiences, and near-death experiences. Research methods were refined and new ones applied or invented. Today there is more information available than the newcomers wish to reckon with.

Second, harmony and agreement in interpreting the database has *not* been reached. Parapsychological journals reveal clashing opinions; a discord of so-called "theories" keeps popping up, often passionately defended; a variety of other explanations are pitted against survival. On both sides I see very intelligent, well-trained colleagues. This confusing variety of interpretations does not help the millions facing death each year and their relatives.

Third, survival of bodily death is not a hypothesis about narrowly limited data, but an overarching concept, a metatheory interpreting a variety of human experiences, like evolution is in the biological sciences. When faced with death, their own or that of a loved one, evidence for life after death is strong enough to give considerable comfort to those who believe in survival, e.g., 70% of Americans. It has social usefulness, but the evidence is not of such a nature that it would shatter the disbeliefs and entrenched ideas of death as extinction of individuality.

I will now take a more detailed look at the good and the not so good developments.

The quest for facts which support the idea of postmortem survival did not appear suddenly. It is rooted in the very beginnings of our Western culture: Plato in *Republic* described the out-of-body journeys of a soldier, Er, who was thought to have been killed in action; the Roman, Pliny the Younger, described a ghost case in Athens where the ghostly information led to the discovery of the bones of a murdered man. Our predecessors thought out the factual base which was needed in order to ground the survival idea in reality and to free it from the overgrowth of superstition, over-belief and exploitation. Thoughtful men and women throughout our history wanted to *know*—not only believe.

The systematic application of scientific method to the collection and evaluation of supportive evidence is only about one hundred years old, but early ideas about it are much older. The inception of Society for Psychical Research (SPR) work came from the famous F.W.H. Myers and H. Sidgwick starry night walk more than a hundred years ago. In retrospect, their seminal idea was right and fruitful, but not all of it. In their time, the scientific method was almost deified as the final arbiter of all things visible and invisible—the researcher who adheres to the right methods will surely gain true insight into things as they are. That over-belief still holds in certain quarters, but at least two serious limitations emerged during the decades which followed.

There is no single "Scientific Method." Methods grow and adapt to the needs of research domains, as H. Margenau and L. LeShan have showed convincingly. Even in the physical sciences, differentiation occurs, e.g., macrophysics and microphysics. For a long time, behavioral sciences were too tightly yoked to methods developed in different domains of enquiry. In recent decades, there has been a breaking loose in various directions, some fruitful, some not. For example, there is now a burgeoning literature of qualitative methods which had been long overlooked in the bulk of parapsychology.

The other limitation was the over-belief that research competently done with acceptable methods is independent of who does it—the researcher is easily replaceable, like a figure on a chessboard. Decades earlier, E. Boring emphasized the influence of cultural climate, which differs from one university to another: not only "zeitgeist" but also "ortsgeist"—the "spirit of the place"—matters. In recent decades, sociological studies of the scientific process have clearly shown the strong influence of the researchers' personality, beliefs, fears, and academic ambitions. Awareness of these extrinsic factors is even more drastically important in research which may vitally affect our lives, our convictions, and our interests—as outlook on death surely does. Researchers have human frailties, too, which often show in spite of the strict discipline maintained by institutions and professional societies. For example, in the May, 1995 issue of the American Psychological Association's review journal, *Contemporary Psychology*, the lead articles are two reviews of a book which had aroused national attention: *The Bell Curve: Intelligence and Class Structure in American Life*. This controversial book was reviewed separately by two highly qualified experts. The first reviewer called it the "most provocative social science book published in many years." The second reviewer likened the two authors of *The Bell Curve* to monkeys punching randomly at the typewriter. Their judgments are so discordant that one feels the human frailties have somehow, somewhere sneaked in.

Unlike building blocks, the phenomena suggestive of afterlife do not come hard and fast. Like all human experiences emerging from our depth, they are not so clear. They often are moldable by the experients, by the writers who publish them, and by the researchers who organize them into theories. But they are not so pliable that they cannot be handled with reasonable objectivity. Reports from the mouths of good experients are reasonably trustworthy. Good researchers don't bend them to fit preconceived theories. We have to know and use methods developed through a hundred years of survival research while remaining open to innovations and new developments in other research areas. Still, equally intelligent scholars have arrived at clashingly different conclusions—the human frailties remain. Meanings alien to the data intrude, coming from cultural fashions and personal beliefs such as materialistic views. In this book we tried hard to make the voices of the dying louder than our own.

The title of a popular book is *I Didn't Believe in Ghosts Until*. Indeed, experients often try to deny the phenomena at first, or explain them away. A Boston woman saw an apparition walking through her living room. The next morning she called the doctor's office and arranged an appointment to get her eyes checked. The problem with her interpretation was that nothing was found to be wrong with her eyes, and her brother experienced an apparition, too—in the living room and fitting the same description. However, once the phenomena are accepted, over-interpretations might follow. I investigated a house in Brooklyn, New York where some phenomena were observed not only by the inhabitants, but also by guests. They also complained about sounds of heavy breathing and moaning. My tape recorder picked it up, too, but when properly amplified, the sounds were easily identified as coming from the washing machine in the basement. Experients often feel the need for reliable clarification and come to us with the request: "Doctor, tell me what it really is." Hopefully, the expert will carefully investigate, rather than inject his or her own beliefs. While the majority of parapsychologists are not well informed on the literature of survival research, a small group of them specialize and are working in phenomena suggestive of survival.

A basic requirement for doing any scientific research is familiarity with the literature of relevant previous work and debates about interpretations. Yet I see publications where researchers report their work on near-death or out-of-body experiences and argue about its relevance for or against survival while leaving out the available evidence from research on other phenomena suggestive of survival, e.g., apparitions, communication, and reincarnation experiences. Human frailties are pervasive, but by being vigilant we can improve our orientation.

Even more important than being well informed is the feel of the basic phenomena—a qualitative awareness of the spiritual, of what is outside the mundane, the admiration or awe in the presence of something greater than ourselves. The sixties ushered in many radical changes in our culture. In retrospect, a lot of it looks exaggerated, distorted, even naive. The significant contributions stuck to our culture as irrevocable changes. The most significant for psychology was rediscovery of experience as a proper focus for its research, theories, and practices of cultivating depth experiences. Aldous Huxley, one of the most wholesome prophets of that time, chided theologians for being non-experients; rationalists telling the experients what their experiences are and how to interpret them, without a qualitative understanding of these life-changing happenings which arise from the human depth. Maybe he located the great divide which separates those of us who see some evidence for life after death and those who deny it.

A British philosopher, Lorimer, tried to predict whether great thinkers would be pro or con survival from their views on mind-body problems. He succeeded in most cases. Later, H. Margenau and R. A. Varghese asked forty top scientists, including twenty-four

Nobel prize winners, six questions about science and religion. The outstanding characteristic of the answers from many of these scientists was again experiential—experiencing admiration, or awe in aspects of the universe with which they grappled in their research. One scientist of high distinction emphasized his motivation: "... a human being who intends to serve his public"—rather than the razzle-dazzle of originality or "theory-building" so seductive in our field.

During the time I was still active in research, I personally knew most researchers in parapsychology, visiting their places of research, having many private discussions. I had the impression that those who had personal experiences, either in themselves or in those they deeply trusted, conducted their research in more effective ways, coming closer to the real. For example, when Margaret Grey, a British clinical psychologist, contacted me during her work on her thesis, I was very reserved because I felt that her grasp of scientific methodologies was poorer than that of her more academic colleagues who were working along the same lines. But she had an asset: personal near-death experience. Later, when I reviewed her thesis book on near-death experiences, I had to change my mind. She had a wealth of good findings and it seemed to me that she had hit the core phenomena better than others in that field. The experiential awareness is important, even though it may detract from the persuasiveness of attained evidence. Without it, research has been less effective, less focused on the essentials and more carried away with the peripheral sides of the phenomena. In my view, there is a need for researchers on survival to gain personal spiritual experience in one way or another. Equally important is the need to abstain from theorizing from an armchair, but rather, interacting with the experients themselves, sympathetically observing their woes and their jewels of experiences until something qualitative from them rubs off on the researcher. Of course, qualitative awareness and a warm heart are not a substitute for careful methods and efficient research designs, nor does it give license for sloppy work. If you work on survival, your research will be scrutinized more—not less—than when working on something less important.

It is true that only a few well qualified parapsychologists have done sustained work on postmortem survival in the second half of our century. It is said that this is a consequence of secularization of our society: postmodern men and women have no room for survival ideas in their well educated world view. That argument is thoroughly discredited by all national polls I know of. In the United States, the level of belief in survival as well as in the spiritual has changed little over the decades.

Others point out the lack of strong phenomena indicative of survival in our times as compared to the golden age of research with mediums in Victorian England. However, those of us, e.g., I. Stevenson, E. Haraldsson and myself, who searched intensively, found them.

The most frequent excuse is the super-ESP hypothesis, which assumes that the psychic capacities of the living are so powerful, so boundless, that they may explain all phenomena which are claimed as signs of existence of the dead. This view was strongly advocated by the Rhines and its shadow still looms large over this field of enquiry. However, Allan Gauld, the noted psychologist of the University of Nottingham, England, analyzed it carefully and thoroughly discredited super-ESP in his book, *Mediumship and Survival*. I have not seen viable refutation of his conclusions. In my own judgment, the psychic powers of the living are not a sufficient explanation of the best evidence accumulated in survival research: super-ESP does not make the dead mute. It is not rational to ascribe to a person enormous psychic powers of a magnitude never observed in a laboratory if he/she has shown no indication of such powers in his/her life other than at the time when a collectively seen apparition was walking in. I refer the reader to Gauld's book for detailed discussion of the super-ESP slogan.

Another basic principle of survival research is also frequently confused. Phenomena suggestive of postmortem existence stem from broad classes of experiences such as apparition experiences, near-death experiences, mediumistic communications, out-of-body experiences, memories of past lives, etc. All of these experiences emerge from our deeper strata of personality shaped by several causative factors where the other-worldly ones may or may not be present. These broader classes, however, contain some smaller subgroups in which something indicating afterlife is traceable and useful for survival research, while the rest of the experiences might not be separable from the broad base of subconscious processes. The broader classes are open to research with the usual sampling and statistical evolution methods and yield relevant information, but be aware that these broadly sampled data will have, so to say, a lot of water mixed with some wine. Examples of useful information coming from broad sampling are Haraldsson's and my cross-cultural study of deathbed visions presented in this book. Stevenson found a large number of cases of reincarnation memories which lacked some essential details or other relevant information to justify careful single case research and detailed reporting. He analyzed this data as a whole and his correlation analysis gave very valuable information supplementing his main work on much smaller samples of the groups of cases where meticulous consideration of every detail was possible.

Out-of-body experiences, when they became fashionable, have been easily inducible in classroom experiments with students. Willed relaxation and suggestion methods can lead a good portion of the class to experience something which students label "out-of-body experiences." In such experiments, researchers found no clear indices that the experients were really out of the body. Some questionnaire surveys also lead to similar conclusions. When I tried to substantiate in the lab the out-of-body-ness of these experiences, I found only six persons, out of one hundred and fifty claimants, who were able to show some indices of really being out of body. Of these six, only two participated for a long time: initially Ingo Swann, and mostly Alex Tanous. We couldn't engage the other four in a long enough series for one reason or another. This smaller group of two were productive and gave us positive results indicating being out of body.

Apparition experiences can powerfully influence the life of the experient, even when seen just by one person and only once. For example, the late president of the American Society for Psychical Research (ASPR), Arthur Twitchell, experienced an apparition while imprisoned in Germany after his plane had been shot down during World War II. That single experience led to a life-long interest and an active participation in the ASPR—but it was of no value for scientific research. We can assess the source of the apparition if it is collectively seen by several persons, especially if animals (cats, dogs, horses) react to it at the same time. But that is only a smaller subclass of apparition experiences. Even more rarely, the apparitions seem to leave physical signs, such as electric lights or gadgets turned on, doors really opened, objects moved. There are more useful indices, e.g., if the apparition experiences stop in a haunted house after the intervention of a psychic—provided factors such as suggestions to the inhabitants of the house are controlled, e.g., the researcher used skillful suggestions before the intervention without resultant stop of the phenomena.

Earlier investigators were impressed by "veridical hallucinations," that is, cases where the apparition told or otherwise exhibited information unknown to the experients. That indeed indicates that something paranormal took place, but the source of the information—whether it's from the living (ESP) or from the dead—remains unclear.

The basic principle emerges: often stronger evidence for postmortem survival emerges from research on subgroups, especially small subgroups, rather than from the broader classes of phenomena, because the source of the phenomena is more clearly traceable. I myself, like many others, preferred the usual sampling methods until the facts bullied me into revision of my views. Undue reliance on the broader classes alone might badly mislead the researcher. Nonparanormal, purely psychological factors are, of course, present in all phenomena, which, after all, happen to human beings while immersed in the flow of psychological processes. In broader classes of phenomena these psychological factors are more dominant, while in the subgroups the indicators of afterlife stand out more clearly. A common mistake is to exaggerate the role of psychological factors ascertained in broad samples at the expense of the spiritual and survival related ones.

Scientific understanding is hierarchically organized. At the base are narrowly focused experiments or observations which either produce or do not produce supportive evidence to the research hypothesis, e.g., believers in ESP (sheep) score higher than disbelievers (goats), while the overall concept of psi encompasses all kinds of ESP and PK phenomena. There is no one "crucial experiment" that establishes or invalidates the hierarchical concept. Postmortem survival is also a roof idea arching over many aspects of our life, based on many phenomena, not one or two. Such metatheories are basic in the processes of scientific enquiry. In astrophysics there is the "Big Bang" metatheory of blind chance processes versus the cosmologies which postulate "intelligence came first." Evolution is metatheory in the biological sciences.

What is needed to support a metatheory is to show its power to organize large arrays of findings in its framework better than the competing metatheories do. For example, the evolution theory makes sense of an enormous mass of data which hang together better in its framework than without it. So does the metatheory of survival.

Metatheories are not static, "proved" or "disproved" forever. They grow and get modified as evolution theory did. Recently it was shown that the subtheory of equilibrium or natural balance, "leave nature alone and it will develop harmoniously," was not on the mark. Catastrophes, such as volcanic eruptions of enormous amounts of ashes, geological changes arising from the shifting of tectonic plates, etc., were formative of evolution processes. The metatheory was reshaped to better cover the new facts.

I expect the metatheory of survival to also develop and grow, often in unexpected ways. We cannot hope to provide more certainties, static "proofs" than the other metatheories do. Very likely the certainty or level of evidence will be less than for other metatheories because of the nature of the reality it reveals: partly of this world, graspable with our capacities and our methods, while part of it transcends this world, bordering the mystery of the spiritual "which passes all understanding." When I was younger I, too, had my vanity, my dreaming of reaching unattainable levels of certainty to satisfy all critical objections. Such caprices are still bubbling in our field. The bubbles might be negative "no evidence" or positive over-claims.

Where does it lead us? In my panorama over decades of search I see modest evidence emerging from well-done research. It is comforting, it is useful—especially when we actually face the mystery of death— our own or those close to us. Beliefs are not enough in our culture. Knowledge helps; the experiences of the spiritual and of the paranormal help. And still the best we can do is "see through the glass darkly" (St. Paul), allowing for surprises when we ourselves arrive at the end. Near-death experiences are basically encounters with the unexpected. With this book we tried to expand and illuminate that which can be expected. We made predictions on the basis of our first American survey. Most of the predictions came true in the second American survey with verification in the Indian survey. Still I expect to experience surprises when I die.

SELECTED REFERENCES which might be helpful to readers in forming a personal panorama of postmortem survival.

Bennett, E. (1939). *Apparitions and Haunted Houses: A Survey of Evidence.* London: Faber & Faber.

Gauld, A. (1977). "Discarnate survival." In B. Wolman (Ed.) *Handbook of Parapsychology.* New York: Van Nostrand, Reinhold, pp. 577–630.

Gauld, A. (1982). *Mediumship and Survival: A Century of Investigation.* London: Heinemann.

Greeley, A.M. (1989). *Religious Change in America.* Cambridge, MA and London: Harvard University Press.

Green, C. & McCreery, C. (1975). *Apparitions.* London: Hamish Hamilton.

Gurney, E., Myers, F.W.H., & Podmore, F. (1886). *Phantasms of the Living.* 2 vols. London: Trubner.

Haraldsson, E. (1987). *Modern Miracles: An Investigative Report on Psychic Phenomena Associated with Sathya Sai Baba.* New York: Ballantine Books. (Will soon be back in print, published by Hastings House Book Publishers.)

Hart, H. (1959). *The Enigma of Survival.* Springfield, IL: Charles C. Thomas.

Jacobson, N.O. (1973). *Life Without Death?* New York: Dell.

Jaffe, A. (1979). *Apparitions: An Archetypal Approach to Death, Dreams, and Ghosts.* Irving, TX: Spring.

Lorimer, D. (1990). *Whole in One. The Near-Death Experience and the Ethic of Interconnectedness.* London: Arcana, a division of Penguin Books.

Margenau, H. & Varghese, R.A. (1992). *Cosmos, Bios, Theos.* La Salle, IL: Open Court.

Morris, R.L., Harrary, S.B., Janis, J., Hartwell, J., & Roll, R.W. (1978) "Studies in communication during out-of-body experiences." *Journal of American Society of Psychical Research,* 72: 1–22.

Murphy, G. (1961). *Challenge of Psychical Research.* New York: Harper & Row.

Myers, F.W.H. (1903/Reprint 1954). *Human Personality and its Survival of Bodily Death.* 2 vols. London: Longman, Green.

Osis, K. (1986). "Apparitions old and new." In K.R. Rao (Ed.) *Case Studies in Parapsychology: Papers Presented in Honor of Dr. Louise E. Rhine.* Jefferson, NC: McFarland, pp. 74–86.

———. (1995). "In search of evidence for life after death—science, experience or both." *The Academy of Religion and Psychical Research Annual Conference 1995 Proceedings.*

Osis, K. & McCormick, D. (1980). "Kinetic effects at the ostensible location of out-of-body projection during perceptual testing." *Journal of American Society for Psychical Research*, 74: 319–29.

Rhine, L.E. (1957). "Hallucinatory psi experiences: The initiative of the percipient in hallucinations of the living, the dying, and the dead." *Journal of Parapsychology*, 21: 13–46.

Siegel, R.K. (1980). "The psychology of life after death." *American Psychologist*, 35: 911–31.

Stevenson, I. (1975–1983). *Cases of the Reincarnation Type*. 4 vols. Charlottesville, VA: University Press of Virginia.

Stevenson, I. (1987). *Children Who Remember Previous Lives*. Charlottesville: University Press of Virginia.

Tart, C.T. (1977). *Psi: Scientific Studies of the Psychic Realm*. New York: E.P. Dutton.

Thouless, R.H. (1984). "Do we survive bodily death?" *Proceedings of the Society for Psychical Research*, 57: 1–52.

Appendix I

QUESTIONNAIRE

This questionnaire is part of a psychological study dealing with observations by physicians and nurses of persons approaching death. We would appreciate your answering the following questions and returning the questionnaire to us at your earliest convenience.

For
Coding
Purposes
Only

(A) In your estimation, about how many times have you actually been with a patient at the moment of death?

1) ☐ 0-10	6) ☐ 51-60
2) ☐ 11-20	7) ☐ 61-70
3) ☐ 21-30	8) ☐ 71-80
4) ☐ 31-40	9) ☐ 81-90
5) ☐ 41-50	10) ☐ more (how many?) _____

11

12

13
14

(B) Approximately how many patients have you treated during a terminal illness?_____

(C) Have you had any patients who, at any time during illness **terminated by death,** seemed to have hallucinations of the following kinds:

(1) Persons: *hallucinations primarily concerned with persons rather than surroundings.*

Did the patients see hallucinations of persons not actually present?
No. of cases _____

15
16

Did the patients, or anyone else, identify the hallucinatory person or persons seen as:

(a) Someone living	No. of cases _____	17 18
(b) Someone dead	No. of cases _____	19 20 21 22
(c) A religious figure or mythological being	No. of cases _____	23 24 25 26
(d) Any combination of these	No. of cases _____	
(e) Unidentified persons	No. of cases _____	

Please describe one characteristic case of such a hallucination of persons:

_____

_____

_____

_____

27

28

29

30

(2) Surroundings: *hallucinations concerned primarily with anything other than persons.*

Of these hallucinations, how many were experienced as "another world," in a religious sense, and how many were of a non-religious nature?

31
32

(a) Hallucinations of "another world"	No. of cases _____
(b) Hallucinations of a non-religious nature	No. of cases _____

33
34

Please describe one characteristic case of such an experience:

_____

_____

_____

_____

35

36

37

38

(D) Have you had any patients who, though they **recovered** from a condition approaching death, seemed to have hallucinations of the following kind:

(1) Persons:

At any time during their illness did the patients see hallucinations of persons not actually present? **No. of cases** _____

Did the patients, or anyone else, identify the hallucinatory person or persons seen as:

    (a) Someone living   **No. of cases** _____

    (b) Someone dead   **No. of cases** _____

    (c) A religious figure or mythological being   **No. of cases** _____

    (d) Any combination of these   **No. of cases** _____

    (e) Unidentified persons   **No. of cases** _____

Please describe one characteristic case of such a hallucination of persons:

_____

_____

_____

_____

(2) Surroundings:

Of these hallucinations, how many were experienced as "another world," in a religious sense, and how many were of a non-religious nature?

    (a) Hallucinations of "another world"   **No. of cases** _____

    (b) Hallucinations of a non-religious nature   **No. of cases** _____

Please describe one characteristic case of such an experience:

_____

_____

_____

(E) Have you ever observed a sudden rise of mood to happiness or serenity in dying patients?

     No. of cases _____

Please describe one characteristic case:

_____

_____

_____

(F) In thinking over these questions, do you have any further comments you would like to make?

_____

_____

_____

YEARS IN
PROFESSIONAL
NAME:_____ DEGREE:_____ PRACTICE:_____

ADDRESS:
Street:_____ City:_____ State:_____

TELEPHONE NUMBER:_____

DATE:_____

**NAMES AND ADDRESSES WILL BE
KEPT STRICTLY CONFIDENTIAL**

39
40

41
43
45
47
49

42
44
46
48
50

51
52
53
54

55
56
57

58

59
60
61
62

63
64
65
66
67
68

69
70
71
72
73

74
75
76
77

Appendix II

TABLE 1

CHARACTERISTICS OF THE APPARITION EXPERIENCE IN TERMINAL PATIENTS

Variables	Characteristics	Number of Cases			Percentage of Total*
		U.S.	India	Total	
a. Duration of apparition	1 sec.–5 min.	85	83	168	48
	6–15 min.	17	43	60	17
	16–60 min.	11	50	61	18
	61 min.–1 day	13	31	44	13
	Longer	4	10	14	4
	No information	86	38	124	—
b. Interval between apparition and death	0–10 min.	17	36	53	12
	11–60 min.	7	59	66	15
	61 min.–6 hr.	26	64	90	20
	7–24 hr.	28	41	69	15
	Longer	117	52	169	38
	No information	21	3	24	—
c. Identity of apparition	Living	30	38	68	18
	Dead	124	54	178	47
	Religious figure	22	93	115	30
	Combination of above	11	7	18	5
	No information	29	63	92	—
d. Sex of apparitional figure	Male	59	103	162	57
	Female	91	30	121	43
	No information	66	122	188	—

TABLE 1

CHARACTERISTICS OF THE APPARITION EXPERIENCE
IN TERMINAL PATIENTS

Variables	Characteristics	U.S.	India	Total	Percentage of Total*
	Taken for visitor	14	28	42	14
	To comfort patient	13	4	17	6
	To take patient away, with consent	40	102	142	47
e. Purpose of apparitional figure	To take patient away, without consent	1	53	54	18
	To send patient back	0	2	2	1
	Threatening	4	13	17	6
	Reliving memories	26	1	27	9
	No information	118	52	170	—
	No effect or relaxation	60	65	125	30
f. Emotional reactions, 1st group	Serenity	46	40	86	20
	Elation	56	32	88	21
	Negative	33	91	124	29
	No information	21	27	48	—
	No effect or relaxation	60	65	125	30
g. Emotional reactions, 2nd group	Negative	33	91	124	29
	Positive, nonreligious	77	36	113	27
	Positive, religious	25	36	61	14
	No information	21	27	48	—

* Percentages do not include cases for which no information was available.

Where the percentages do not total 100, it is because decimals were rounded off.

TABLE 2

IDENTITY OF APPARITIONAL FIGURES*

Variables	Identity	Number of Figures			Percent-age of Total
		U.S.	India	Total	
	Mother	60	16	76	23
	Father	15	16	31	9
	Spouse	49	10	59	18
	Sibling	27	15	42	13
	Offspring	27	17	44	13
a. Secular	Other relatives, pre-vious generation	5	7	12	4
	Other relatives, same generation	2	10	12	4
	Other relatives, next generation	0	4	4	1
	Unidentified relatives	9	14	23	7
	Friends, acquaintances	21	8	29	9
	Unidentified persons	25	61	86	—
	Totals:	240	178	418	
	God or Jesus	13	17	30	28
	Shiva, Rama, Krishna	0	13	13	12
	Mary, Kali, Durga	5	4	9	8
b. Religious	God of death and messengers	0	18	18	17
	Saints and gurus	3	5	8	8
	Angels, Devi, etc.	9	17	26	24
	Demons and devils	1	2	3	3
	Other religious figures, unidentified	2	31	33	—
	Totals:	33	107	140	

* Totals include cases in which several figures were seen by the same patient.

TABLE 3

MEDICAL STATUS OF TERMINAL PATIENTS
SEEING APPARITIONS

Variables	Medical Status	Number of Patients U.S.	India	Total	Percentage of Total
	Cancer	79	28	107	23
	Heart and circulatory disease	61	39	100	22
a. Primary diagnosis	Injury and post-operative	10	62	72	16
	Respiratory disease	9	26	35	8
	Brain injury or disease, uremia	28	26	54	12
	Miscellaneous	25	64	89	19
	No information	4	10	14	—
b. Secondary diag-	Present	68	40	108	25
nosis, possibly	Absent	137	187	324	75
hallucinogenic	No information	11	28	39	—
	Less than 100°	128	129	257	58
c. Body temperature	100°–103°	55	94	149	34
(oral)	Above 103°	16	20,	36	8
	No information	17	12	29	—
	None	94	165	259	61
d. Medication	Medication, no effect	39	40	79	19
affecting con-	Mildly affected	31	18	49	11
sciousness	Moderately affected	22	10	32	8
	Strongly affected	5	1	6	1
	No information	25	21	46	—
	Clear	98	100	198	43
e. Clarity of	Mildly impaired	31	103	134	29
consciousness	Severely impaired	36	39	75	17
	Fluctuating	38	12	50	11
	No information	13	1	14	—

TABLE 4

CHARACTERISTICS OF TERMINAL PATIENTS
SEEING APPARITIONS

Variables	Characteristics	Number of Patients U.S.	India	Total	Percentage of Total
a. Age	1–30	19	68	87	19
	31–50	22	97	119	25
	Over 50	174	90	264	56
	No information	1	0	1	—
b. Sex	Male	99	175	274	58
	Female	117	80	197	42
	None, preschool	13	77	90	21
	Primary	57	59	116	27
c. Education	High school	73	65	138	32
	College	45	38	83	20
	No information	28	16	44	—
	Professional, manager, clergy	56	29	85	30
d. Occupation	Clerical, sales, crafts	9	40	49	17
	Farmers, laborer, services, housewife	70	83	153	53
	No information	81	103	184	—
	Hindu		214	214	48
	Christian (India)		26	26	6
	Muslim		12	12	3
e. Religion	Protestant (U.S.)	97		97	22
	Catholic (U.S.)	68		68	15
	Jewish	12		12	3
	Other or none	14		14	3
	No information	25	3	28	—
	No involvement	12	3	15	5
f. Degree of involvement in religion	Slight	27	12	39	14
	Moderate	44	48	92	33
	Deep	64	65	129	47
	No information	69	127	196	—
g. Belief in afterlife	Belief	69	70	139	92
	No belief	6	6	12	8
	No information	141	179	320	—

TABLE 5

CHARACTERISTICS OF THE APPARITIONAL EXPERIENCE IN NONTERMINAL CASES

Variables	Characteristics	Number of Cases U.S.	India	Total	Percentage of Total
a. Duration of apparition	Up to 5 min.	16	9	25	35
	6–15 min.	2	6	8	11
	16–60 min.	5	14	19	27
	61 min.–1 day	5	6	11	15
	Longer	4	4	8	11
	No information	24	25	49	—
b. Identity of apparition	Living	11	8	19	20
	Dead	25	14	39	40
	Religious figure	9	27	36	37
	Combination of above	3		3	3
	No information	8	15	23	—
c. Sex of apparitional figure	Male	22	29	51	70
	Female	14	8	22	30
	No information	20	27	47	—
d. Purpose of apparitional figure	Taken for visitor	3	7	10	11
	To comfort patient	9	1	10	11
	To take patient away, with consent	6	15	21	24
	To take patient away, without consent	2	16	18	20
	To send patient back	5	13	18	20
	Threatening	2	4	6	7
	Reliving memories	5	1	6	7
	No information	24	7	31	—
e. Emotional reactions, 1st group	No effect or relaxation	8	11	19	17
	Serenity	19	14	33	29
	Elation	14	14	28	25
	Negative	12	20	32	29
	No information	3	5	8	—
f. Emotional reactions, 2nd group	No effect or relaxation	8	11	19	17
	Negative	12	20	32	29
	Positive, nonreligious	23	11	34	30
	Positive, religious	10	17	27	24
	No information	3	5	8	—

TABLE 6

MEDICAL STATUS OF NONTERMINAL PATIENTS
SEEING APPARITIONS

Variables	Medical Status	Number of Cases U.S.	India	Total	Percentage of Total
a. Primary diagnosis	Cancer	4	2	6	5
	Heart and circulatory diseases	14	8	22	19
	Injury and post-operative	12	14	26	22
	Brain injury or disease, uremia	7	2	9	8
	Infections and respiratory diseases	9	18	27	23
	Miscellaneous	9	17	26	22
	No information	1	3	4	—
b. Secondary diagnosis, possibly hallucinogenic	Present	15	4	19	18
	Absent	37	49	86	82
	No information	4	11	15	—
c. Body temperature (oral)	Less than 100°	24	28	52	46
	100°–103°	18	24	42	38
	Over 103°	7	11	18	16
	No information	7	1	8	—
d. Medication affecting consciousness	None	29	34	63	57
	Medication, no effect	12	16	28	25
	Mildly affected	7	4	11	10
	Moderately affected	2	4	6	5
	Strongly affected	1	2	3	3
	No information	5	4	9	—
e. Clarity of consciousness	Clear	18	24	42	36
	Mildly impaired	17	15	32	27
	Severely impaired	9	21	30	25
	Fluctuating	11	3	14	12
	No information	1	1	2	—

TABLE 7

CHARACTERISTICS OF NONTERMINAL PATIENTS SEEING APPARITIONS

Variables	Characteristics	Number of Patients			Percentage of Total
		U.S.	India	Total	
a. Age	1–30	8	21	29	24
	31–50	11	28	39	33
	Over 50	37	15	52	43
	No information	0	0	0	—
b. Sex	Male	23	30	53	44
	Female	33	34	67	56
c. Education	None, preschool	4	16	20	18
	Primary	13	18	31	28
	High school	18	16	34	31
	College	16	10	26	23
	No information	5	4	9	—
d. Occupation	Professional, manager, clergy	15	8	23	27
	Clerical, sales, craft	1	4	5	6
	Farmer, laborer, services	8	21	29	35
	Housewife	8	19	27	32
	No information	24	12	36	
e. Religion	Hindu		45	45	38
	Christian (India)		16	16	14
	Muslim		3	3	3
	Protestant (U.S.)	27		27	23
	Catholic (U.S.)	19		19	16
	Jewish	4		4	3
	Other or none	3		3	3
	No information	3		3	—
f. Degree of involvement in religion	No involvement	3	1	4	5
	Slight	5	2	7	8
	Moderate	20	16	36	43
	Deep	16	21	37	44
	No information	12	24	36	—
g. Belief in afterlife	Belief	26	21	47	90
	No belief	2	3	5	10
	No information	28	40	68	—

TABLE 8

CHARACTERISTICS OF MOOD ELEVATION PRIOR TO DEATH

Variables	Characteristics	Number of Cases U.S.	India	Total	Percentage of Total
a. Duration of mood elevation	Up to 10 min.	17	11	28	17
	11–60 min.	19	18	37	22
	61 min.–1 day	34	26	60	36
	Longer	30	11	41	25
	No information	6	2	8	—
b. Interval from end of mood elevation until death	Up to 10 min.	49	20	69	41
	11–60 min.	7	14	21	13
	61 min.–1 day	29	23	52	31
	Longer	17	9	26	15
	No information	4	2	6	—
c. Nature of mood changes, group 1	No change or relaxation	11	1	12	7
	Serenity	65	29	94	57
	Elation	21	28	49	30
	Negative mood changes	8	2	10	6
	No information	1	8	9	—
d. Nature of mood changes, group 2	No changes or relaxation	11	1	12	7
	Negative mood changes	8	2	10	6
	Positive, nonreligious	57	40	97	59
	Positive, religious	29	17	46	28
	No information	1	8	9	—

TABLE 8

CHARACTERISTICS OF MOOD ELEVATION
PRIOR TO DEATH

Variables	Characteristics	Number of Cases			Percentage of Total
		U.S.	India	Total	
e. Patient's verbal expression of mood change	Serene, peaceful	62	18	80	49
	Elated, cheerful	17	28	45	27
	Optimistic, making plans	17	16	33	20
	Other	5	1	6	4
	No information	5	5	10	—
f. Activity increase expressing mood change	Physical strength	10	6	16	18
	More talkative	9	18	27	31
	Less agitated	31	8	39	45
	Other	3	2	5	6
	None or no information	53	34	87	—
g. Social interactions expressing mood change	More cooperative	21	6	27	36
	Benevolent	8	12	20	27
	Enjoys company more	6	10	16	22
	Self-control	5	5	10	14
	Others	0	1	1	1
	None or no information	66	34	100	—
h. Religious activities expressing mood change	Praying, singing	13	8	21	100
	None or no information	93	60	153	—

TABLE 9

MEDICAL STATUS OF TERMINAL PATIENTS EXPERIENCING MOOD ELEVATION

Variables	Medical Status	Number of Cases U.S.	India	Total	Percentage of Total
a. Primary diagnosis	Cancer	47	15	62	36
	Heart and circulatory diseases	29	14	43	25
	Injury and postoperative	10	12	22	13
	Brain injury or disease, uremia	3	4	7	4
	Infections and respiratory diseases	6	4	10	6
	Miscellaneous	9	17	26	15
	No information	2	2	4	—
b. Secondary diagnosis, possibly hallucinogenic	Present	17	6	23	15
	Absent	81	52	133	85
	No information	8	10	18	—
c. Body temperature (oral)	Less than 100°	63	47	110	69
	100°–103°	27	17	44	28
	Over 103°	4	1	5	3
	No information	12	3	15	—
d. Medication affecting consciousness	None	43	43	86	54
	Medication, no effect	20	14	34	21
	Mildly affected	18	3	21	13
	Moderately affected	12	3	15	9
	Strongly affected	1	2	3	2
	No information	12	3	15	—
e. Clarity of consciousness	Clear	87	51	138	80
	Mildly impaired	11	16	27	16
	Severely impaired	3	1	4	2
	Fluctuating	4	0	4	2
	No information	1	0	1	—

TABLE 10

CHARACTERISTICS OF PATIENTS EXPERIENCING MOOD ELEVATION

Variables	Characteristics	Number of Cases U.S.	India	Total	Percentage of Total
a. Age	1–30	8	8	16	9
	31–50	19	33	52	30
	Over 50	78	27	105	61
	No information	1	0	1	—
b. Sex	Male	51	50	101	58
	Female	55	18	73	42
c. Education	None, preschool	5	13	18	11
	Primary	33	16	49	30
	High school	35	23	58	36
	College	23	13	36	22
	No information	10	3	13	—
d. Occupation	Professional, manager, clergy	38	10	48	33
	Clerical, sales, crafts	9	12	21	14
	Farmer, laborer, services	21	20	41	28
	Housewife	19	16	35	24
	No information	19	10	29	—
e. Religion	Hindu		56	56	34
	Christian (India)		7	7	4
	Muslim		3	3	2
	Protestant (U.S.)	39		39	24
	Catholic (U.S.)	38		38	23
	Jewish	11		11	7
	Other or none	9	1	10	6
	No information	9	1	10	—
f. Degree of involvement in religion	No involvement	4	0	4	4
	Slight	11	5	16	16
	Moderate	25	9	34	34
	Deep	30	16	46	46
	No information	36	38	74	—
g. Belief in afterlife	Belief	35	17	52	93
	No belief	3	1	4	7
	No information	68	50	118	—

TABLE 11

CHARACTERISTICS OF VISIONS OF ENVIRONMENT IN TERMINAL AND NONTERMINAL PATIENTS

Variables	Characteristics	Number of Cases			Percentage of Total
		U.S.	India	Total	
a. Duration of visions	Up to 5 min.	18	11	29	52
	6–15 min.	5	8	13	23
	16–60 min.	2	3	5	9
	Longer than 1 hr.	5	4	9	16
	No information	34	22	56	—
b. Subject matter	This-world places or objects	23	9	32	32
	Heaven, gates, etc.	12	29	41	41
	Gardens, landscapes	16		16	16
	Symbolic architecture	5		5	5
	Music, sounds	5	1	6	6
	No information	3	9	12	—
c. Appearance of surroundings	Threatening	7		7	10
	Everyday	6	4	10	14
	Beautiful but natural	4	11	15	21
	Extraordinary beauty, beyond reality	11	16	27	37
	Images of the other world	13		13	18
	No information	23	17	40	—
d. Emotional qualities expressed in visions	Beauty	24	12	36	72
	Peace	4	3	7	14
	Negative, threatening, etc.	6	1	7	14
	None or no information	30	32	62	—

TABLE 11

CHARACTERISTICS OF VISIONS OF ENVIRONMENT IN TERMINAL AND NONTERMINAL PATIENTS

Variables	Characteristics	Number of Cases			Percent-age of Total
		U.S.	India	Total	
e. Visions express-ing symbolism of death	Death as transition to gratifying existence	17	19	36	84
	Death as neutral or frightening existence	3	1	4	9
	Other symbolisms	2	1	3	7
	None or no infor-mation	42	27	69	—
f. Emotional reac-tions to visions, group 1	No effect or relaxa-tion	14	12	26	25
	Serenity	24	16	40	38
	Elation	9	15	24	23
	Negative	11	4	15	14
	No information	6	1	7	—
g. Emotional reac-tion to visions, group 2	No effect or relaxa-tion	14	12	26	25
	Negative	11	4	15	14
	Positive, non-religious	19	9	28	27
	Positive, religious	14	22	36	34
	No information	6	1	7	—

TABLE 12

MEDICAL STATUS OF TERMINAL AND NONTERMINAL PATIENTS SEEING VISIONS OF ENVIRONMENT

Variables	Medical Status	Number of Cases			Percentage of Total
		U.S.	India	Total	
a. Primary diagnosis	Cancer	12	5	17	17
	Heart and circulatory diseases	17	8	25	24
	Injury and post-operative	12	10	22	21
	Brain injury or disease, uremia	10	0	10	10
	Infections and respiratory diseases	10	13	23	22
	Miscellaneous		6	6	6
	No information	3	6	9	—
b. Secondary diagnosis, possibly hallucinogenic	Present	17	4	21	21
	Absent	42	35	77	79
	No information	5	9	14	—
c. Body temperature (oral)	Less than 100°	31	22	53	53
	100°–103°	20	20	40	40
	Over 103°	4	3	7	7
	No information	9	3	12	—
d. Medication affecting consciousness	None	25	31	56	60
	Medication, no effect	16	5	21	22
	Mildly affected	6	2	8	9
	Moderately affected	2	4	6	6
	Strongly affected	2	1	3	3
	No information	13	5	18	—
e. Clarity of consciousness	Clear	23	11	34	32
	Mildly impaired	11	15	26	25
	Severely impaired	14	22	36	34
	Fluctuating	9		9	9
	No information	7		7	—

TABLE 13

CHARACTERISTICS OF TERMINAL AND NONTERMINAL PATIENTS SEEING VISIONS OF ENVIRONMENT

Variables	Characteristics	Number of Cases			Percent-age of Total
		U.S.	India	Total	
a. Age	1–30	7	11	18	16
	31–50	10	22	32	29
	Over 50	47	15	62	55
	No information				—
b. Sex	Male	31	28	59	55
	Female	33	20	53	45
c. Education	None, preschool	1	13	14	15
	Primary	14	11	25	26
	High school	21	15	36	38
	College	13	7	20	21
	No information				—
d. Occupation	Professional, manager, clergy	18	8	26	30
	Clerical, sales, crafts	14	4	18	21
	Farmer, laborer, services	4	16	20	23
	Housewife	13	10	23	26
	No information	15	10	25	—
e. Religion	Hindu		35	35	36
	Christian (India)		11	11	11
	Muslim		2	2	2
	Protestant (U.S.)	31		31	32
	Catholic (U.S.)	15		15	15
	Jewish	1		1	1
	Other or none	2		2	2
	No information	15		15	—
f. Degree of involvement in religion	No involvement	1	1	2	3
	Slight	6	1	7	11
	Moderate	14	9	23	35
	Deep	17	17	34	52
	No information	26	20	46	—
g. Belief in after-life	Belief	21	22	43	96
	No belief		2	2	4
	No information	43	24	67	—

Notes

Chapter One. The Mystery of Death: What We Believe versus What We Know

1. H. Carrington and J. R. Meader, *Death: Its Causes and Phenomena with Special Reference to Immortality* (London: W. Rider and Son, 1911).

Chapter Two. Is the Idea of Postmortem Survival Testable?

1. For those interested in follow-up reading, we have listed useful works in the Bibliography. Those references can be traced from the main text by the year given in parentheses after the author's name.

2. Osis (1961) defines hallucinations of an apparitional nature as "seeing" somebody deceased while at the same time maintaining proper awareness of and response to the actual environment.

3. G. Murphy (1961) defines a cross correspondence as ". . . a series of fragmentary phrases or sentences each essentially without significance, but which, when put together, give a clear message."

Chapter Three. Research on Deathbed Visions: Past and Present

1. Sir William Barrett, *Death-bed Visions* (London: Methuen, 1926), pp. 11–12.

2. *Ibid.*, p. 14.

3. Available for $1.75 from the Parapsychology Foundation, 29 West 57th Street, New York, N.Y. 10019.

4. However, see John Fuller's book about James Kidd's will and how it was probated in the courts, *The Great Soul Trial* (New York: Macmillan, 1969). It includes lucid descriptions of expert testimony on evidence of life after death.

5. *Ibid.*, p. 300.

Chapter Four. The Pilot Survey: A Most Encouraging Start

1. K. Osis, *Deathbed Observations by Physicians and Nurses* (New York: Parapsychology Foundation, Inc., 1961).

2. *Ibid.*, p. 53.

Chapter Seven. Apparitions: Hallucinations of Persons as Seen by Terminal Patients

1. Theories of hallucinations vary. A wide spectrum of thoughtful explanations of hallucinations is presented in R. K. Siegel and L. J. West (eds.), *Hallucinations: Behavior, Experience and Theory* (New York: John Wiley & Sons, 1975).

Chapter Eight. General Characteristics of Apparition Cases in Terminal Patients

1. This figure, 73%, is for the whole adult population. Belief in life after death may be considerably higher among older persons such as are the majority of our sample. In Iceland Haraldsson (1976) found that belief in survival increases with age. Among persons in their thirties, 10% did not expect survival; 20% considered it a possibility, and 62% expected it. On the other hand, among persons in their sixties, the same percentages were 1, 7 and 77 respectively. (Some had no opinion.)

Chapter Nine. Getting at the Roots of the Apparition Experience I

1. The proportions are significant in the U.S. sample, p = .04 (53 percent versus 18 percent).

2. K. Osis, *Deathbed Observations by Physicians and Nurses* (New York: Parapsychology Foundation, Inc., 1961), p. 67.

3. *Ibid.*, pp. 67–68.

Chapter Ten. Getting at the Roots of the Apparition Experience II

1. K. Osis, *Deathbed Observations by Physicians and Nurses* (New York: Parapsychology Foundation, Inc., 1961), p. 71.

2. We included negative emotions in this group despite some overlap in responses to survival-related apparitions. The overlap would blunt, not exaggerate, any contrasts with otherworldly emotions. We feel safe in assuming this conservative position.

Chapter Fourteen. The Meaning of Death: What We Learned from This Study

1. R. A. Moody, *Life After Life* (Atlanta: Mockingbird Books, 1975), pp. 43–44.

2. *Ibid.*, pp. 45–46.

3. R. A. Moody, *Reflections on Life After Life* (Atlanta: Mockingbird Books, 1977).

4. C. Garfield, "Consciousness Alteration and Fear of Death," *Journal of Transpersonal Psychology* 7 (1975):172.

5. Moody, *Life After Life*, p. 68.

Bibliography

Barrett, W. F. *Death-Bed Visions.* London: Methuen, 1926.

Blackmore, S. J. *Beyond the Body: An Investigation of Out-of-the-Body Experiences.* London: Heinemann, 1982.

Carr, D. B. Pathophysiology of stress-induced limbic lobe dsyfunction: a hypothesis relevant to near-death experiences. In B. Greyson and C.P. Flynn, eds., *The Near-Death Experience: Problems, Prospects, Perspectives.* Springfield, Ill.: Charles C. Thomas, 1984, 125–139.

Clark, W. H. *Chemical Ecstasy, Psychedelic Drugs and Religion.* New York: Sheed and Ward, 1969.

Cohen, S. *The Beyond Within.* New York: Atheneum, 1964.

Collins, H. M. *Changing Order: Replication and Induction in Scientific Practice.* Beverly Hills, CA: Sage Publications, 1985.

Cummins, G. *Swan on a Black Sea.* London: Routledge and Kegan Paul, Ltd., 1965.

Deikman, A. J. "Experimental Meditation." *Journal of Nervous and Mental Disease* 1963, 136, 329–342.

Ducasse, C. J. *A Critical Examination of the Belief in a Life After Death.* Springfield, Ill.: Charles C. Thomas, 1961.

Gabbard, G. O. and Twemlow, S.W. *With the Eyes of the Mind: An Empirical Analysis of Out-of-Body States.* New York: Praeger, 1984.

Gallup, G., Jr. with Practor, W. *Adventures in Immortality: A Look Beyond the Threshold of Death.* New York: McGraw-Hill, 1982.

Garfield, C. "Consciousness Alteration and Fear of Death." *Journal of Transpersonal Psychology* 7 (1975): 147–75.

Gauld, A. "A Series of 'Drop In' Communicators." *Proceedings of the Society for Psychical Research* 55 (1966–72): 273–340.

Gauld, A. *Mediumship and Survival: A Century of Investigations.* London: Heinemann, 1982.

Greeley, A. M. *Sociology of the Paranormal: A Reconnaissance.* Beverly Hills, Calif.: Sage Publications, 1975.

Green, C., and McCreery, C. *Apparitions.* London: Hamish Hamilton, Ltd., 1975.

Grey, M. *Return from Death: An Exploration of the Near-Death Experience.* London: Arkana, an insignia of Routledge and Kegan Paul, 1985.

Greyson, B. and Flynn, C.P., eds. *The Near-Death Experience: Problems, Prospects, Perspectives.* Springfield, Ill.: Charles C. Thomas, 1984.

Haraldsson, E., *et al.* "National Survey of Psychical Experiences and Attitudes Towards the Paranormal in Iceland." In: W. G. Roll, R. L. Morris, and J. D. Morris, eds., *Research in Parapsychology 1976.* New Jersey: Scarecrow Press, 1977.

Haraldsson, E. Representative national surveys of psychic phenomena: Iceland, Great Britain, Sweden, USA, and Gallup's multinational survey. *Journal of the Society for Psychical Research*, 1985, *53*, 145–158.

Hart, H. *The Enigma of Survival.* Springfield, Ill.: Charles C. Thomas, 1959.

———. "ESP Projection: Spontaneous Cases and the Experimental Method." *Journal of the American Society for Psychical Research* 48 (1954): 121–46.

———. "Six Theories About Apparitions." *Proceedings of the Society for Psychical Research* 50 (1953–56): 153–239.

Heywood, R. *Beyond the Reach of Sense.* New York: E. P. Dutton and Co., 1961.

Huxley, A. *Heaven and Hell.* New York: Harper & Row, 1955.

———. *The Perennial Philosophy.* Cleveland: World Publishing Co., 1962.

Hyslop, J. H. *Psychical Research and the Resurrection.* Boston: Small, Maynard and Co., 1908.

Jacobson, N. O. *Life Without Death.* New York: Dell Publishing Co., 1973.

James, W. *Varieties of Religious Experience.* New York: Longmans, Green and Co., 1902.

Keene, M. L. *The Psychic Mafia.* As told by A. Spraggett. New York: St. Martin's Press, 1976.

Kübler-Ross, E. *Death: The Final Stage of Growth.* Englewood Cliffs, N.J.: Prentice-Hall, Inc., 1975.

———. *On Death and Dying.* New York: Macmillan Co., 1969.

———. Personal communication, 1976.

———. *Questions and Answers on Death and Dying.* New York: Macmillan Co., 1974.

———. *On Children and Death.* New York: Macmillan, 1983.

Kung, H. *Eternal Life? Life After Death as a Medical, Philosophical and Theological Problem.* Garden City, NY: Image Books, a division of Doubleday and Co., 1985.

Lewis, C. S. *The Great Divorce.* London: Macmillan Co., 1946.

Ludahl, C. R., ed. *A Collection of Near-Death Research Readings, Scientific Inquiries into the Experiences of Persons Near Physical Death.* Chicago: Nelson-Hall Publishers, 1982.

McClelland, D. C. *The Roots of Consciousness.* New York: D. Van Nostrand Co., 1964.

MacKenzie, A. *Apparitions and Ghosts: A Modern Study.* London: Barker, 1971.

MacKenzie, A. *Hauntings and Apparitions.* London: Heinemann, 1982.

Maslow, A. H. *The Farther Reaches of Human Nature.* New York: Viking Press, 1971.

———. *Religions, Values and Peak Experiences.* New York: Viking Press, 1970.

McClenon, J. *Deviant Science: The Case of Parapsychology.* Philadelphia, PA: University of Pennsylvania Press, 1984.

Monroe, R. *Journeys Out of the Body.* Introduction by C. T. Tart. New York: Doubleday and Co., 1971.

Moody, R. A. *Life After Life.* Atlanta: Mockingbird Books, 1975.

———. *Reflections on Life After Life.* Atlanta: Mockingbird Books, 1977.

Murphy, Gardner. *Challenge of Psychical Research.* New York: Harper & Row, 1961.

Murphy, G., and Ballou, R. O., eds. *William James on Psychical Research.* New York: Viking Press, 1961.

Myers, F. W. H. *Human Personality and Its Survival of Bodily Death.* 2 vols. London: Longmans, Green, 1903.

Noyes, R. "The Experience of Dying." *Psychiatry* 35 (1972): 174–83.

Noyes, R., and Kletti, R. "The Experience of Dying From Falls." *Omega* 3 (1972): 45–52.

Noyes, R., Jr. and Slymen, D. J. The subjective response to life-threatening danger. In B. Greyson and C. P. Flynn, eds., *The Near-Death Experience: Problems, Prospects, Perspectives.* Springfield, Ill.: Charles C. Thomas, 1984, 19–29.

———. "Depersonalization in the Face of Life-Threatening Danger: A Description." *Psychiatry* 39 (1976): 19–27.

Osis, K. *Deathbed Observations by Physicians and Nurses.* New York: Parapsychology Foundation, Inc., 1961.

Osis, K.; Bokert, E.; and Carlson, M. L. "Dimensions of the Meditative Experience." *Journal of Transpersonal Psychology* 5 (1973):109–135.

Osis, K., and Haraldsson, E. "Five Out-of-Body Cases of Sri Sathya Sai Baba." Unpublished.

————. "Deathbed Observations by Physicians and Nurses: A Cross-Cultural Survey." *Journal of American Society for Psychical Research*, 71 (1977): 237–259.

Osis, K. and McCormick, D. Kinetic effects at the ostensible location of an out-of-body projection during perceptual testing. *Journal of the American Society for Psychical Research*, 1980, *74*, 319–329.

Osis, K. and Mitchell J. L. Physiological correlates of reported out-of-body experiences. *Journal of the Society for Psychical Research*, 1977, *49*, 525–536.

Otto, R. *The Idea of the Holy*. New York: Oxford University Press, 1958.

Pahnke, W. N. "Drugs and Mysticism: An Analysis of the Relationship between Psychedelic Drugs and Mystical Consciousness." Harvard University Dissertation, Cambridge, 1964.

Palmer, J. "Scoring in ESP Tests as a Function of Belief in ESP. Part 1. The Sheep-Goat Effect." *Journal of the American Society for Psychical Research* 65 (1971): 373–408.

Palmer, J., and Dennis, M. "A Community Mail Survey of Psychic Experiences." In W. G. Roll, R. L. Morris, and J. D. Morris, eds., *Research in Parapsychology 1974*. Metuchen, N.J.: Scarecrow Press, 1975, pp. 130–33.

Pearce-Higgins, C. J. D., and Whitby, S. *Life, Death and Psychical Research*. London: Rider & Co., 1973.

Price, H. H. "What Kind of Next World?" In A. Toynbee *et al.*, *Man's Concern with Death*. New York: McGraw-Hill, 1969, pp. 251–58.

Rees, W. D. "The Hallucinations of Widowhood." *British Medical Journal* 4 (1971): 37–41.

Rhine, J. B. "Incorporeal Personal Agency: The Prospects of a Scientific Solution." *Journal of Parapsychology*, 24 (1960): 279–309.

————. "Comments: Psi Methods Reexamined." *Journal of Parapsychology*, 39 (1975): 38–58.

Rhine, L. E. *Hidden Channels of the Mind*. New York: Sloane, 1961.

————. "Subjective Forms of Spontaneous Psi Experiences." *Journal of Parapsychology*, 17 (1953): 77–114.

Richmond, K. *Evidence of Identity*. London: G. Bell, 1939.

Richmond, Z. *Evidence of Purpose*. London: G. Bell, 1938.

Ring, K. *Life at Death. A Scientific Investigation of Near-Death Experience.* New York: Coward, McCann and Geoghegan, 1980.

———. *Heading Toward Omega. In Search of the Meaning of the Near-Death Experience.* New York: Quil, William Morrow, 1984.

Roll, W. G. "A New Look at the Survival Problem." In J. Beloff, *New Directions in Parapsychology.* London: Elek Science, 1974, pp. 144–64.

———. "Survival Research: Problems and Possibilities." In E. D. Mitchell and J. White, eds., *Psychic Exploration : A Challenge for Science.* New York: G. P. Putnam's Sons, 1974, pp. 397–424.

Sabom, M. B. *Recollections of Death: A Medical Investigation.* New York: Harper and Row, 1982.

Salter, W. H. *Zoar: Or The Evidence of Psychical Research Concerning Survival.* London: Sidgwick and Jackson, 1961.

Saltmarsh, H. F. *Evidence of Personal Survival from Cross Correspondences.* London: G. Bell, 1939.

Schmeidler, G. R., and McConnell, R. A. *ESP and Personality Patterns* New Haven: Yale University Press, 1958.

Sidwick, H., *et al.* "Report on the Census of Hallucinations." *Proceedings of the Society for Psychical Research* 10 (1894): 25–422.

Siegel, R. K., and West, L. J., eds. *Hallucinations: Behavior, Experience and Theory.* New York: John Wiley & Sons, 1975.

Siegel, R. K. The psychology of life after death. *American Psychologist,* 1980, *35*, 911–931.

Smith, H. *The Religions of Man.* New York: Harper & Row, 1958.

———. *Forgotten Truth: The Primordial Tradition.* New York: Harper and Row, 1976.

———. *Beyond the Post-Modern Mind.* New York: Crossroad Publishing, Co., 1982.

Stace, W. T. *Mysticism and Philosophy.* New York: J. B. Lippincott, 1960.

Stevenson, I. *Twenty Cases Suggestive of Reincarnation.* 2nd rev. ed. Charlottesville: University Press of Virginia, 1974. (a)

———. *Xenoglossy: A Review and Report of a Case.* Charlottesville: University Press of Virginia, 1974. (b)

———. *Cases of the Reincarnation Type, Volume 1. Ten Cases in India.* Charlottesville, VA: University Press of Virginia, 1975.

———. *Cases of the Reincarnation Type, Volume 2. Ten Cases in Sri Lanka.* Charlottesville, VA: University Press of Virginia, 1977.

———. *Cases of the Reincarnation Type, Volume 3, Twelve Cases in Lebanon and Turkey.* Charlottesville, VA: University Press of Virginia, 1980.

———. *Cases of the Reincarnation Type, Volume 4. Twelve Cases in Thailand and Burma.* Charlottesville, VA: University Press of Virginia, 1983.

———. *Unlearned Language. New Studies in Xenoglossy.* Charlottesville, VA: University Press of Virginia, 1984.

Tart, C. "Out-of-Body Experiences." In E. D. Mitchell and J. White, eds., *Psychic Exploration: A Challenge for Science.* New York: G. P. Putnam's Sons, 1974, pp. 349–73.

———. *States of Consciousness.* New York: E. P. Dutton & Co., 1975.

———. ed. *Transpersonal Psychologies.* New York: Harper & Row, 1975.

Tart, C. T. *Psi, Scientific Studies of the Psychic Realm.* New York: E. P. Dutton, 1977.

Toynbee, A., *et al. Man's Concern with Death.* New York: McGraw-Hill, 1968.

Tyrrell, G. N. M. *Apparitions.* New York: Macmillan Co., 1962.

West, D. J. "A Mass Observation Questionnaire on Hallucinations." *Journal of the Society for Psychical Research* 34 (1948): 187–96.

West, L. J., ed., *Hallucinations.* New York: Grune and Stratton, 1962.

Whiteman, J. H. M. *The Mystical Life.* London: Faber and Faber, 1961.

Index

Afterlife, *see* Life after death
American Society for Physical
    Research:
  Chester F. Carlson and, 19–20
  Indian studies by, 22–24
  James Kidd and, 21–22
  U.S. studies by, 19
Anoxia, 190
Apparitions, 13, 18, 54–61
  bargaining with, 45
  emotional reponses to, 69–72,
    108–117, 110–119
  hallucinations and, 29–30, 56–68
    103
  "not-so-loved ones" and, 203
  reliving memories and, 55
  reluctance to discuss, 69–70
  roots of the experience, 58–61
    analyses, 83–84
    cross-cultural comparison,
      90–92
    different generations and,
      97–100
    identity of apparition, 93–97
    interactions of various factors,
      81–83
    medical factors, 84–85
    psychological factors, 85–86
    purpose of apparition, 84–92
    respondents, 119–121
    severe stress and, 86–90
    sex and, 100–102
    total hallucinations and,
      103–110

terminal patients and, 62–80
  background of patient, 72–79
  education and, 78–79
  how close to death did vision
    occur?, 63, 64, 186
  how did patient react?, 69–72
  how long did vision last?, 63
  medical conditions and, 72–75
  nature of experience, 63–72
  religion and beliefs and, 76–78
  sex and age and, 75–76
  summary, 79–80
  what was its purpose?, 67–69
  whom did they see? 64–67
  three types of, 54–56
  with a will of its own, 45, 89,
    187

Contact with the dead, 13–14
Core phenomena, 186–189

Deathbed visions:
  contents of, 48–49
  cultural factors and, 50, 60–61,
    76–78, 90–97, 109,
    158–159, 190–193
  described, 2, 16–17
  of God, 38–41, 45, 60, 66–67,
    96, 104, 150, 152–153,
    178, 183
  of light and brightness, 16–17,
    29, 37, 39–40
  model of, 46–53
  nearness to death of, 63–44, 186

Deathbed visions: *(continued)*
  pathological, 35
  procedure of study of, 50–53
  psychological factors and, 49
  religion and, 116–118
  research on, 16–27
  source of, 48
  See also Apparitions;
    Hallucinations
Death quota, 97–100
Depersonalization syndrome,
    197–198
Destruction hypothesis, 35–36
  models of deathbed visions and,
    48–50
Drugs:
  apparitions and, 31, 45, 59,
    72–75, 114–115
  bizarre experiences and, 5
  hallucinations and, 162
  mood elevation and, 136
  near-death patients and, 158
  visions of another world and,
    174, 189

ESP, 30, 31, 39, 41, 56
  duration of apparitions, 63, 186
  hallucinations, 56, 57, 104, 106
  of life after death, 123, 141–142,
    173, 186
  model of deathbed visions and,
    48, 49, 96, 169, 188–189
Ethical argument for life after
    death, 6

"Good death," 2, 122
  death of a Yogi and, 134–136

Hallucinations:
  afterlife-oriented, 56–58, 59–60
  apparitional, 30–32, 40, 56–58, 103
  cause of death and, 73–75
  defined, 56–57
  high fever and, 73
  mirages and, 88
  models of deathbed visions and,
    48–50

near-death, 148–161
predictions of death and, 3–4,
    16–17, 38–46, 92
psychological factors and, 59–60,
    85–86
"sick brain" hypothesis and,
    31–32, 56, 59, 73–75, 93,
    106–107, 158, 173–174,
    189–190
state of consciousness and, 73,
    115–116, 118, 175
study interviews and, 52–53
study questionnaire and, 50–52
this-life oriented, 31, 34, 37–39,
    82
"totai," 40–41, 103–110
See also Apparitions
Hallucinogenic index, 75
Historical argument for life after
    death, 6

"Laws of Parsimony," 10
Life after death:
  belief in, 5–6, 77–78, 117, 139
  clear mind and, 133
  come-back cases and, 160–161
  evidence for, 3, 6
  explanations other than, 189–193
  hallucinations and, 54–56,
    63–67, 82–83
    culture and, 93–97
    emotional reaction to, 110–119
  mood elevation, and, 122–124
  out-of-body experiences and,
    170–171
  science and, 7, 8
  testability of the idea, 9–15
    crucial experiments and, 11
    literature on, 12–13
  visions of another world and,
    175

Meaning of death, 185–211
  after deathbed visions, 203–204
  core phenomena, 186–189
    closeness of death and vision,
    186

Meaning of death *(continued)*
   dead and religious figures,
      186–187
   emotional responses, 187–188
   ESP and, 186
   intent of apparition, 187
   mood elevation, 188–189
   serenity and peace, 188
   subject matter of visions, 188
   willingness to "go," 187
explanations other than afterlife,
      189–193
   brain malfunctions, 189–190
   cultural background, 190–193
   drugs, 189
   medical factors, 189, 190
   psychological factors, 190
the other world: how certain are
      we?, 193–197
   checks and balances, 195
   patients bias, 196
   pattern consistency, 193–194
   research bias, 194–197
   sampling technique, 195–196
   time lapse, 195
support by other researchers,
      197–209
   depersonalization syndrome,
      197–198
   dream-world theory, 207–208
   literature and, 204
   mediums and, 204–207
   mystics and, 203–204
   semiphysical reality theory,
      207–208
Medical conditions:
   deathbed visions caused by, 48,
      72–75, 84–85, 106–107,
      114, 189–190
   mood elevation caused by,
      136–137
   visions of another world and,
      173–174
Medical profession:
   concept of death, 1–2
   deathbed visions explained by,
      48

destruction hypothesis and,
   35–36
hallucinations and, 56
Mediums, 7, 13, 204–207
Mood elevation, *see* Pre-death peace
   and serenity
Mystics, 6, 13, 32, 203–204

Near-death patients, reports from,
   148–161
   brain malfunctions and, 158
   compared to terminal cases,
      148–150, 157
   demographics and, 158–159
   drugs and, 158
   duration of visions, 157
   Indian, 154–156
   negative reactions, 157
   patients expectations and,
      159–160
   psychological factors and, 159
   rejection cases, 151–154, 157
   religion and, 152–154
   roots of visions in, 156–161
   this-world apparitions and,
      150–151

Ontological argument for life after
   death, 6
Out-of-body experiences, 13,
   40–41, 105, 170–171,
   180–181, 204

Pain, disappearance of, 130–132
Panoramic memory, 29
Parapsychology, 10, 43
   hallucinations and, 56
Parapsychology Foundation, 19–20
   pilot study by, 27–33
Physical phenomena, 43–44
Postmortem survival, *see* Life after
   death
Pre-death peace and serenity, 2, 4,
   30, 32–33, 37, 42, 44, 46,
   59, 60, 69, 82–83, 110–119,
   122–147
   age and, 124

Pre-death peace and serenity
  (continued)
  belief in afterlife and, 125
  disappearance of pain and,
    130–132
  education and, 125–127
  ESP and, 141–142
    of life after death and, 123
  facial expression and, 121–128
  Indian patients and, 133–136
  mood elevation and, 136–141
  nearness to death of, 123–124
  negative emotions and, 129
  religion and, 124–125, 137–139
  respondent bias and, 142–147
  soul and, 131
  state of consciousness and, 124,
    132
Predictions of death:
  hallucinations and, 3–4, 16–17,
    38–46, 92
  "no-consent" cases and, 89–90,
    92, 95
  peace and serenity and, 129–130
  by persons expected to recover,
    37–39, 88–90, 134, 135

Reliving memories, 55

Science, 7–10
Seers, 13
Soul, 131
Stress, schizoid reaction to, 86–90

Teleological argument for life after
    death, 6
Thanatology, 7–8, 82
Transcendental reality, 59
Transcultural study, procedure of,
    50–53

Visions of another world, 161–184
  age and sex and, 175
  belief in life after death and, 175
  brain malfunctions and, 173–174
  drugs and, 174
  education and, 175
  emotional reactions to, 177
  hallucinations of people and,
    162–163
  of heaven, 164–172
    Indian and American experi-
      ences, 176–184
  of hell, 169
  medical conditions and, 174
  music and, 169–170
  patients expectations and, 176
  peace and, 171
  religion and, 172, 175–176
  state of consciousness and, 175
  subject matter of, 163
  summary of, 173
  symbolism of death in, 172,
    175–176

Will to live, 4

Yogis, 134–136

About the Authors

KARLIS OSIS, Ph.D., was born in Riga, Latvia, in 1917, and is one of the few psychologists to have obtained a Ph.D. with a thesis dealing with extrasensory perception (University of Munich, 1950).

As research associate of the Parapsychology Laboratory at Duke University from 1951 to 1957, Osis was a colleague of Dr. J. B. Rhine. In his research there, Osis pioneered experiments on ESP in animals and worked with humans to study ESP over the dimensions of space and time. Then, widening the scope of his activities, he served as director of research at the Parapsychology Foundation in New York City, where he conducted novel experiments with mediums and a large-scale survey of deathbed observations by physicians and nurses (1957–62). Cases of apparitions seen by several persons, and cases of poltergeist phenomena were also studied.

From 1962 to 1975, Osis was director of research at the American Society for Psychical Research in New York. He is presently a Chester F. Carlson Research Fellow emeritus of the ASPR. During this time, Osis conducted a number of pioneering efforts in parapsychology. He conducted his second survey on deathbed observations by physicians and nurses to collect data suggestive of life after death. In an interview with creative artists, Osis found altered states of consciousness to be related to states conducive to ESP. Altered states of consciousness induced by meditation were studied in a four-year project. Osis also explored the relationship between mediumship and ESP by laboratory work with small, carefully selected groups of experienced meditators. Basic dimensions of the meditation experience were worked out by means of factor analysis.

Osis is well known for his long-distance ESP experiments—up to ten thousand miles—and for his research on the ESP channel—that is, an unknown energy which transmits ESP.

In the 1970s, Osis conducted extensive laboratory experiments on out-of-body experiences. These involved perceptual, physiological (EEG), and physical measurements. Together with Dr. Erlendur Haraldsson, he conducted a large-scale survey of the experiences of dying patients in India, which provided data for cross-cultural comparison between India and the United States. They also studied psychic phenomena in selected Yogis, particularly Sri Sathya Sai Baba, in southern India.

Osis is past president of the Parapsychological Association and a member of the American Psychological Association, Eastern Psychological Association, American Association for the Advancement of Science, Society for Scientific Study of Religion, and various organizations concerned with the study of psychic phenomena and human personality.

ERLENDUR HARALDSSON, Ph.D., was born in Reykjavik, Iceland, in 1931. After finishing his studies at the gymnasium (college), he worked for some years as a journalist and writer, traveling extensively in western Asia and India. During that time, he wrote a book on the Kurdish uprising in Iraq, which was published in both Iceland and Germany.

Having studied psychology at the German universities of Freiburg and Munich, Haraldsson received the diploma of psychology, a degree which is equivalent to the M.A. in the United States. From 1969 to 1970, he was a research fellow at Dr. J. B. Rhine's Institute of Parapsychology in Durham, North Carolina.

Haraldsson underwent his internship in clinical psychology from 1970 to 1971 in the Department of Psychiatry at the University of Virginia in Charlottesville. In 1972 he obtained his Ph.D. from the University of Freiburg in Germany for work on "Vasomotoric Indicators of ESP." He was a research associate at the American Society for Psychical Research in New York in 1972 and 1973. Since that time he has been on the Faculty of Social Science at the University of Iceland in Reykjavik, and a full professor since 1989, apart from three years which he spent as a visiting professor in Charlottesville and Freiburg.

Haraldsson is a member of several professional organizations, among them the American Psychological Association. He has conducted numerous research projects, has published widely in scholarly journals in America and Europe, and written four books. *At the Hour of Death*, which he wrote with Dr. Karlis Osis, has appeared in over twenty editions. Over a period of ten years he made several journeys to India to study the famous "man of miracles" Sathya Sai Baba. Haraldsson's thorough study of Sai Baba resulted in *Modern Miracles* (the English edition is titled *Miracles Are My Visiting Cards*) which has been highly acclaimed by critics and appeared in fourteen editions.